D0978785

The Crisis of Global Capitalism

ALSO BY GEORGE SOROS

Soros on Soros: Staying Ahead of the Curve

The Alchemy of Finance: Reading the Mind of the Market

GEORGE SOROS

THE CRISIS OF GLOBAL CAPITALISM

[*Open Society Endangered*]

PublicAffairs

New York

Copyright © 1998 by George Soros.

Published in the United States by PublicAffairs™,
a member of the Perseus Books Group.

All rights reserved.

Printed in the United States of America

No part of this book may be reproduced in any manner whatsoever without written permis-
sion except in the case of brief quotations embodied in critical articles and reviews. For information, address PublicAffairs, 250 West 57th Street, Suite 1825, New York, NY 10107.

Book design by Jenny Dossin.

Library of Congress Cataloging-in-Publication Data
Soros, George.
The crisis of global capitalism : open society endangered / George Soros.
p. cm.
Includes index.
ISBN 1-891620-27-4 (hc)
1. Financial crises.
2. Capitalism.
3. International finance.
4. Economic history—1990-
I. Title.
HB3722 .S67   1998
332' .042—dc21
98-48634
CIP

5 7 9 10 8 6 4

Acknowledgments

Several people took a great interest in the manuscript and helped me enormously. Anatole Kaletsky acted as my de facto editor helping me to organize the material and make it more accessible; Roman Frydman was particularly helpful on the conceptual framework; Leon Botstein raised many interesting points and we had several animated discussions; Anthony Giddens commented on more than one version of the manuscript; William Newton-Smith put me right on some philosophical points; and John Gray made me re-read Karl Polanyi's *Great Transformation*. Others who made helpful comments include Robert Kuttner, John Simon, Jeffrey Friedman, Mark Malloch Brown, Arminio Fraga, Tom Glaessner, Aryeh Neier, Daniel Kahneman, Byron Wien, and Richard Medley. My apologies to those whom I have forgotten to mention.

This book could not have been published at such a breakneck speed without the tireless assistance of my devoted secretary, Yvonne Sheer. Believe it or not, I first contacted my publisher, Peter Osnos, on September 22, 1998, and finished books will be shipped on November 18, 1998. Geoff Shandler worked overtime as my instant editor. Hats off to Peter and his team and thanks to Kris Dahl for suggesting him.

Contents

Preface

My original aim in writing this book was to expound the philosophy that has guided me through life. I had become known as a successful money manager and later on as a philanthropist. Sometimes I felt like a gigantic digestive tract, taking in money at one end and pushing it out at the other, but in fact a considerable amount of thought connected the two ends. A conceptual framework, which I had formulated in my student days long before I became engaged in the financial markets, governed both my money making and my philanthropic activities.

I was greatly influenced by Karl Popper, the philosopher of science, whose book *Open Society and Its Enemies* made sense of the Nazi and communist regimes that I had experienced first hand as an adolescent in Hungary. Those regimes had a common feature: They laid claim to the ultimate truth and they imposed their views on the world by the use of force. Popper proposed a different form of social organization, one that recognized that nobody has access to the ultimate truth. Our understanding of the world in which we live is inherently imperfect and a perfect society is unattainable. We must content ourselves with the second best: an imperfect society that is, however, capable of infinite improvement. He called it open society, and totalitarian regimes were its enemies.

I absorbed Popper's ideas about critical thinking and scientific method. I did it critically and I came to differ with him on an important point. Popper claimed that the same methods and criteria apply to both natural and social sciences. I was struck by a vital difference: In the social sciences, thinking forms part of the subject matter whereas the natural sciences deal with phenomena that occur independently of what anybody thinks. This makes natural phenomena amenable to Popper's model of scientific method, but not social phenomena.

I developed the concept of *reflexivity:* a two-way feedback mechanism between thinking and reality. I was studying economics at the time and reflexivity did not fit into economic theory, which operated with a concept borrowed from Newtonian physics, namely, equilibrium.

The concept of reflexivity came in very useful to me when I became engaged in managing money. In 1979, when I had made more money than I had use for, I established a foundation, called the Open Society Fund. I defined its objectives as helping to open up closed societies, helping to make open societies more viable, and fostering a critical mode of thinking. Through the foundation, I became deeply involved in the disintegration of the Soviet system.

Partly as a result of that experience and partly on the basis of my experience of the capitalist system, I came to the conclusion that the conceptual framework I had been working with was no longer valid. I sought to reformulate the concept of open society. In Popper's formulation, it stood in contrast with closed societies based on totalitarian ideologies, but recent experience taught me that it could be threatened from the opposite direction as well: from the lack of social cohesion and the absence of government.

I expressed my views in an article titled "The Capitalist Threat," published in the February 1997 issue of *The Atlantic Monthly*. This book, which I started writing shortly thereafter, was meant to be a more thorough elaboration of those ideas. In my previous books, I had relegated my conceptual framework to an appendix or served it up buried in personal reminiscences. Now I felt that it deserved a direct hearing. I had always been passionately interested in understanding the world in which I lived. Rightly or wrongly, I felt I had made some progress and I wanted to share it.

The original plan for this book was, however, disrupted by the global financial crisis that began in Thailand in July 1997. I was exploring the flaws of the global capitalist system but I was doing it in a leisurely fashion. I was fully cognizant of the Asian crisis—indeed my fund management company anticipated it six months before it happened—but I had no idea how far-reaching it would turn out to be. I was explaining why the global capitalist system was unsound and unsustainable, but until the Russian meltdown in August 1998, I did not realize that it was in fact disintegrating. Suddenly my book took on a new sense of urgency. Here I had a ready-made conceptual framework in terms of which the rapidly evolving global financial crisis could be understood. I decided to rush into print.

My view of the current situation was summed up in the congressional testimony I delivered on September 15, 1998, where I said, in part, as follows:

The global capitalist system which has been responsible for the remarkable prosperity of this country in the last decade is coming apart at the seams. The current decline in the U.S. stock market is only a symptom, and a belated symptom at that, of the more profound problems that are afflicting the world economy. Some Asian stock markets have suffered worse declines than the Wall Street crash of 1929 and in addition their currencies have also fallen to a fraction of what their value was when they were tied to the U.S. dollar. The financial collapse in Asia was followed by an economic collapse. In Indonesia, for instance, most of the gains in living standards that accumulated during 30 years of Suharto's regime have disappeared. Modern buildings, facto-ries and infrastructure remain, but so does a population that has been uprooted from its rural origins. Currently Russia has under-gone a total financial meltdown. It is a scary spectacle and it will have incalculable human and political consequences. The conta-gion has now also spread to Latin America.

It would be regrettable if we remained complacent just because most of the trouble is occurring beyond our borders. We are all part of the global capitalist system which is characterized not only by free trade but more specifically by the free movement of capital. The system is very favorable to financial capital which is free to pick and choose where to go and it has led to the rapid growth of global financial markets. It can be envisaged as a gigan-tic circulatory system, sucking up capital into the financial mar-kets and institutions at the center and then pumping it out to the periphery either directly in the form of credits and portfolio investments, or indirectly through multinational corporations.

Until the Thai crisis in July 1997 the center was both sucking in and pumping out money vigorously, financial markets were growing in size and importance and countries at the periphery could obtain an ample supply of capital by opening up their cap-ital markets. There was a global boom in which the emerging markets fared especially well. At one point in 1994 more than half the total inflow into U.S. mutual funds went into emerging market funds.

The Asian crisis reversed the direction of the flow. Capital started fleeing the periphery. At first, the reversal benefited the financial markets at the center. The U.S. economy was just on the verge of overheating and the Federal Reserve was contem-plating raising the discount rate. The Asian crisis rendered such a move inadvisable and the stock market took heart. The econ-omy enjoyed the best of all possible worlds with cheap imports keeping domestic inflationary pressures in check and the stock market made new highs. The buoyancy at the center raised hopes that the periphery might also recover and between February and April of this year most Asian markets recovered roughly half their previous losses measured in local currencies. That was a classic bear market rally.

There comes a point when distress at the periphery cannot be good for the center. I believe that we have reached that point with the meltdown in Russia. I have three main reasons for saying so.

One is that the Russian meltdown has revealed certain flaws in the international banking system which had been previously disregarded. In addition to their exposure on their own balance sheets, banks engage in swaps, forward transactions and derivative trades among each other and with their clients. These transactions do not show up in the balance sheets of the banks. They are constantly marked to market, that is to say, they are constantly revalued and any difference between cost and market made up by cash transfers. This is supposed to eliminate the risk of any default. Swap, forward and derivative markets are very large and the margins razor thin; that is to say, the value of the underlying amounts is a manifold multiple of the capital employed in the business. The transactions form a daisy chain with many intermediaries and each intermediary has an obligation to his counterparties without knowing who else is involved. The exposure to individual counterparties is limited by setting credit lines.

This sophisticated system received a bad jolt when the Russian banking system collapsed. Russian banks defaulted on their obligations, but the Western banks remained on the hook to their own clients. No way was found to offset the obligations of one bank against those of another. Many hedge funds and other speculative accounts sustained large enough losses that they had to be liquidated. Normal spreads were disrupted and professionals who arbitrage between various derivatives, i.e., trade one derivative against another, also sustained large losses. A similar situation arose shortly thereafter when Malaysia deliberately shut down its financial markets to foreigners but the Singapore Monetary Authority in cooperation with other central banks took prompt action. Outstanding contracts were netted out and the losses were shared. A potential systemic failure was avoided.

These events led most market participants to reduce their exposure all round. Banks are frantically trying to limit their exposure, deleverage, and reduce risk. Bank stocks have plummeted. A global credit crunch is in the making. It is already restricting the flow of funds to the periphery, but it has also begun to affect the availability of credit in the domestic economy. The junk bond market, for instance, has already shut down.

This brings me to my second point. The pain at the periphery has become so intense that individual countries have begun to opt out of the global capitalist system, or simply fall by the wayside. First Indonesia, then Russia, have suffered a pretty complete breakdown but what has happened in Malaysia and to a lesser extent in Hong Kong is in some ways even more ominous. The collapse in Indonesia and Russia was unintended, but Malaysia opted out deliberately. It managed to inflict considerable damage on foreign investors and speculators and it managed to obtain some temporary relief, if not for the economy, then at least for the rulers of the country. The relief comes from being able to lower interest rates and to pump up the stock market by isolating the country from the outside world. The relief is bound to be temporary because the borders are porous and money will leave the country illegally; the effect on the economy will be disastrous but the local capitalists who are associated with the regime will be able to salvage their businesses unless the regime itself is toppled. The measures taken by Malaysia will hurt the other countries which are trying to keep their financial markets open because it will encourage the flight of capital. In this respect Malaysia has embarked on a beggar-thy-neighbor policy. If this makes Malaysia look good in comparison with its neighbors, the policy may easily find imitators, making it harder for others to keep their markets open.

The third major factor working for the disintegration of the global capitalist system is the evident inability of the international monetary authorities to hold it together. IMF [International Monetary Fund] programs do not seem to be working; in addition, the IMF has run out of money. The response of the G7 governments to the Russian crisis was woefully inadequate, and the loss of control was quite scary. Financial markets are rather peculiar in this respect: they resent any kind of government interference but they hold a belief deep down that if conditions get really rough the authorities will step in. This belief has now been shaken.

These three factors are working together to reinforce the reverse flow of capital from the periphery to the center. The initial shock caused by the meltdown in Russia is liable to wear off, but the strain on the periphery is liable to continue. The flight of capital has now spread to Brazil and if Brazil goes, Argentina will be endangered. Forecasts for global economic growth are being steadily scaled down and I expect they will end up in negative territory. If and when the decline spreads to our economy, we may become much less willing to accept the imports which are necessary to feed the reverse flow of capital and the breakdown in the global financial system may be accompanied by a breakdown in international free trade.

This course of events can be prevented only by the intervention of the international financial authorities. The prospects are dim, because the G7 governments have just failed to intervene in Russia, but the consequences of that failure may serve as a wake-up call. There is an urgent need to rethink and reform the global capitalist system. As the Russian example has shown, the problems will become progressively more intractable the longer they are allowed to fester.

The rethinking must start with the recognition that financial markets are inherently unstable. The global capitalist system is based on the belief that financial markets, left to their own devices, tend towards equilibrium. They are supposed to move like a pendulum: they may be dislocated by external forces, so-called exogenous shocks, but they will seek to return to the equilibrium position. This belief is false. Financial markets are given to excesses and if a boom/bust sequence progresses beyond a certain point it will never revert to where it came from. Instead of acting like a pendulum financial markets have recently acted more like a wrecking ball, knocking over one economy after another.

There is much talk about imposing market discipline, but if imposing market discipline means imposing instability, how much instability can society take? Market discipline needs to be supplemented by another discipline: maintaining stability in financial markets ought to be the objective of public policy. This is the general principle that I should like to propose.

Despite the prevailing belief in free markets this principle has already been accepted and implemented on a national scale. We have the Federal Reserve System and other financial authorities whose mandate is to prevent a breakdown in our domestic financial markets and if necessary act as lenders of last resort. I am confident that they are capable of carrying out their mandate. But we are sadly lacking in the appropriate financial authorities in the international arena. We have the Bretton Woods institutions—the IMF and the World Bank—which have tried valiantly to adapt themselves to rapidly changing circumstances. Admittedly the IMF programs have not been successful in the current global financial crisis; its mission and its methods of operation need to be reconsidered. I believe additional institutions may be necessary. At the beginning of this year I proposed establishing an International Credit Insurance Corporation, but at that time it was not yet clear that the reverse flow of capital would become such a serious problem and my proposal fell flat. I believe its time has now come. We also have to establish some kind of international supervision over the national supervisory authorities. Moreover, we have to reconsider the workings of the international banking system and the functioning of the swap and derivative markets.

This book is divided in two parts. Part I contains the conceptual framework. I shall not try to summarize it here, but in this age of keywords it can be represented by three keywords: fallibility, reflexivity, and open society. It contains a critique of the social sciences in general and economics in particular. I interpret financial markets in terms of reflexivity rather than equilibrium and I seek to develop a reflexive theory of history, treating financial markets as a laboratory where the theory can be tested.

In Part II, I apply the conceptual framework described in the first part to the present moment in history. Although the financial crisis looms understandably large, the analysis goes much deeper. I deal with the discrepancy between a global economy and a political and social organization that is still basically national in scope. I explore the unequal relationship between center and periphery and the unequal treatment of debtors and creditors. I examine the unhealthy substitution of monetary values for intrinsic human values. I interpret global capitalism as an incomplete and distorted form of open society.

Having identified the main features of the global capitalist system in Chapter 6, I try to predict its future in terms of a boom/bust sequence in Chapter 7. Chapter 8 contains some practical proposals on how the financial disintegration of the system could be prevented. In Chapter 9, I discuss the prospects for a less distorted and more complete form of open society and, in Chapter 10, the international context. Chapter 11 outlines some practical steps that could be taken to achieve it. I had meant this to be the definitive statement of my philosophy. Due to the intervention of history, it has become what I would call an instant book.

Introduction

This book seeks to lay the groundwork for a global open society. We live in a global economy, but the political organization of our global society is woefully inadequate. We are bereft of the capacity to preserve peace and to counteract the excesses of the financial markets. Without these controls, the global economy is liable to break down.

The global economy is characterized not only by free trade in goods and services but even more by the free movement of capital. Interest rates, exchange rates, and stock prices in various countries are intimately interrelated, and global financial markets exert tremendous influence on economic conditions. Given the decisive role that international financial capital plays in the fortunes of individual countries, it is not inappropriate to speak of a global capitalist system.

Financial capital enjoys a privileged position. Capital is more mobile than the other factors of production and financial capital is even more mobile than direct investment. Financial capital moves wherever it is best rewarded; as it is the harbinger of prosperity, individual countries compete to attract it. Due to these advantages, capital is increasingly accumulated in financial institutions and publicly traded multinational corporations; the process is intermediated by financial markets.

The development of a global economy has not been matched by the development of a global society. The basic unit for political and social life remains the nation-state. International law and international institutions, insofar as they exist, are not strong enough to prevent war or the large-scale abuse of human rights in individual countries. Ecological threats are not adequately dealt with. Global financial markets are largely beyond the control of national or international authorities.

I argue that the current state of affairs is unsound and unsustainable. Financial markets are inherently unstable and there are social needs that cannot be met by giving market forces free rein. Unfortunately these defects are not recognized. Instead there is a widespread belief that markets are self-correcting and a global economy can flourish without any need for a global society. It is claimed that the common interest is best served by allowing everyone to look out for his or her own interests and that attempts to protect the common interest by collective decision making distort the market mechanism. This idea was called laissez faire in the nineteenth century but it may not be such a good name today because it is a French word and most of the people who believe in the magic of the marketplace do not speak French. I have found a better name for it: market fundamentalism.

It is market fundamentalism that has rendered the global capitalist system unsound and unsustainable. This is a relatively recent state of affairs. At the end of the Second World War, the international movement of capital was restricted and the Bretton Woods institutions were set up to facilitate trade in the absence of capital movements. Restrictions were removed only gradually and it was only when Margaret Thatcher and Ronald Reagan came to power around 1980 that market fundamentalism became the dominant ideology. It is market fundamentalism that has put financial capital into the driver's seat.

This is, of course, not the first time that we have had a global capitalist system. Its main features were first identified in rather prophetic fashion by Karl Marx and Friedrich Engels in the *Communist Manifesto*, published in 1848. The system that prevailed in the second half of the nineteenth century was in some ways more stable than the contemporary version. First, there were imperial powers, Great Britain foremost among them, that derived large enough benefits from being at the center of the system to find it worthwhile to preserve it. Second, there was a single international currency in the form of gold; today there are three major currencies—the dollar; the German mark, which is soon to become the euro; and the yen—which are rubbing against each other like tectonic plates, often creating earthquakes, crashing minor currencies in the process. Third, and most important, there were certain shared beliefs and ethical standards, which were not necessarily practiced but were nevertheless quite universally accepted as desirable. These values combined a faith in reason and a respect for science with the Judeo-Christian ethical tradition and on the whole provided a more reliable guide to what is right and what is wrong than the values that prevail today. Monetary values and transactional markets do not provide an adequate basis for social cohesion. This sentence may not make much sense to the reader as it stands, but it will be expounded in the book.

The nineteenth-century incarnation of the global capitalist system, in spite of its relative stability, was destroyed by the First World War. After the end of the war, there was a feeble attempt to reconstruct it, which came to a bad end in the crash of 1929 and the subsequent Great Depression. How much more likely is it, then, that the current version of global capitalism will also come to a bad end, given that the elements of stability that were present in the nineteenth century are now missing?

Yet a calamity could be avoided if we recognized the deficiencies of our system and corrected them in time. How did these deficiencies arise and how could they be corrected? These are the questions

I propose to address. I argue that the global capitalist system is a distorted form of an open society and its excesses could be corrected if the principles of open society were better understood and more widely supported.

The term open society was given currency by Karl Popper in his book *Open Society and Its Enemies*. At the time the book was published, in 1944, open society was threatened by totalitarian regimes such as Nazi Germany and the Soviet Union, which used the power of the state to impose their will on the people. The concept of open society could be readily understood by contrasting it with the closed societies that totalitarian ideologies fostered. This remained true right up to the collapse of the Soviet empire in 1989. The open societies of the world—commonly referred to as the West—exhibited considerable cohesion in the face of a common enemy. But after the collapse of the Soviet system, open society, with its emphasis on freedom, democracy, and the rule of law, lost much of its appeal as an organizing principle and global capitalism emerged triumphant. Capitalism, with its exclusive reliance on market forces, poses a different kind of danger to open society. The central contention of this book is that market fundamentalism is today a greater threat to open society than any totalitarian ideology.

This statement is rather shocking. A market economy is an integral part of an open society. Friedrich Hayek, the greatest twentieth-century ideologist of laissez faire economics, was a firm believer in the concept of an open society. How can market fundamentalism threaten open society?

Let me make myself clear. I am not saying that market fundamentalism is diametrically opposed to the idea of open society the way fascism or communism were. Quite the contrary. The concepts of open society and market economy are closely linked and market fundamentalism can be regarded as merely a distortion of the idea of the open society. That does not make it any less dangerous. Market fundamentalism endangers the open society inadvertently by misinterpreting how markets work and giving them an unduly large role to play.

My critique of the global capitalist system falls under two main headings. One concerns the defects of the market mechanism. Here I am talking primarily about the instabilities built into financial markets. The other concerns the deficiencies of what I have to call, for lack of a better name, the nonmarket sector. By this I mean primarily the failure of politics and the erosion of moral values on both the national and the international level.

I want to say at the outset that I consider the failures of politics much more pervasive and debilitating than the failures of the market mechanism. Individual decision making as expressed through the market mechanism is much more efficient than collective decision making as practiced in politics. This is particularly true in the international arena. The disenchantment with politics has fed market fundamentalism and the rise of market fundamentalism has, in turn, contributed to the failure of politics. One of the great defects of the global capitalist system is that it has allowed the market mechanism and the profit motive to penetrate into fields of activity where they do not properly belong.

The first part of my critique concerns the inherent instability of the global capitalist system. Market fundamentalists have a fundamentally flawed conception of how financial markets operate. They believe that financial markets tend toward equilibrium. Equilibrium theory in economics is based on a false analogy with physics. Physical objects move the way they move irrespective of what anybody thinks. But financial markets attempt to predict a future that is contingent on the decisions people make in the present. Instead of just passively reflecting reality, financial markets are actively creating the reality that they, in turn, reflect. There is a two-way connection between present decisions and future events, which I call reflexivity.

The same feedback mechanism interferes with all other activities that involve cognizant human participants. Human beings respond to the economic, social, and political forces in their environment, but unlike the inanimate particles of the physical sciences humans have perceptions and attitudes that simultaneously transform the forces acting on them. This two-way reflexive interaction between what participants expect and what actually happens is central to an understanding of all economic, political, and social phenomena. This concept of reflexivity lies at the heart of the arguments presented in this book.

Reflexivity is absent from natural science, where the connection between scientists' explanations and the phenomena they are trying to explain runs only one way. If a statement corresponds to the facts, it is true; if not, it is false. In this way, scientists can establish knowledge. But market participants do not have the luxury of basing their decisions on knowledge. They must make judgments about the future and the bias they bring to bear influences the outcome. These outcomes, in turn, reinforce or weaken the bias with which the market participants began.

I contend that the concept of reflexivity is more relevant to financial markets (and to many other economic and social phenomena) than the concept of equilibrium, on which conventional economics is based. Instead of knowledge, market participants start with a bias. Either reflexivity works to correct the bias, in which case you have a tendency toward equilibrium, or the bias can be reinforced by a reflexive feedback, in which case markets can move quite far from equilibrium without showing any tendency to return to the point from which they started. Financial markets are characterized by booms and busts and it is quite amazing that economic theory continues to rely on the concept of equilibrium, which denies the possibility of these phenomena, in face of the evidence. The potential for disequilibrium is inherent in the financial system; it is not just the result of external shocks. The insistence on exogenous shocks as a kind of deus ex machina to explain away the frequent refutation of economic theory in the behavior of financial markets reminds me of the ingenious contrivances of spheres within spheres and divine forces that pre-Copernican astronomers used to explain the position of the planets instead of accepting that the earth moves around the sun.

Reflexivity is not a widely accepted concept, at least in mainstream thinking, and it will take more than a few sentences to explore all its implications. It will occupy much of Part I of the book. In Part II of the book, I then use this framework to draw some practical conclusions—about financial markets; about the world economy; and about such broader issues as international politics, social cohesion, and the instability of the global capitalist system as a whole.

My second main line of argument is more complex and more difficult to summarize. I believe that the failures of the market mechanism pale into insignificance compared to the failure of what I call the nonmarket sector of society. When I speak of the nonmarket sector, I mean the collective interests of society, the social values that do not find expression in markets. There are people who question whether such collective interests exist at all. Society, they maintain, consists of individuals, and their interests are best expressed by their decisions as market participants. For instance, if they feel philanthropic they can express it by giving money away. In this way, everything can be reduced to monetary values.

It hardly needs saying that this view is false. There are things we can decide individually; there are other things that can only be dealt with collectively. As a market participant, I try to maximize my profits. As a citizen, I am concerned about social values: peace, justice, freedom, or whatever. I cannot give expression to those values as a market participant. Let us suppose that the rules that govern financial markets ought to be changed. I cannot change them unilaterally. If I impose the rules on myself but not on others, it would effect my own performance in the market but it would have no effect on what happens in the markets because no single participant is supposed to be able to influence the outcome.

We must make a distinction between making the rules and playing by those rules. Rule making involves collective decisions, or politics. Playing by the rules involves individual decisions, or market behavior. Unfortunately the distinction is rarely observed. People seem largely to vote their pocketbooks and they lobby for legislation that serves their personal interests. What is worse, elected representatives also frequently put their personal interests ahead of the common interest. Instead of standing for certain intrinsic values, political leaders want to be elected at all costs—and under the prevailing ideology of market fundamentalism, or untrammeled individualism, this is regarded as a natural, rational, and even perhaps desirable way for politicians to behave. This attitude toward politics undermines the postulate on which the principle of representative democracy was built. The contradiction between politicians' personal and public interests was, of course, always present, but it has been greatly aggravated by prevailing attitudes that put success as measured by money ahead of intrinsic values such as honesty. Thus the ascendancy of the profit motive and the decline in the effectiveness of the collective decision-making process have reinforced each other in a reflexive fashion. The promotion of self-interest to a moral principle has corrupted politics and the failure of politics has become the strongest argument in favor of giving markets an ever freer reign.

The functions that cannot and should not be governed purely by market forces include many of the most important things in human life, ranging from moral values to family relationships to aesthetic and intellectual achievements. Yet market fundamentalism is constantly attempting to extend its sway into these regions, in a form of ideological imperialism. According to market fundamentalism, all social activities and human interactions should be looked at as transactional, contract-based relationships and valued in terms of a single common denominator, money. Activities should be regulated, as far as possible, by nothing more intrusive than the invisible hand of profit-maximizing competition. The incursions of market ideology into fields far outside business and economics are having destructive and demoralizing social effects. But market fundamentalism has become so powerful that any political forces that dare to resist it are branded as sentimental, illogical, and naive.

Yet the truth is that market fundamentalism is itself naive and illogical. Even if we put aside the bigger moral and ethical questions and concentrate solely on the economic arena, the ideology of market fundamentalism is profoundly and irredeemably flawed. To put the matter simply, market forces, if they are given complete authority even in the purely economic and financial arenas, produce chaos and could ultimately lead to the downfall of the global capitalist system. This is the most important practical implication of my argument in this book.

There is a widespread presumption that democracy and capitalism go hand in hand. In fact the relationship is much more complicated. Capitalism needs democracy as a counterweight because the capitalist system by itself shows no tendency toward equilibrium. The owners of capital seek to maximize their profits. Left to their own devices, they would continue to accumulate capital until the situation became unbalanced. Marx and Engels gave a very good analysis of the capitalist system 150 years ago, better in some ways, I must say, than the equilibrium theory of classical economics. The remedy they prescribed—communism—was worse than the disease. But the main reason why their dire predictions did not come true was because of countervailing political interventions in democratic countries.

Unfortunately we are once again in danger of drawing the wrong conclusions from the lessons of history. This time the danger comes not from communism but from market fundamentalism. Communism abolished the market mechanism and imposed collective control over all economic activities. Market fundamentalism seeks to abolish collective decision making and to impose the supremacy of market values over all political and social values. Both extremes are wrong. What we need is a correct balance between politics and markets, between rule making and playing by the rules.

But even if we recognized this need, how could we achieve it? The world has entered a period of profound imbalance in which no individual state can resist the power of global financial markets and there are practically no institutions for rule making on an international scale. Collective decision-making mechanisms for the global economy simply do not exist. These conditions are widely acclaimed as the triumph of market discipline, but if financial markets are inherently unstable, imposing market discipline means imposing instability—and how much instability can society tolerate?

Yet the situation is far from hopeless. We must learn to distinguish between individual decision making as expressed in market behavior and collective decision making as expressed in social behavior in general and politics in particular. In both cases, we are guided by self-interest; but in collective decision making we must put the common interest ahead of our individual self-interest *even if others fail to do so.* That is the only way the common interest can prevail.

Today the global capitalist system still stands near the height of its powers. It is certainly endangered by the present global crisis, but its ideological supremacy knows no bounds. The Asian crisis has swept away the autocratic regimes that combined personal profits with Confucian ethics and replaced them with more democratic, reform-minded governments. But the crisis has also undermined the ability of the international financial authorities to prevent and resolve financial crises. How long before the crisis starts sweeping away reform-minded governments? I am afraid that the political developments triggered by the financial crisis may eventually sweep away the global capitalist system itself. It has happened before.

I want to make it clear that I do not want to abolish capitalism. In spite of its shortcomings, it is better than the alternatives. Instead, I want to prevent the global capitalist system from destroying itself. For this purpose, we need the concept of open society more than ever.

The global capitalist system is a distorted form of open society. Open society is based on the recognition that our understanding is imperfect and our actions have unintended consequences. All our institutional arrangements are liable to be flawed and just because we find them wanting we should not abandon them. Rather we should create institutions with error-correcting mechanisms built in. These mechanisms include both markets and democracy. But neither will work unless we are aware of our fallibility and willing to recognize our mistakes.

At present there is a terrific imbalance between individual decision making as expressed in markets and collective decision making as expressed in politics. We have a global economy without a global society. The situation is untenable. But how can it be corrected? This book is quite specific with regard to the deficiencies of financial markets. With regard to the moral and spiritual fields where market fundamentalism is squeezing its way into the nonmarket sector, my views are, of necessity, much more tentative.

To stabilize and regulate a truly global economy, we need some global system of political decision making. In short, we need a global society to support our global economy. A global society does not mean a global state. To abolish the existence of states is neither feasible nor desirable; but insofar as there are collective interests that transcend state boundaries, the sovereignty of states must be subordinated to international law and international institutions. Interestingly, the greatest opposition to this idea is coming from the United States, which, as the sole remaining superpower, is unwilling to subordinate itself to any international authority. The United States faces a crisis of identity: Does it want to be a solitary superpower or the leader of the free world? The two roles could be blurred as long as the free world was confronting an "evil empire," but the choice now presents itself in much starker terms. Unfortunately we have not even started to consider it. The popular inclination in the United States is to go it alone, but that would deprive the world of the leadership it so badly needs. Isolationism could be justified only if the market fundamentalists were right and the global economy could sustain itself without a global society.

The alternative is for the United States to forge an alliance with like-minded nations to establish the laws and institutions that are necessary to the preservation of peace, freedom, prosperity, and stability. What these laws and institutions are cannot be decided once and for all; what we need is to set in motion a cooperative, iterative process that defines the open society ideal—a process in which we openly admit the imperfections of the global capitalist system and try to learn from our mistakes. It cannot happen without the United States. But conversely, there has never been a time when a strong lead from the United States and other like-minded countries could achieve such powerful and benign results. With the right sense of leadership and with clarity of purpose, the United States and its allies could begin to create a global open society that could help to stabilize the global economic system and to extend and uphold universal human values. The opportunity is waiting to be grasped.

PART I

Conceptual Framework

CHAPTER 1

Fallibility and Reflexivity

Strange as it may seem for someone who has made his reputation and his fortune in the very practical world of business, my financial success and my political outlook have rested largely on a number of abstract philosophical ideas. Until these are understood, none of the other arguments presented in this book, whether on financial markets, geopolitics, or economics, can make much sense. This is why the rather abstract discussion of the next two chapters is required. Specifically, it is necessary to explain in detail the three key concepts on which all my other ideas—and most of my actions in business and philanthropy—are founded. These concepts are fallibility, reflexivity, and open society. Such abstract nouns may seem far removed from the everyday world of politics and finance. One of the main purposes of this book is to convince the reader that these concepts go to the heart of the real world of affairs.

Thinking and Reality

I must start at the beginning, with an old philosophical question that seems to lie at the root of many other problems. What is the relationship between thinking and reality? This is, I admit, a very roundabout way of approaching the world of affairs but it cannot be avoided. Fallibility means that our understanding of the world in which we live is inherently imperfect. Reflexivity means that our thinking actively influences the events in which we participate and about which we think. Because there is always a divergence between reality and our understanding of it, the gap between the two, which I call the participants' bias, is an important element in shaping the course of history. The concept of open society is based on the recognition of our fallibility. Nobody is in possession of the ultimate truth. This may seem obvious enough to ordinary readers, but it is a fact that political and economic decision makers, and even academic thinkers, are often unwilling to accept. This refusal to accept the inherent gap between reality and our thinking has had a far-reaching, and historically very dangerous, impact.

The relationship between thinking and reality has been, in one form or another, at the center of philosophical discourse ever since people became aware of themselves as thinking beings. The discussion proved to be very fertile. It has allowed the formulation of basic concepts such as truth and knowledge and it has provided the foundations of scientific method.

It is no exaggeration to say that the distinction between thinking and reality is necessary for rational thought. But beyond a certain point, the separation of thought and reality into independent categories runs into difficulties. Although it is desirable to separate statements and facts, it is not always possible. In situations that have thinking participants, the thoughts of these participants are part of the reality about which they have to think. It would be foolish not to distinguish between thinking and reality and to treat our view of the world as if it were the same as the world itself; but it is just as wrong to treat thinking and reality as if they were totally separate and independent. People's thinking plays a dual role: It is both a passive reflection of the reality they seek to understand and an active ingredient in shaping the events in which they participate.

There are, of course, events that occur independently of what anybody thinks; these phenomena, such as the movement of planets, form the subject matter of natural science. Here thinking plays a purely passive role. Scientific statements may or may not correspond to the facts of the physical world, but in either case the facts are separate and independent of the statements that refer to them.* Social events, however, have thinking participants. Here the relationship between thinking and reality is more complicated. Our thinking is part of reality; it guides us in our actions and our actions have an impact on what happens. The situation is contingent on what we (and others) think and how we act. The events in which we participate do not constitute some sort of independent criterion by which the truth or falsehood of our thoughts could be judged. According to the rules of logic, statements are true if, and only if, they correspond to the facts. But in situations that have thinking participants, the facts do not occur independently of what the participants think; they reflect the impact of the participants' decisions. As a result, they may not qualify as an independent criterion for determining the truth of statements. That is the reason why our understanding is inherently imperfect. This is not an abstruse philosophical debating point, comparable to Berkeley's question about whether the cow in front of him ceases to exist when he turns his back. When it comes to decision making, there is an inherent lack of correspondence between thinking and reality because the facts lie somewhere in the future and are contingent on the participants' decisions.

*But the existence of a material world independent of human observation has been a matter of heated dispute among philosophers since Berkeley.

The lack of correspondence is an important factor in making the world the way it is. It has far-reaching implications both for our thinking and for the situations in which we participate—implications that are deliberately ignored in standard economic theory, as we shall see in Chapter 2. The point I want to make here is that participants in social events cannot base their decisions on knowledge for the simple reason that such knowledge does not exist at the time they make their decisions. Of course people are not bereft of *all* knowledge; they have the whole body of science (including social science, for what it is worth) at their disposal as well as the practical experience accumulated through the ages, but this knowledge is not enough to reach decisions. Let me cite an obvious example from the world of finance. If people could act on the basis of scientifically valid knowledge, then different investors would not be buying and selling the same stocks at the same time. Participants cannot predict the outcome of their decisions the way scientists can predict the movement of celestial bodies. The outcome is liable to diverge from their expectations, introducing an element of indeterminacy that is peculiar to social events.

The Theory of Reflexivity

The best way to approach the relationship between the participants' thinking and the social events in which they participate is to examine first the relationship between scientists and the phenomena they study.

In the case of scientists, there is only a one-way connection between statements and facts. The facts about the natural world are independent of the statements that scientists make about them. That is a key characteristic that renders the facts suitable to serve as the criterion by which the truth or validity of statements can be judged. If a statement corresponds to the facts, it is true; if not, it is false. Not so in the case of thinking participants. There is a two-way connection. On the one hand, participants seek to understand the situation in which they participate. They seek to form a picture that corresponds to reality. I call this the passive or *cognitive function*. On the other hand, they seek to make an impact, to mold reality to their desires. I call this the active or *participating function*. When both functions are at work at the same time, I call the situation reflexive. I use the word in the same way as the French do when they describe a verb as reflexive when it has its subject as its object: *Je me lave* (I wash myself).

When both functions are at work at the same time, they may interfere with each other. Through the participating function, people may influence the situation that is supposed to serve as an independent variable for the cognitive function. Consequently, the participants' understanding cannot qualify as objective knowledge. And because their decisions are not based on objective knowledge, the outcome is liable to diverge from their expectations.

There are vast areas where our thoughts and reality are independent of each other and keeping them separate poses no problem. But there is an area of overlap where the cognitive and participating functions can interfere with each other and when they do our understanding is rendered imperfect and the outcome uncertain.

When we think about events in the outside world, the passage of time can provide some degree of insulation between thought and reality. Our present thoughts can influence future events, but future events cannot influence present thinking; only at a future date will those events be converted into an experience that may change the participants' thinking. But this insulation is not fool proof, because of the role of expectations. Our expectations about future events do not wait for the events themselves; they may change at any time, altering the outcome. That is what happens in financial markets all the time. The essence of investment is to anticipate or "discount" the future. But the price investors are willing to pay for a stock (or currency or commodity) today may influence the fortunes of the company (or currency or commodity) concerned in a variety of ways. Thus changes in current expectations affect the future they discount. This reflexive relationship in financial markets is so important that I deal with it later at much greater length. But reflexivity is not confined to financial markets; it is present in every historical process. Indeed, it is reflexivity that makes a process truly historical.

Not all social actions qualify as reflexive. We may distinguish between humdrum, everyday events and historical occasions. In everyday events, only one of the two reflexive functions is at work; either the cognitive or the participating function remains idle. For instance, when you register to vote in a local election, you do not alter your views about the nature of democracy; when you read in the newspaper about a rigged election in Nigeria, your changed perception does not affect what is actually going on in that part of the world, unless you are an oil executive or a human rights activist engaged in Nigeria. But there are occasions when the cognitive and participating functions operate simultaneously so that neither the participants' views nor the situation to which they relate remain the same as before. That is what justifies describing such developments as historic.

A truly historic event does not just change the world; it changes our understanding of the world—and that new understanding, in turn, has a new and unpredictable impact on how the world works. The French Revolution was such an event. The distinction between humdrum and historic events is, of course, tautological, but tautologies can be illuminating. Party congresses in the Soviet Union were rather humdrum, predictable affairs, but Khrushchev's speech to the Twentieth Congress was a historic occasion. It changed people's perceptions and, even if the communist regime did not change immediately, the speech had unpredictable consequences: The outlook of the people who were in the forefront of Gorbachev's glasnost was shaped in their youth by Khrushchev's revelations.

Of course, people think not only about the outside world but also about themselves and about other people. Here the cognitive and participation functions may interfere with each other without any lapse of time. Consider statements like "I love you" or "He is my enemy." They are bound to affect the person to which they refer, depending on how they are communicated. Or look at marriage. It has two thinking participants, but their thinking is not directed at a reality that is separate and independent of what they think and feel. One partner's thoughts and feelings affect the behavior of the other and vice versa. Both feelings and behavior can change out of all recognition as the marriage evolves.

If the passage of time can insulate the cognitive and participating functions, reflexivity can be envisaged as a kind of short circuit between thinking and its subject matter. When it occurs, it affects the participants' thinking directly, but the outside world only indirectly. The effect of reflexivity in shaping the participants' self-images, their values, and their expectations is much more pervasive and instantaneous than its effect on the course of events. It is only intermittently, in special cases, that a reflexive interaction significantly affects not only the participants' views but also the outside world. These occasions take on special significance because they demonstrate the importance of reflexivity as a real-world phenomenon. By contrast, the endemic uncertainty in people's values and self-images is primarily subjective.

Indeterminacy

The next step in analyzing the impact of reflexivity on social and economic phenomena is to point out that the element of indeterminacy I speak about is not produced by reflexivity on its own; reflexivity must be accompanied by imperfect understanding on the part of the participants. If by some fluke people were endowed with

9

perfect knowledge, the two-way interaction between their thoughts and the outside world could be ignored. Because the true state of the world was perfectly reflected in their views, the outcome of their actions would perfectly correspond to their expectations. Indeterminacy would be eliminated, as it derives from the feedback between inaccurate expectations and the unintended consequences of people's perhaps changing but always biased expectations.

The contention that situations that have thinking participants contain an element of indeterminacy is amply supported by everyday observation. Yet it is not a conclusion that has been generally accepted in economics or social science. Indeed, it has rarely even been proposed in the direct form in which I have put it here. On the contrary, the idea of indeterminacy has been vehemently denied by social scientists who assert their ability to explain events by scientific method. Marx and Freud are prominent examples, but the founders of classical economic theory have also gone out of their way to exclude reflexivity from their field of study, despite its importance for financial markets. It is easy to see why. Indeterminacy, the lack of firm predictions and satisfactory explanations, can be threatening to the professional status of a science.

The concept of reflexivity is so basic that it would be hard to believe that I was the first to discover it. The fact is, I am not. Reflexivity is merely a new label for the two-way interaction between thinking and reality that is deeply ingrained in our common sense. If we look outside the realm of social science, we find a widespread awareness of reflexivity. The predictions of the Delphic oracle were reflexive and so was Greek drama. Even in social science, there are occasional acknowledgments: Machiavelli introduced an element of indeterminacy into his analysis and called it fate; Robert K. Merton drew attention to self-fulfilling prophesies and the bandwagon effect; and a concept akin to reflexivity was introduced into sociology by Alfred Schutz under the name of intersubjectivity.

I do not want people to think that I am discussing some mysterious new phenomenon. Yes, there are some aspects of human affairs that have not been properly accounted for, but that is not because reflexivity has only just been discovered; it is because the social sciences in general and economics in particular have gone out of their way to cover it up.

Reflexivity in the History of Ideas

Let me try to position the concept of reflexivity in the history of ideas. The fact that statements may affect the subject matter to which they refer was first established by Epimenides the Cretan when he posed the paradox of the liar. Cretans always lie, he said, and by saying it he brought into question the truth of his statement. Being a Cretan, if the meaning of what he said was true, then his statement had to be false; conversely, if his statement was true, then the meaning it conveyed would have to be false.

The paradox of the liar was treated as an intellectual curiosity and neglected for the longest time because it interfered with the otherwise successful pursuit of truth. Truth came to be recognized as the correspondence of statements to external facts. The so-called correspondence theory of truth came to be generally accepted at the beginning of the twentieth century. That was a time when the study of facts yielded impressive results and the achievements of science enjoyed widespread admiration.

Emboldened by the success of science, Bertrand Russell tackled the paradox of the liar head on. His solution was to distinguish between two classes of statements: a class that included statements that referred to themselves and a class that excluded such statements. Only statements belonging to the latter class could be considered well-formed statements with a determinate truth value. In the case of self-referent statements, it may not be possible to distinguish whether they are true or false. Logical positivists carried Bertrand Russell's argument further and declared that statements whose truth value cannot be determined are meaningless. Remember, that was the time when science was providing determinate explanations for an ever-expanding range of phenomena, while philosophy had become ever more removed from reality. Logical positivism was a dogma that exalted scientific knowledge as the sole form of understanding worthy of the name and outlawed metaphysics. "Those who have understood my argument," to paraphrase Ludwig Wittgenstein in the conclusion of his *Tractatus Logico Philosophicus*, "must realize that everything I have said in the book is meaningless." It seemed to be the end of the road for metaphysical speculations and the total victory of the fact-based, deterministic knowledge that characterized science.

Soon thereafter Wittgenstein realized that his judgment had been too severe and he started to study the everyday use of language. Even natural science became less deterministic. It encountered boundaries beyond which observations could not be kept apart from their subject matter. Scientists managed to penetrate the barrier, first with Einstein's theory of relativity, then with Heisenberg's uncertainty principle. More recently, investigators using evolutionary systems theory, also known as chaos theory, started exploring complex phenomena whose course cannot be determined by timelessly valid laws. Events follow an irreversible path in which even slight variances become magnified with the passage of time. Chaos theory has been able to shed light on many phenomena, such as the weather, that had previously proved impervious to scientific treatment, and it has made the idea of an indeterminate universe, where events follow a unique, irreversible path, more acceptable.

It so happens that I started to apply the concept of reflexivity to understanding finance, politics, and economics in the early 1960s, before evolutionary systems theory was born. I arrived at it, with the help of Karl Popper's writings, through the concept of self-reference. The two concepts are closely related but they should not be confused. Self-reference is a property of statements; it belongs entirely in the realm of thinking. Reflexivity connects thinking with reality; it belongs to both realms. Perhaps that is why it was ignored for such a long time.

What reflexivity and self-reference have in common is the element of indeterminacy. Logical positivism outlawed self-referent statements as meaningless, but by introducing the concept of reflexivity I am setting logical positivism on its head. Far from being meaningless, I claim that statements whose truth value is indeterminate are *even more* significant than statements whose truth value is known. The latter constitute knowledge: They help us understand the world as it is. But the former, expressions of our inherently imperfect understanding, help to shape the world in which we live.

At the time I reached this conclusion, I considered it a great insight. Now that natural science no longer insists on a deterministic interpretation of all phenomena and logical positivism has faded into the background, I feel as if I were beating a dead horse. Indeed, intellectual fashion has turned to the opposite extreme: The deconstruction of reality into the subjective views and prejudices of the participants has become all the rage. The very basis on which differing views can be judged, namely the truth, is being questioned. I consider this other extreme equally misguided. Reflexivity should lead to a reassessment, not a total rejection, of our concept of truth.

A Reflexive Concept of Truth

Logical positivism classified statements as true, false, or meaningless. After dismissing meaningless statements, it was left with two categories: true or false. The scheme is eminently suitable to a universe that is separate and independent of the statements that refer to it, but it is quite inadequate for understanding the world of thinking agents. Here we need to recognize an additional category: reflexive statements whose truth value is contingent on the impact they make.

It was always possible to attack the logical positivist position at the margin by conjuring up certain statements whose truth value could be disputed; for instance, "The present King of France is bald." But such statements are either nonsensical or contrived; either way, we can live without them. By contrast, reflexive statements are indispensable. We cannot live without reflexive statements because we cannot avoid decisions that have a bearing on our fate; and we cannot reach decisions without relying on ideas and theories that can affect the subject matter to which they refer. To ignore such statements or to force them into the categories of "true" and "false" pushes the discourse in a misleading direction and places our interpretation of human relations and history in the wrong framework.

All value statements are reflexive in character: "Blessed are the poor, for theirs is the kingdom of heaven"—if this statement is believed, then the poor may indeed be blessed, but they will be less motivated to get themselves out of their misery. By the same token, if the poor are held to be guilty of their own misery, then they are less likely to lead blessed lives. Most generalizations about history and society are similarly reflexive in character; consider, "The proletarians of the world have nothing to lose but their chains" or "The common interest is best served by allowing people to pursue their own interests." It may be appropriate to assert that such statements have no truth value but it would be misleading (and has historically been very dangerous) to treat them as meaningless. They affect the situation to which they refer.

I am not claiming that a third category of truth is indispensable for dealing with reflexive phenomena. The crucial point is that in reflexive situations *the facts do not necessarily provide an independent criterion of truth*. We have come to treat correspondence as the hallmark of truth. But correspondence can be brought about in two ways: either by making true statements or by making an impact on the facts themselves. Correspondence is not the guarantor of truth. This caveat applies to most political pronouncements and economic forecasts.

I hardly need to emphasize the profound significance of this proposition. Nothing is more fundamental to our thinking than our concept of truth. We are accustomed to thinking about situations that have thinking participants in the same way as we do about natural phenomena. But if there is a third category of truth, we must thoroughly revise the way we think about the world of human and social affairs.

I should like to give a minor illustration from the field of international finance. The IMF has come under increasing pressure to operate in a more transparent manner and to disclose its internal deliberations and views on individual countries. These demands ignore the reflexive nature of these statements. If the IMF disclosed its concerns about certain countries, they would affect the countries to which they refer. Recognizing this, IMF officials would be inhibited from expressing their true opinions and internal debate would be stifled. If truth is reflexive, the search for the truth sometimes requires privacy.

An Interactive View of Reality

We may be justified in drawing a distinction between statements and facts, our thoughts and reality, but we must recognize that this distinction has been introduced *by us* in an attempt to make sense of the world in which we live. Our thinking belongs in the same universe that we are thinking about. This makes the task of making sense of reality (i.e., reason) much more complicated than it would be if thinking and reality could be neatly separated into watertight compartments (as they can be in natural science). Instead of separate categories, we must treat thinking as part of reality. This gives rise to innumerable difficulties, of which I should like to discuss only one.

It is impossible to form a picture of the world in which we live without distortion. In a literal sense, when we form a visual image of the world we have a blind spot where our optic nerve is attached to the nerve stem. The image made in our brain replicates the outside world remarkably well, and we can even fill in the blind spot by extrapolating from the rest of the picture, though we cannot actually see what is in the area covered by the blind spot. This may be taken as a metaphor for the problem we confront. But the fact that I rely on a metaphor to explain the problem is an even more powerful metaphor.

The world in which we live is extremely complicated. To form a view of the world that can serve as a basis for decisions, we must simplify. Using generalizations, metaphors, analogies, comparisons, dichotomies, and other mental constructs serves to introduce some order into an otherwise confusing universe. But every mental construct distorts to some extent what it represents and every distortion adds something to the world that we need to understand. The more we think, the more we have to think about.* This is because reality is not given. It is formed in the same process as the

---

*This point was brought home to me by Kurt Gödel. He proved mathematically that there are always more laws in mathematics than the ones that can be proved mathematically. The technique he used was to denote the laws of mathematics by so-called Gödel numbers. By adding the laws to the universe to which they relate, namely, the laws of mathematics, Gödel has been able to prove not only that the number of laws is infinite but also that it exceeds the number of laws that can be known because there are laws about laws about laws ad infinitum, and what is to be known expands in step with our knowledge.

The same line of reasoning could be applied to situations that have thinking participants. To understand such situations, we need to construct a model that contains the views of all the participants. These views also constitute a model that must contain the views of all the participants. So we need a model of model builders whose models incorporate the models of model builders and so on, ad infinitum. The more levels the models recognize, the more levels there are to be recognized—and if the models fail to recognize them, as they must sooner or later, they no longer reproduce reality. If I had Gödel's mathematical skills, I ought to be able to prove along these lines that participants' views cannot correspond to reality.

16

participants' thinking: The more complex the thinking, the more complicated reality becomes. Thinking can never quite catch up with reality: Reality is always richer than our comprehension. Reality has the power to surprise thinking, and thinking has the power to create reality.

That said, I have little sympathy with those who seek to deconstruct reality. Reality is unique and uniquely important. It cannot be reduced or broken down to the views and beliefs of the participants because there is a *lack of correspondence* between what people think and what actually happens. This lack of correspondence stands in the way of reducing events to the participants' views just as it thwarts the prediction of events on the basis of universally valid generalizations. There *is* a reality, even if it is unpredictable and unexplainable. This may be difficult to accept but it is futile or downright dangerous to deny it, as any participant in the financial markets who has tried it can testify. Markets rarely gratify people's subjective expectations; yet their verdict is real enough to cause anguish and loss—and there is no appeal. Reality exists. But the fact that reality incorporates inherently imperfect human thinking makes it logically impossible to explain and predict.

As a child, I lived in a house that had an elevator with two mirrors facing each other. Every day I looked into the mirrors and I saw myself reproduced. It seemed like infinity, but it was not. This experience made a lasting impression on me. The view of the world confronting thinking participants is very much like what I saw in those elevator mirrors. Thinking participants must impose some interpretative patterns on what they see. The reflexive process would never end if they did not end it deliberately. The most effec-

---

It has been pointed out to me by William Newton-Smith that my interpretation of Gödel numbers differs from Gödel's own. Apparently, Gödel envisaged a platonic universe in which Gödel numbers existed before he discovered them, whereas I think that Gödel numbers were invented by him, thereby enlarging the universe in which he was operating. I think my interpretation makes more sense. It certainly makes Gödel's theorem more relevant to the thinking participant's predicament.

tive way to bring closure is to settle on a pattern and emphasize it until the actual picture recedes into the background. The pattern that emerges may be far removed from the underlying sensory perception but it has the great attraction of being understandable and clear. That is why religions and dogmatic political ideologies have so much appeal.

This is not the place to discuss the many ways in which thinking both distorts reality and alters it. The way I have tried to make some sense out of a complex and confusing reality is by recognizing my own fallibility. I have been practicing a critical attitude based on that insight most of my life—certainly since I read Popper—and this has been absolutely fundamental to my professional success in financial markets. It has only recently dawned on me how unusual this critical attitude is. It has surprised me that other people were surprised by my way of thinking. If this book has something original to say, it is on this subject.

Two Versions of Fallibility

I offer two versions of fallibility: first, a more moderate, better substantiated "official" version that accompanies the concept of reflexivity and justifies a critical mode of thinking and an open society; and, second, a more radical, idiosyncratic version that has actually guided me through life.

The public, moderate version has already been discussed. Fallibility means that there is a lack of correspondence between the participants' thinking and the actual state of affairs; as a result actions have unintended consequences. Events do not necessarily diverge from expectations, but they are liable to do so. There are many humdrum, everyday events that play out exactly as expected, but those events that show a divergence are more interesting. They may alter people's view of the world and set in motion a reflexive process as a result of which neither the participants' views nor the actual state of affairs remains unaffected.

Fallibility has a negative sound, but it has a positive aspect that can be very inspiring. What is imperfect can be improved. The fact that our understanding is inherently imperfect makes it possible to learn and to improve our understanding. All that is needed is to recognize our fallibility. That opens the way to critical thinking and there is no limit to how far our understanding of reality may go. There is infinite scope for improvement not only in our thinking but also in our society. Perfection eludes us; whatever design we choose, it is bound to be defective. We must therefore content ourselves with the next best thing—a form of social organization that falls short of perfection but is open to improvement. That is the concept of the open society: a society open to improvement. The concept rests on the recognition of our fallibility. I explore it further later on, but first I want to introduce a more radical, idiosyncratic version of fallibility.

Radical Fallibility

At this point, I shall change my tack. Instead of discussing fallibility in general terms, I shall try to explain what it means to me personally. It is the cornerstone not only of my view of the world but also of my behavior. It is the foundation of my theory of history and it has guided me in my actions both as a participant in the financial markets and as a philanthropist. If there is anything original in my thinking, it is my radical version of fallibility.

I take a more stringent view of fallibility than the one I could justify by the arguments I have presented so far. I contend that all constructs of the human mind, whether they are confined to the inner recesses of our thinking or find expression in the outside world in the form of disciplines, ideologies, or institutions, are deficient in some way or another. The flaw may manifest itself in the form of internal inconsistencies or inconsistencies with the external world or inconsistencies with the purpose that our ideas were designed to serve.

This proposition is, of course, much stronger than the recognition that all our constructs *may* be wrong. I am not speaking of a mere lack of correspondence but of an actual flaw in all human constructs and an actual divergence between outcomes and expectations. As I explained earlier, the divergence really matters only in historic events. That is why the radical version of fallibility can serve as the basis for a theory of history.

The contention that all human constructs are flawed sounds very bleak and pessimistic, but it is no cause for despair. Fallibility sounds so negative only because we cherish false hopes. We yearn for perfection, permanence, and the ultimate truth, with immortality thrown in for good measure. Judged by those standards, the human condition is bound to be unsatisfactory. In fact, perfection and immortality elude us and permanence can only be found in death. But life gives us a chance to improve our understanding exactly because it is imperfect and also to improve the world. When all constructs are deficient, the variations become all important. Some constructs are better than others. Perfection is unattainable but what is inherently imperfect is capable of infinite improvement.

For good order's sake, I note that my claim that all human and social constructs are deficient does not qualify as a scientific hypothesis because it cannot be properly tested. I can claim that the participants' views always diverge from reality but I cannot prove it because we cannot know what reality would be in the absence of our views. I can wait for events to show a divergence from expectations, but, as I have indicated, subsequent events do not serve as an independent criterion for deciding what the correct expectations would have been because different expectations could have led to a different course of events. Similarly, I can claim that all human constructs are flawed but I cannot demonstrate what the flaw is. The flaws usually manifest themselves at some future date, but that is no evidence that they were present at the time the constructs were formed. The shortcomings of dominant ideas and institutional arrangements become apparent only with the passage of time, and the concept of reflexivity justifies only the claim that all human constructs are *potentially* flawed. That is why I present my proposition as a working hypothesis, without logical proof or scientific status.

I call it a working hypothesis because it has worked well both in my financial activities and in my involvement in philanthropy and international affairs. It has encouraged me to look for the flaws in every situation and, when I found them, to benefit from the insight. On the subjective level, I recognized that my interpretation was bound to be distorted. This did not discourage me from having a view; on the contrary, I sought out situations where my interpretation was at variance with the prevailing wisdom. But I was always on the lookout for my error; when I discovered it, I grasped it with alacrity. In my financial dealings, the discovery of error would often present an opportunity to take whatever profits I had made from my flawed initial insight—or to cut my losses if the insight had not yielded even a temporarily profitable result. Most people are reluctant to admit that they are wrong; it gave me positive pleasure to discover a mistake because I knew it could save me from financial grief.

On the objective level, I recognized that the companies or industries in which I invested were bound to be flawed and I preferred to know what the flaws were. This did not stop me from investing; on the contrary, I felt much safer when I knew the potential danger points because that told me what signs to look for to sell my investment. No investment can offer superior returns indefinitely. Even if a company has superior market position, outstanding management, and exceptional profit margins, the stock may become overvalued, management may become complacent, and the competitive or regulatory environment may change. It is wise to be constantly looking for the fly in the ointment. When you know what it is, you are ahead of the game.

I developed my own variant of Popper's model of scientific method for use in financial markets. I would formulate a hypothesis on the basis of which I would invest. The hypothesis had to differ from the accepted wisdom and the bigger the difference the greater the profit potential. If there was no difference, there was no point in taking a position. This corresponded to Popper's contention—much criticized by philosophers of science—that the more severe the test, the more valuable the hypothesis that survives it. In science, the value of a hypothesis is intangible; in financial markets it can be readily measured by the profit it yields. In contrast to science, a financial hypothesis does not have to be true to be profitable; it is enough that it should come to be generally accepted. But a false hypothesis cannot prevail forever. That is why I liked to invest in flawed hypotheses that had a chance of becoming generally accepted, provided I knew what the flaw was: It allowed me to sell in time. I called my flawed hypotheses fertile fallacies and I built my theory of history, as well as my success in financial markets, around them.

My working hypothesis—that all human constructs are always flawed—is not only unscientific but it has a more radical defect: *It is probably not true.* Every construct develops a defect with the passage of time, but this does not mean that it was inappropriate or ineffective at the time it was constructed. I think it is possible to refine my working hypothesis and cast it in a form that can lay a stronger claim to be true. For this purpose, I must appeal to my theory of reflexivity. In a reflexive process, neither the participants' thinking nor the actual state of affairs remains unaffected. Therefore even if a decision or interpretation was correct at the beginning of the process, it is bound to be inappropriate at a later stage. So I must add an important proviso to the claim that all human constructs are flawed: It is true only if we expect theories or policies to be timelessly valid like the laws of science.

Constructs, like actions, have unintended consequences and those consequences cannot be properly anticipated at the time of their creation. Even if the consequences could be anticipated, it might still be appropriate to proceed because those consequences would arise only in the future. So my working hypothesis is not incompatible with the idea that one course of action is better than another, that there is indeed an optimum course of action. It does imply, however, that the optimum applies only to a particular moment of history and what is optimum at one point may cease to be so at the next. This is a difficult concept to work with, particularly for institutions that cannot avoid some degree of inertia. The longer any form of taxation is in effect, the more likely it is that it will be evaded; that may be a good reason for changing the form of taxation after a while, but not a good reason for having no taxation. To take an example from a different field, the Catholic Church has evolved into something quite different from what Jesus intended, but that is not sufficient ground for dismissing his teachings.

In other words, theories or policies may be temporarily valid at a certain point in history. It is to bring this point home that I call them *fertile fallacies:* flawed constructs with initially beneficial effects. How long the beneficial effects last depends on whether the flaws are recognized and corrected. In this way, constructs may become increasingly sophisticated. But no fertile fallacy is likely to last forever; eventually the scope for refining it and developing it will be exhausted and a new fertile fallacy captures people's imagination. What I am about to say may be a fertile fallacy, but I am inclined to interpret the history of ideas as composed of fertile fallacies. Other people may call them paradigms.

The combination of these two ideas—that all mental constructs are flawed but some of them are fertile—lies at the core of my own, radical version of fallibility. I apply it to the outside world and to my own activities with equal vigor and it has served me well both as a fund manager and more recently as a philanthropist. Whether it will also serve me well as a thinker is being tested right now, for this radical version of fallibility serves as the foundation for the theory of history and the interpretation of financial markets that I lay out in the rest of this book.

A Personal Postscript

My radical version of fallibility is not only an abstract theory but also a personal statement. As a fund manager, I depended a great deal on my emotions. That was because I was aware of the inadequacy of knowledge. The predominant feelings I operated with were doubt, uncertainty, and fear. I had moments of hope or even euphoria, but they made me feel insecure. By contrast, worrying made me feel safe. So the only genuine joy I experienced was when I discovered what I had to worry about. By and large, I found managing a hedge fund* extremely painful. I could never acknowledge my success, because that might stop me from worrying, but I had no trouble recognizing my mistakes.

Only when others pointed it out to me did I realize that there may be something unusual in my attitude to mistakes. It made so much sense to me that discovering an error in my thinking or in my position should be a source of joy rather than regret that I thought that it ought to make sense to others as well. But that is not the case. When I looked around, I found that most people go to great lengths to deny or cover up their mistakes. Indeed, their misconceptions and misdeeds become an integral part of their personality. I will never forget an experience I had when I visited Argentina in 1982 to look at the mountain of debt that country had accumulated. I sought out a number of politicians who had served in previous governments and asked them how they would handle the situation.

---

*Hedge funds engage in a wide variety of investment activities. They cater to sophisticated investors and are not subject to the regulations that apply to mutual funds. The managers are compensated on the basis of performance rather than as a fixed percentage of assets. Performance funds would be a more accurate description.

To a man, they said they would apply the same policies they followed when they were in government. Rarely had I met so many people who learned so little from experience.

I carried my critical attitude into my philanthropic activities. I found philanthropy riddled with paradoxes and unintended consequences. For instance, charity may turn the recipients into objects of charity. Giving is supposed to help others, but in reality it often serves for the ego gratification of the giver. What is worse, people frequently engage in philanthropy because they want to feel good, not because they want to do good.

Holding these views, I had to take a different approach. I found myself behaving not very differently from the way I behave in business. For instance, I subordinated the interests of the foundation personnel and of the individual applicants to the mission of the foundation. I used to joke that ours is the only misanthropic foundation in the world. I remember explaining at a staff meeting in Karlovi Vari, Czechoslovakia, around 1991, my views about foundations, and I am sure that those who were there will never forget it. I said that foundations are hothouses of corruption and inefficiency and I would consider it a greater accomplishment to wind up a foundation that failed than to set up a new one. I also remember telling a gathering in Prague of staff members from European foundations that networking means not working.

I must confess that I have mellowed with the passage of time. There is a difference between running a hedge fund and a foundation. The external pressures are largely absent and it is only internal discipline that keeps a critical attitude alive. Moreover, heading a large foundation requires people skills and leadership qualities and people do not like critical remarks—they want praise and encouragement. Not many people share my predilection for identifying error and even fewer share my joy in it. To be an effective leader, one has to gratify people. I am learning the hard way what seems to come naturally to politicians and heads of corporations.

There is another influence as well. I have to make some public appearances, and when I do I am expected to exude self-confidence. In reality I am consumed by self-doubt and I cherish the feeling. I would hate to lose it. There is a wide gap between my public persona and what I consider my real self, but I am aware of a reflexive connection between the two. I have been watching with amazement how the development of a public persona has affected me. I have become a "charismatic" personality. Fortunately I do not quite believe in myself as others do. I try to remember my limitations even if I do not feel them as acutely as I used to. But other charismatic personalities have not arrived at their leadership position following the same route as I did. They do not have the same memories. They probably remember that they always tried to get others to believe in them and eventually they succeeded. They are not consumed by self-doubt and they do not need to repress the urge to express it. No wonder that their attitude to fallibility is different.

It is fascinating to consider how my current "charismatic" personality relates to the financial markets and to my previous self as a fund manager. It qualifies me to make deals or even to manipulate markets but disqualifies me from managing money. My utterances can move markets, although I make great efforts not to abuse that power. At the same time, I have lost the ability to operate within the confines of the market as I used to. I have dismantled the mechanism of pain and anxiety that used to guide me. This is a long story, which I recounted elsewhere. The change happened long before I acquired my "charisma." When I was an active fund manager, I used to shun publicity. I considered it the kiss of death to be on the cover of a financial magazine. This amounted to a superstition, but it was well supported by the evidence. It is easy to see why. The publicity would engender a feeling of euphoria and, even if I fought it, it would throw me off my stride. And if I expressed a market view in public, I found it more difficult to change my mind.

It can be seen that operating in the financial markets requires a different mind-set from that required for operating in a social, political, or organizational setting or, indeed, for acting like a normal human being. This is also borne out by the evidence. There is considerable tension in most financial institutions between profit producers and the managers of the organization, or at least there used to be when I was familiar with these institutions, and the most gifted producers often preferred to go out on their own. That was the genesis of the hedge fund industry.

The radical version of fallibility I have adopted as a working hypothesis certainly proved effective in the financial markets. It has outperformed the random walk hypothesis* by a convincing margin. Does it also apply to other aspects of human existence? That depends on what our goal is. If we want to understand reality, I believe it is helpful; but if our aim is to manipulate reality, it does not work so well—charisma works better.

Coming back to my personal feelings, I have learned to adjust to the new reality in which I am operating. I used to find public expressions of praise and gratitude positively painful, but I have come to realize that this is a reflex left over from the days when I was actively managing money and I had to be guided by the results of my actions, not by what other people thought of them. I am still embarrassed by gratitude and I still believe that philanthropy, if it is deserving of praise, should put the interests of society ahead of ego gratification, but I am willing to accept praise because my philanthropy has in fact met this condition. Whether it can continue to do so in the light of my changed attitude toward praise is a question that troubles me, but as long as I am troubled the answer will probably remain in the affirmative.

---

*Rational expectations theory maintains that in an efficient market individual guesses deviate from the actual course of prices in a random manner.

CHAPTER 2

A Critique of Economics

There is a prevailing belief that economic affairs are subject to irresistible natural laws comparable to the laws of physics. This belief is false. What is more important, decisions and structures that are based on this belief are destabilizing economically and dangerous from a political point of view. I am convinced that the market system, like every other human arrangement, is inherently flawed. This conviction lies at the foundation of this book's entire analysis, as well as of my personal philosophy and of my funds' financial success. Because this critical view about economics and other social arrangements is so fundamental to everything else in this book, I must now apply the general discussion of reflexivity in Chapter 1 to explain why all theories about economic, political, and financial arrangements are qualitatively different from the laws of natural science. Only when it is acknowledged that social constructs in general and financial markets in particular are inherently unpredictable can the arguments in the rest of this book be understood.

Everyone realizes that economic analysis does not have the same universal validity as the physical sciences. But the most important reason for the failure of economic analysis—and for the inevitable instability of all social and political institutions that assume the absolute validity of market economics—is not properly understood. The failures of economics are not simply due to our imperfect understanding of economic theory or to a lack of adequate statistics. These problems could in principle be remedied by better research. But economic analysis, and the free-market ideology that it supports, are subverted by a far more fundamental and irredeemable flaw. Economic and social events, unlike the events that preoccupy physicists and chemists, involve thinking participants. And thinking participants can change the rules of economic and social systems by virtue of their own ideas about these rules. The claims of economic theory to universal validity become untenable once this principle is properly understood. This is not just an intellectual curiosity. For if economic forces are not irresistible and if economic theories are not scientifically valid—and never can be—the entire ideology of market fundamentalism is undermined.

Reflexivity poses two distinct but interrelated problems for economics and all other social sciences. One relates to the subject matter, the other to the scientific observer. I deal first with reflexivity as it affects the subject matter and then with its impact on the scientific observer. We shall see that the first problem is serious for the conventional view about economic theory and the second is fatal.

Reflexivity in Social Phenomena

For the purposes of this discussion, I invoke Karl Popper's theory of scientific method. Popper's simple and elegant model con-

tains three components and three operations. The three components are specific initial conditions and specific final conditions in a
scientific experiment and generalizations of a hypothetical character. The initial and final conditions can be verified by direct observation; the hypothesis cannot be verified, it can only be falsified.
The three basic scientific operations are prediction, explanation,
and testing. A hypothetical generalization can be combined with
initial conditions to provide a specific prediction. It can be combined with specific final conditions to provide an explanation. The
hypothesis is assumed to be timelessly valid, and this allows testing.
Testing involves comparing specific initial and final conditions to
establish whether they conform to the hypothesis. No amount of
testing will verify a hypothesis, but as long as a hypothesis has not
been falsified, it can be accepted as valid.

The asymmetry between verification and falsification is, in my
opinion, Popper's greatest contribution not only to the philosophy
of science but to our understanding of the world. It eliminates the
pitfalls of inductive argument. We do not need to insist that the sun
will *always* rise in the east just because it has done so every day; it is
enough if we accept the hypothesis provisionally, until it is falsified.
This is an elegant solution to what would be otherwise an insuperable logical problem. It allows unverifiable hypotheses to provide
determinate predictions and explanations.

It has perhaps not been sufficiently emphasized that hypotheses must
be timelessly valid to make testing possible. If a particular result cannot be replicated, the test cannot be considered conclusive. But
reflexivity gives rise to irreversible, historical processes and therefore
it does not lend itself to timelessly valid generalizations. More exact,
the generalizations that can be made about reflexive events cannot be
used for determinate predictions and explanations.* This contention

---

*It will be noted that the generalization I have just made is meant to be timelessly valid but
it cannot be used for explaining and predicting reflexive events in a deterministic fashion.
Therefore it is internally consistent.

does not invalidate Popper's model of scientific method in any way. The model remains as elegant and as close to perfection as before; it merely fails to apply to reflexive phenomena. The contention does, however, create a cleavage between the natural and the social sciences, because reflexivity occurs only when a situation has thinking participants.

It is, of course, dangerous to introduce hard-and-fast dividing lines into the understanding of reality. Am I falling into this error when I try to divide the humanities from the natural sciences? Social phenomena are not always reflexive. Even in those situations in which both the participating and the cognitive functions are at work, they do not necessarily set in motion a reflexive feedback mechanism that affects both the situation and the participants' thinking. And even if there is a feedback process at work, it may be possible to ignore it without greatly distorting reality. Applying the methods of the natural sciences to social phenomena can produce worthwhile results. That is what classical economic theory sought to do, and in many situations it works quite well.

Nevertheless there is a fundamental difference between the natural and social sciences that has not been sufficiently recognized. To understand it better, we must consider the second problem, scientific observers' relation to their subject matter.

Reflexivity and Social Scientists

Science is itself a social phenomenon and as such it is potentially reflexive. Scientists are linked to their subject matter both as participants and as observers, but the distinctive feature of scientific method, as exemplified in Popper's model, is that the two functions do not interfere with each other. The scientists' theories have no effect on their experiments. On the contrary, the experiments provide the facts by which scientific hypotheses can be judged.

31

As long as the separation between statements and facts remains watertight, there can be no doubt about the purpose of scientific activities: It is to acquire knowledge. The goals of individual participants may differ. Some may pursue knowledge for its own sake, others for the benefits it may bring, and yet others may seek personal advancement. Whatever the motivation, the yardstick of success is knowledge, and it is an objective criterion. Those who are seeking personal advancement can do so only by making true statements; if they falsify experiments they are liable to be found out. Those who are trying to bend nature to their will can do so only by acquiring knowledge first. Nature follows its course irrespective of any theories that relate to it; therefore we can make nature serve our needs only by understanding the laws that govern its behavior. There are no shortcuts.

It took a long time before this was recognized. For thousands of years, people have tried every form of magic, ritual, and wishful thinking to try to influence nature more directly; they were reluctant to accept the harsh discipline scientific method imposed. The conventions of science took a long time to prove their superiority, but eventually, as science continued to produce powerful discoveries, it attained a status that equaled that of magic and religion in earlier times. The agreement on purpose, the acceptance of certain conventions, the availability of an objective criterion, and the possibility of establishing timelessly valid generalizations combined to make science successful. It is recognized today as the crowning achievement of the human intellect.

This beautiful combination is disrupted when the subject matter is reflexive. For one thing, positive results are more difficult to attain, because the subject matter does not readily lend itself to the discovery of timelessly valid and therefore testable hypotheses that carry the authority of scientific laws. Looking at the evidence, we can see that the achievements of the social sciences do not compare well with those of the natural sciences. For another thing, the independence of the objective criterion, namely, the facts, is impaired. This renders the conventions of science difficult to enforce. Facts can be influenced by making statements about them. That is true not only for the participants but also for the scientists. Reflexivity implies a short circuit between statements and facts and that short circuit is available to scientists as well as participants.

This is an important point. Let me drive it home by comparing the indeterminacy involved in reflexivity with the indeterminacy observed in the behavior of quantum particles. The indeterminacy is similar but the relation of the observer to the subject matter is not. The behavior of quantum particles is the same whether Heisenberg's uncertainty principle is recognized or not. But the behavior of human beings can be influenced by scientific theories just as it can be influenced by other beliefs. For instance, the scope of the market economy has expanded because people believe in "the magic of the marketplace." In natural science, theories cannot change the phenomena to which they relate; in social science they can. This gives rise to an additional element of uncertainty, which is absent from Heisenberg's uncertainty principle. It is this additional element of uncertainty that is responsible for the cleavage between the natural and social sciences.

I admit that scientists could take special precautions to insulate their statements from their subject matter, for instance by keeping their predictions secret. But why should they? Is the purpose of science to acquire knowledge for its own sake or for some other benefits? In natural science, the question does not arise because the benefits can be realized only by first attaining knowledge. Not so in social science: Reflexivity offers a shortcut. A theory does not need to be true to affect people's behavior.

The classic example of pseudoscientific observers trying to impose their will on their subject matter was the attempt to convert base metal into gold. Alchemists struggled long and hard until they were finally persuaded to abandon their enterprise by their lack of success. Their failure was inevitable because the behavior of base metals is governed by laws of universal validity that cannot be modified by any statements, incantations, or rituals. The prestige accorded to modern economists, especially in politics and financial markets, shows that medieval alchemists were barking up the wrong tree. Base metals cannot be turned into gold by incantation, but people can get rich in financial markets and powerful in politics by propounding false theories or self-fulfilling prophecies. Moreover, their chances of success are increased if they can present themselves in scientific guise. It is noteworthy that both Marx and Freud were vocal in claiming their scientific status for their theories and based many of their conclusions on the authority they derived from being "scientific." Once this point sinks in, the very expression "social science" becomes suspect. It is often a magic phrase employed by social alchemists in their effort to impose their will on their subject matter by incantation.

Social scientists have in fact gone to great lengths to imitate the natural sciences but with remarkably little success. Their endeavors often yield little more than a parody of natural science. But there is a crucial difference between the failures of the social scientists and the failures of alchemists. Although the failure of the alchemists was well-nigh total, social scientists usurping the authority of natural science have managed to make a considerable social and political impact. The behavior of people, exactly because it is not governed by reality, is easily influenced by theories. In the field of natural phenomena, scientific method is effective only when theories are valid; but in social, political, and economic matters, theories can be effective without being valid. Although alchemy failed as science, social science can succeed as alchemy.

Karl Popper saw the danger of political ideologies exploiting the prestige of science to influence the course of history; the danger was particularly acute in the case of Marxism. To protect scientific method against this kind of abuse, he proclaimed that theories that cannot be falsified do not qualify as scientific. But even with the best will in the world, we cannot fit reflexive phenomena into the mold of Popper's model, and even theories designed to meet its requirements can be exploited for political purposes. For instance, economists have gone out of their way to avoid introducing value judgments, but because of that very fact their theories have been appropriated by the advocates of laissez faire and used as the basis for the most pervasive value judgment imaginable—that no better social outcomes than those available under market competition can ever be achieved.

There is a better way to protect scientific method. All we need do is to declare that the social sciences are not entitled to the status that we accord the natural sciences—and never can be, regardless of whatever breakthroughs might be claimed in social and statistical research. This would stop pseudoscientific social theories from parading with borrowed feathers; it would also discourage the slavish imitation of natural science in areas where that is not appropriate. It would not prevent attempts to establish universally valid laws governing human behavior, but it would help to scale down our expectations about the results. It could do more. It could allow us to come to terms with the limitations of our knowledge and liberate social science from the straitjacket into which it has been forced by its adherents' ambition to attain scientific status. That is what I advocated in my book *The Alchemy of Finance* when I called social science a false metaphor. Popper's model works with timelessly valid generalizations. Reflexivity is a time-bound, irreversible process—why should it fit Popper's model?

Recognizing the limitations of social science does not mean that we must give up the pursuit of truth in exploring social phenomena. It means only that the pursuit of truth requires us to recognize that some aspects of human behavior are not governed by timelessly valid laws. This should encourage us to explore other avenues to understanding. The pursuit of truth also forces us to recognize that social phenomena may be influenced by the theories put forward to explain them. As a consequence, the study of social phenomena may be motivated by objectives other than the pursuit of truth. The best way to guard against the abuse of scientific method is to recognize that social theories may affect the subject to which they relate.

A Critique of Economic Theory

Economic theory is the most far-reaching attempt to emulate the natural sciences and it has been by far the most successful. Classical economists were inspired by Newtonian physics. They aimed to establish universally valid laws that could be used both to explain and to predict economic behavior and hoped to achieve this goal by relying on the concept of equilibrium. The concept allowed economic analysis to focus on the ultimate outcome and to disregard temporary disturbances. A pendulum comes to rest at the same point however wide it swings; it is this "ergodic" principle that allowed economic theorists to establish timelessly valid rules about the equilibrating role of markets.

The concept of equilibrium is very useful, but it can also be very deceptive. It has the aura of something empirical. That is not the case. Equilibrium itself has rarely been observed in real life—market prices have a notorious habit of fluctuating. The process that can be observed is supposed to move toward equilibrium, but equilibrium may never be reached. It is true that market participants adjust to market prices, but they may be adjusting to a constantly moving target. In that case, calling the participants' behavior an adjustment process may be a misnomer.

Equilibrium is the product of an axiomatic system. Economic theory is constructed like logic or mathematics: It is based on certain postulates and all of its conclusions are derived from them by logical manipulation. The possibility that equilibrium is never reached need not invalidate the logical construction, but when a hypothetical equilibrium is presented as a model of reality a significant distortion is introduced. Euclidean geometry was and remains a perfectly valid axiomatic system, but it was amenable to false interpretations of reality, such as the belief that the earth was flat.

Equilibrium is not always a moving target. There are many humdrum situations in which the cognitive function is constant and the intersection of the demand and supply curves does determine the equilibrium point. But there are also numerous developments that are excluded from consideration by taking the demand and supply curves as given. The omission has been justified on methodological grounds: It is argued that economics is not concerned with either demand or supply on its own but only with the relationship between the two.* Behind this claim lies a hidden assumption, namely, that the price mechanism works only in one direction by passively reflecting the conditions of demand and supply. When sellers know how much they are willing to supply at each price and buyers know how much they are willing to buy, all that needs to happen to achieve equilibrium is for the market to find the unique price that matches demand and supply. But what if price movements themselves change the willingness of buyers and sellers to trade their goods at given prices, for example, because they expect the price to rise further in the near future? This possibility, which is the dominant fact of life in financial markets and also in industries with rapidly advancing technologies, is simply assumed away.

The assumption that demand and supply curves are independently given is needed to determine market prices. Without independently given demand and supply curves, prices would cease to be uniquely determined. Economists would be deprived of their ability to provide generalizations comparable to those of natural science. The idea that the conditions of supply and demand may be

*Lionel Robbins, *An Essay on the Nature and Significance of Economic Science* (London: Macmillan, 1969).

in some ways interdependent or dependent on market events may seem incongruous to those who have been reared on economic theory; yet that is exactly what the concept of reflexivity implies and the behavior of financial markets demonstrates.

The assumption of independently given conditions of supply and demand eliminates the possibility of any reflexive interaction. How significant is the omission? How important is reflexivity in the behavior of markets and economies? Let us look at the evidence. In *The Alchemy of Finance*, I identified and analyzed several cases of reflexivity that cannot be properly accounted for by equilibrium theory. In the case of the stock market, I focused on the phenomenon of equity leveraging. When a company or industry is overvalued, it can issue stock and use the proceeds to justify inflated expectations—up to a point. Conversely, when a fast-growing company is undervalued it may not be able to exploit the opportunities confronting it, thereby justifying the undervaluation—but, again, only up to a point. Based on these examples, I developed a boom/bust theory for the stock market, which has produced good results (and which I discuss in greater detail in the next chapter).

Looking at currency markets, I discerned the prevalence of vicious and virtuous circles in which exchange rates and the so-called fundamentals that they are supposed to reflect are interconnected in a self-reinforcing fashion, creating trends that sustain themselves for prolonged periods until they are eventually reversed. I identified a vicious circle for the dollar that culminated in 1980 and analyzed a virtuous circle that unfolded in the 1980–1985 period. I called it Reagan's imperial circle. Had I written the book later, I could have analyzed a similar imperial circle in Germany, touched off by German reunification in 1990. It unfolded differently because of its effect on the European Exchange Rate Mechanism: It led to the devaluation of sterling in 1992. The presence of such long-lasting, well-identifiable trends encourages trend-following speculation and the instability tends to be cumulative.

Studying the banking system and credit markets in general, I observed a reflexive connection between the act of lending and the value of the collateral that determines the creditworthiness of the borrower. This gives rise to an asymmetrical boom/bust pattern in which credit expansion and economic activity gather speed gradually and may come to an abrupt end. The reflexive connection and the asymmetrical pattern were clearly visible in the great international lending boom of the 1970s that culminated in the Mexican crisis of 1982. A similar process is unfolding in 1998 while I am writing these lines.

These examples should be sufficient to demonstrate the inadequacy of equilibrium theory and to justify the attempt to develop a general theory of reflexivity in which equilibrium becomes a special case. After all, a single sunspot experiment was sufficient to demonstrate the deficiency of Newtonian physics and to establish the credentials of Einstein's theory of relativity. But there is a big difference between Einstein's theory and mine. Einstein could predict a specific event—the Michelson-Morley experiment, which proved the invariance of the speed of light, or the perihelion of Mercury, which confirmed general relativity. I cannot predict anything except unpredictability. We must lower our expectations about our ability to explain and predict social and historical events before a theory of reflexivity becomes acceptable.

Before moving on, I want to clarify a couple of theoretical points.

First, about equilibrium. There are other factors besides reflexivity that can interfere with the tendency toward equilibrium. Innovation is one. Brian Arthur and others have developed the concept of increasing returns, which justifies increasing production beyond the classical equilibrium in the hopes that technological advances will push the costs of production steeply downward and thereby generate large profits from market dominance. This theory has undermined one of the most hallowed normative conclusions of economic theory, namely, the optimality of free trade.

Second, about reflexivity. Reflexivity manifests itself in changes in people's values and expectations. But it is not enough for those perceptions to vary; the perceptions must also have a significant effect on actual conditions or the variations could be dismissed as mere noise and the eventual equilibrium would remain the same. Generally speaking, I do not believe that any great violence is done to reality when microeconomic analysis leaves reflexivity out of account. One possible exception is advertising and marketing, which are intended to modify the demand curve rather than to satisfy an existing demand. But even these activities are not always reflexive in the sense in which I just defined the term and they do not prevent an equilibrium being established in which firms devote some resources to enhancing demand and some to satisfying it.

The situation is different when it comes to financial markets and macroeconomic issues. Expectations play an important role and the role they play is reflexive. Participants base their decisions on their expectations, and the future they are trying to anticipate is, in turn, dependent on the decisions they are taking today. Different decisions produce a different future. So the decisions do not relate to something independently given. This gives rise to an element of uncertainty both in the decisions and in their consequences. The uncertainty could, in theory, be eliminated by introducing the heroic assumption of perfect knowledge. But this postulate is untenable because it ignores the fact that people are free to make choices. Perfect knowledge of what? Of all the choices of all the participants? This is impossible when those choices relate to an outcome that is, in turn, dependent on the choices. So not only must the participants know what the eventual equilibrium is, they must also will it; and they must know that all the others know it and will it. This is a rather far-fetched set of assumptions, but it has been put forward in all seriousness.

We must recognize that perfect knowledge is unattainable and an element of uncertainty is unavoidable. Does that mean the concept of equilibrium is irrelevant to the real world? Not necessarily.

Something else has to happen to turn equilibrium into a moving target: Expectations must influence the future to which they relate. Moreover, the influence must be such as to bring about changes in those expectations that, in turn, alter the future. Such self-referring, self-affecting feedback mechanisms do not spring into action every time, but they occur often enough not to be ignored. They are endemic in financial markets where changes in present prices can change the future that present prices are supposed to discount. They are also characteristic of macroeconomic policy making, which is influenced by events in financial markets and, in turn, exerts its influence through the financial markets. Thus, to try to explain the behavior of financial markets and macroeconomic developments through equilibrium analysis seems misguided. Yet that is exactly what economic theory has attempted to do by attributing all manifestations of disequilibrium to so-called exogenous shocks. This endeavor reminds me of Ptolemy's efforts to explain the movement of heavenly bodies by drawing extra circles when the planets failed to follow their prescribed course.

In practice, both market practitioners and regulators are aware that equilibrium is an illusion. It is rare to find a field in which theory and practice are so far apart, leaving ample room for alchemy and other forms of magic. I know, because I have been endowed with the reputation of a magician, particularly in Asian countries, which would allow me to manipulate markets unless I deliberately avoid it. Federal Reserve Chairman Alan Greenspan's testimonies, particularly his warning on the "irrational exuberance of markets" invoked reflexivity in everything but name. The greatest practitioners of reflexive alchemy in the past were to be found in the Ministry of Finance in Japan; currently their bag of tricks is empty.

I have to confess that I am not familiar with the prevailing theories about efficient markets and rational expectations. I consider them irrelevant and I never bothered to study them because I seemed to get along quite well without them—which was perhaps just as well, judging by the recent collapse of Long-Term Capital Management, a hedge fund whose managers aimed to profit from the application of modern equilibrium theory and whose arbitrage strategies were inspired, in part, by the joint winners of the 1997 economics Nobel Prize—a prize they won for their theoretical work on options pricing. The fact that some successful participants in financial markets have found modern theories supposedly explaining how financial markets function completely useless may be considered a scathing criticism in itself but it does not quite amount to a formal demonstration of their inadequacy. The failure of Long-Term Capital Management is much more conclusive.

I regard the concept of equilibrium as very helpful in illuminating the deficiencies of the real world. We would not be able to construct a dynamic disequilibrium theory if the concept of equilibrium were not available as a foil. I have no quarrel with economics itself, as far as it goes, except that it does not go far enough. It leaves out of account the reflexive connections between market developments and the conditions of demand and supply.

To understand financial markets and macroeconomic developments we need a new paradigm. We need to supplement the concept of equilibrium with the concept of reflexivity. Reflexivity does not invalidate the conclusions of equilibrium theory as an axiomatic system, but it adds a dimension that equilibrium theory has left out of account. It is like combining plane geometry with the notion that the earth is round. Equilibrium theory is meant to provide timelessly valid generalizations. Reflexivity adds a historical dimension. The arrow of time introduces a historical process which may or may not tend toward equilibrium. This makes all the difference in the real world.

I shall put forward a reflexive, historical interpretation of financial markets in the next chapter; but first I want to complete my critique of economic theory by examining the question of values.

The Question of Values

Economic theory takes market participants' values and preferences as given. Under the guise of this methodological convention, it tacitly introduces certain assertions about values. The most important of these is that only market values should be taken into account; that is to say, only those considerations that enter into a market participant's mind when he or she decides what he or she is willing to pay another participant in free exchange. This assertion is justified when the objective is to determine the market price, but it ignores a wide range of individual and social values that do not find expression in market behavior. They ought not to be ignored in deciding issues other than the market price. How society should be organized; how people ought to live their lives—these questions ought not to be answered on the basis of market values.

Yet this is happening. The scope and influence of economic theory has expanded beyond the confines that the postulates of an axiomatic system ought to impose. Market fundamentalists have transformed an axiomatic, value-neutral theory into an ideology, which has influenced political and business behavior in a powerful and dangerous way. How market values penetrate into areas of society where they do not properly belong is one of the key questions I want to address in this book.

The values taken as given by economic theory always involve a choice between alternatives: So much of one thing can be equated to so much of another. The idea that some values may not be negotiable is not recognized or, more exactly, such values are excluded from the realm of economics. Generally speaking, only individual preferences are included, whereas collective needs are disregarded. This means that the entire social and political realm is left out of account. If the argument of market fundamentalists that the common interest is best served by the untrammeled pursuit of self-interest were valid, no great harm would be done; but the fact that the conclusion was reached by disregarding collective needs does beg the question.

Empirical studies in decision making have shown that even in matters of individual preference people's behavior does not conform to the requirements of economic theory. The evidence indicates that instead of being consistent and constant, people's preferences vary depending on how they frame their decision problems. For example, economic theory has assumed ever since Bernoulli (circa 1738) that economic agents evaluate the outcomes of their choices in terms of final states of wealth. In fact, agents generally frame outcomes as gains and losses relative to some reference point. Furthermore, these variations of framing can have a profound effect on decisions: Agents who frame their outcomes in terms of wealth will tend to be less averse to risk than agents who think in terms of losses.*

I go further. I contend that people behave differently depending on the frame of reference they employ. While there is some consistency in the choice of frames, it is far from dependable and there is often a noticeable discontinuity between different frames. I can speak from personal experience. I have often felt as if I had multiple personalities: one for business, one for social responsibility, and one (or more) for private use. Often the roles got confused, causing me no end of embarrassment. I have made a conscious effort to integrate the various aspects of my existence and I am happy to report that I have been successful. When I say that I am happy to report it, I really mean it: Integrating the various facets of my personality has been a source of great satisfaction to me. I must confess, however, that I could not have achieved it if I had remained an active participant in financial markets. Managing money requires a single-minded devotion to the cause of making money and all other considerations must be sub-

*Daniel Kahneman and Amos Tversky, "Prospect theory: An analysis of decision under risk," *Econometrica*, Vol. 47 (1979): 263–291.

ordinated to it. In contrast to other forms of employment, managing a hedge fund can produce losses as well as profits; you cannot afford to take your eye off of the ball. It is noteworthy that the values that guided me in my money-making activities did resemble the values postulated by economic theory: They involved a careful weighing of alternatives, they were cardinal rather than ordinal in character,* they were continuous and gradual, and they were single-mindedly directed at optimizing the ratio between risk and reward—including accepting higher risks at times when the ratio was favorable.

I am ready to generalize from my personal experience and admit that the values postulated by economic theory are, in fact, relevant to economic activities in general and the behavior of market participants in particular. The generalization is justified because market participants who do not abide by those values are liable to be eliminated or reduced to insignificance by the pressures of competition.

By the same token, economic activity represents only one facet of human existence. Undoubtedly it is very important, but there are other aspects that cannot be ignored. For present purposes, I distinguish between the economic, political, social, and individual spheres, but I do not want to attribute any great importance to these categories. It would be easy to introduce others. For instance, I could mention peer pressure, family influences, or public opinion; or I could distinguish between the sacred and the profane. The point I am trying to make is that economic behavior is only one kind of behavior and the values that economic theory takes as given are not the only kind of values that prevail in society. It is difficult to see how the values pertaining to these other spheres could be subjected to differential calculus like indifference curves.

How do economic values relate to other kinds of values? That is

---

*This is an important point. In contrast to most fund managers, who are concerned with relative performance, I was guided by and rewarded according to absolute performance. The pursuit of relative performance is a source of instability in financial markets that economic theory has failed to identify.

Bias is a difficult concept to work with. It cannot be properly measured, because we cannot know what an unbiased world would look like. Different people work with different biases but it is impossible to work without a bias. That holds true even in the limiting case when a participant anticipates the future accurately. Fortunately there is a norm in the outside world that provides an indication—but not a measurement—of the participants' bias, namely, the actual course of events. Although there is no reality independent of the participants' thinking, there is a reality that is dependent on it. In other words, there is a sequence of events that actually occurs and that sequence incorporates the impact of the participants' bias. The actual course of events is likely to differ from the participants' expectations and the divergence can be taken as an indication of the bias at play. Unfortunately it can be taken only as an indication—not the full measure of the bias—because the actual course of events already contains the effects of the participants' bias. A phenomenon that is partially observable and partially submerged in the course of events is of limited value as an instrument of scientific investigation. We can now appreciate why economists were so anxious to eliminate it from their universe. Nevertheless, I consider it the key to understanding financial markets.

The course of events that participants in financial markets seek to anticipate consists of market prices. These are readily observable but they do not, by themselves, reveal anything about the participants' bias. To identify the bias, we need some other variable that is not contaminated by the bias. The conventional interpretation of financial markets posits such a variable: It consists of the fundamentals that market prices are supposed to reflect. For the sake of simplicity, I shall stick to the stock market. Companies have balance sheets and earnings and they pay dividends. Market prices are supposed to express prevailing expectations about those fundamentals. I disagree with this interpretation, but it provides an excellent starting point for studying the participants' bias.

For purposes of this discussion, I define equilibrium as a correspondence between the participants' views and the fundamentals. I believe this accords with the concept as it is used in economic theory. The fundamentals that matter are in the future. It is not last year's earnings, balance sheets, and dividends that stock prices are supposed to reflect but the future stream of earnings, dividends, and asset values. That stream is not given; therefore it is not an object of knowledge but of guessing. The important point is that the future, when it occurs, will have been influenced by the guessing that has preceded it. The guessing finds expression in the stock prices and stock prices have ways of affecting the fundamentals. Similar arguments apply to currencies, credit, and commodities, as we shall see later. (For simplicity, I focus the initial discussion on the stock market.) A company can raise capital by selling stock and the price at which it sells will influence earnings per share. The price of the stock also has an influence on the terms at which the company can borrow. The company can also motivate its management by issuing options. There are other ways in which the image of the company as represented by its stock price can affect the substance. Whenever that happens, the possibility of a two-way reflexive interaction arises and equilibrium becomes a deceptive concept because the fundamentals cease to provide an independent variable to which the stock price could correspond. Equilibrium becomes a moving target and the reflexive interaction may render it altogether elusive because the movement in stock prices may push the fundamentals in the same direction in which the stock is moving.

The future that market participants seek to anticipate consists primarily of stock prices, not of fundamentals. The fundamentals matter only insofar as they affect stock prices. When stock prices find a way to affect the fundamentals, a self-reinforcing process may be set in motion that may carry both the fundamentals and stock prices quite far from what would be the conventional equilibrium. This would justify trend-following behavior that can carry financial markets into what I call far-from-equilibrium territory. Eventually the divergence between image and reality, expectations and outcome, is bound to become unsustainable and the process is reversed. The important point to realize is that trend-following behavior is not necessarily irrational. Just as certain animals have good reasons to move in herds, so do investors. Only at inflection points will mindless trend followers get hurt and if they are alert enough they are likely to survive. By the same token, lone investors who hitch their fortune to the fundamentals are liable to get trampled by the herd.

It is only occasionally that the price of an individual company's stock can affect that company's fundamentals like a dog chasing its own tail. We need to look at the larger picture to find reflexive interactions that occur as a rule rather than as an exception. For instance, currency movements tend to be self-validating; credit expansion and contraction tend to follow a cyclical pattern. Self-reinforcing—but eventually self-defeating—processes are endemic in financial markets, but it is not often that they can be properly documented.

I want to use for illustration one particular case from *The Alchemy of Finance:* the so-called conglomerate boom, which reached its apogee in the late 1960s. At the time, investors were willing to pay a high multiple of earnings for companies that could produce fast per-share earnings growth. This consideration, earnings growth, loomed larger in investors' minds than the other so-called fundamentals, such as dividends or balance sheets, and investors were not terribly discriminating about the way per-share earnings growth was achieved. Certain companies managed to exploit this bias. Typically, conglomerates were high-tech defense companies that had enjoyed fast earnings growth in the recent past and a correspondingly high multiple of earnings. They decided to use their high-priced stock to acquire other companies whose stock was selling at a lower multiple of earnings resulting in higher earnings per-share. Investors appreciated the earnings growth and accorded high multiples to the shares, which enabled the companies to continue the process. Soon there were many imitators. Even companies whose stock started with a low multiple of earnings could attain a higher multiple simply by announcing their intention to become a conglomerate. The boom was launched.

At first, the record of each company was judged on its own merit, but gradually conglomerates became recognized as a group. A new breed of investor emerged, the so-called go-go fund managers, or gunslingers, who developed a special affinity with the managements of conglomerates. Direct lines of communication were opened between them, and conglomerates learned to manage their stock prices as well as their earnings. The stocks climbed, but eventually reality could not sustain expectations. Acquisitions had to get larger and larger to maintain the momentum and in the end they ran into the limits of size. The climactic event was the attempt by Saul Steinberg to acquire Chemical Bank: It was fought and defeated by the establishment.

When stock prices started to fall, the decline fed on itself. The internal problems that had been swept under the carpet during the period of rapid external growth began to surface. Earnings reports revealed unpleasant surprises. Investors became disillusioned and, after the heady days of acquisitions-based success, few managers were willing to buckle down to the burdens of running their companies. The situation was aggravated by a recession and many of the high-flying conglomerates literally disintegrated. By then investors were prepared to believe the worst and in some cases the worst actually occurred. But in other cases, reality turned out to be better than expectations and eventually the situation stabilized, with surviving companies, often under new management, slowly working themselves out from under the debris.*

Using the conglomerate boom as my paradigm, I devised an ideal type of boom/bust sequence. It starts with a prevailing bias and a pre-

The Alchemy of Finance: Reading the Mind of the Market (New York: John Wiley & Sons, 1987), p. 57.

vailing trend. In the case of the conglomerate boom, the prevailing bias was a preference for rapid earnings growth per share without much attention to how it was brought about; the prevailing trend was the ability of companies to generate high earnings growth per share by using their stock to acquire other companies selling at a lower multiple of earnings. In the initial stage (1), the trend is not yet recognized. Then comes the period of acceleration (2) when the trend is recognized and reinforced by the prevailing bias. A period of testing (3) may intervene when prices suffer a setback. If the bias and trend are maintained, both emerge stronger than ever (4). Then comes the moment of truth (5) when reality can no longer sustain the exaggerated expectations, followed by a twilight period (6) when people continue to play the game although they no longer believe in it. Eventually a crossover point (7) is reached when the trend turns down and the bias is reversed, which leads to a catastrophic acceleration in the opposite direction (8), commonly known as the crash.

This is illustrated in Graph 3.1. The graph presents an ideal case, but the charts of various conglomerates conformed to it quite

Graph 3.1

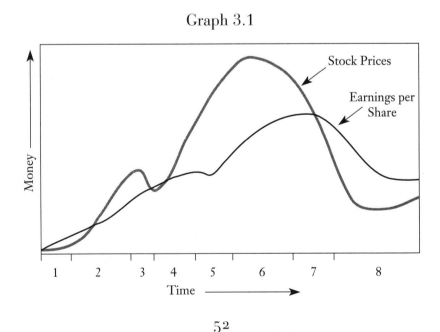

closely. Not every boom/bust process follows the same pattern. In *The Alchemy of Finance*, I described another ideal case in which the upside and the downside are more symmetrical. It is typical of currency markets, where upside and downside are more or less reversible. In reality, various reflexive processes interact, creating a weird and unique pattern. Every case is different and the curves have as many shapes as there are cases. The sudden collapse of confidence in Far Eastern financial markets in 1997, which transformed the fundamentals throughout Asia and even the rest of the world, is an obvious case in point (one that I analyze later).

There is nothing determinate about the ideal case I described above. The various stages may be of various amplitudes and duration. There seems to be some logic in the sequence of the various stages: It would be strange to encounter a period of acceleration after the moment of truth or a crossover point before the moment of truth. But the process may abort at any time; indeed, it may never get started. It is brought about by a mutually self-reinforcing interaction between bias and trend, thinking and reality. In more cases than not, the reflexive feedback mechanism is self-correcting rather than self-reinforcing. A full-fledged boom/bust sequence is the exception rather than the rule, but reflexivity—whether self-reinforcing or self-correcting—*is* the rule and it is ignored by the prevailing wisdom. For instance, there is a reflexive element in the current boom in Internet stocks: The popularity of the Internet and of Internet stocks were mutually self-reinforcing. There is a similar reflexive connection between corporate earnings and the use of stock options to reward management. It is particularly strong in the banking industry.

In fact, to understand financial markets, the concept of reflexivity is much more appropriate than the concept of equilibrium. But the concept of equilibrium has its uses. Indeed, as we have seen, it would be difficult to shed much light on the feedback mechanism without invoking the concept. Equilibrium, like the fundamentals, is a fertile fallacy. After all, we could not say much about the participants' bias without introducing the fundamentals, even though I contend that the so-called fundamentals can be influenced by the participants' bias. The chart of the conglomerate boom would not make much sense without a line denoting earnings per share (i.e., "the fundamentals"), even if these are influenced by market prices.

So what is equilibrium? I define it as the state in which there is a correspondence between expectations and outcomes. Equilibrium is unattainable in financial markets, but it may be possible to establish whether a prevailing trend is leading toward equilibrium or away from it. Knowing that much would be a major advance in our understanding. If we can identify a prevailing trend and a divergence between expectations and outcomes, this may enable us to predict whether the trend is toward or away from equilibrium. It is not easy to do and it cannot be done scientifically, although I have found that adapting Popper's theory of scientific method can be helpful. I do so by establishing a hypothesis (or thesis for short) as the basis of my expectations and testing it against the future course of events. In my days of actively managing money, I used to get particularly excited when I picked up the scent of an initially self-reinforcing but eventually self-defeating process. My mouth began to water as if I was one of Pavlov's dogs. Just as economists have been said to predict ten out of the last three recessions, I did the same with boom/bust sequences. I was wrong most of the time, because not every situation lends itself to the formation of a reflexive thesis, but the few occasions when I was right made the effort worthwhile because the profit potential was so much greater than in near-equilibrium situations. That is how I operated as a fund manager. It required imagination, intuition, and a relentlessly critical attitude.

I documented one particular instance in *The Alchemy of Finance*: the case of real estate investment trusts (REITs) in the early 1970s. The case was remarkable in many ways. I published a brokerage report that forecast a boom/bust process, and afterward the scenario played out, like a Greek drama, exactly as predicted. I was a major player myself, benefiting fully from the scenario both on the upside and the downside. Persuaded by my own analysis that most REITs would end up in bankruptcy, I continued to sell the stocks short as they declined, ending up making more than 100 percent on my short positions—a seemingly impossible feat.

Even on those occasions when my thesis turned out to be false, I could often exit with a profit because my critical attitude enabled me to identify earlier than others the flaws in my thesis. When I picked up the scent, I followed the rule of investing first and investigating afterward. When the thesis was plausible, this usually gave me a chance to turn around with a profit because there were other people ready to believe in it. Recognizing a flaw in a thesis gave me comfort; not knowing all potential weaknesses kept me on the alert, as I firmly believed that every thesis must be inherently flawed.

Based on my own experience, I established a rather interesting hypothesis about the stock market: I postulated that the stock market acts out an adaptation of Popper's theory of scientific method very much along the same lines as me, with the difference that it does not know that it is doing so. In other words, it adopts a thesis and tests it; when it fails, as it usually does, it tries out another thesis. That is what produces market fluctuations. It occurs at various levels of significance and the patterns produced are recursive, very much like Mandelbrot's fractals.*

The thesis adopted by the market is often trivial; it may not amount to much more than saying that the prices of certain companies, groups, or entire markets ought to move up or down. In these cases, by the time a participant figures out why the market adopted a certain thesis it may be too late—the thesis has already been discarded. It is much better to anticipate the fluctuations by studying market patterns. That is what technical analysts do. I was never par-

---

*Recursive structures in which irregular configurations are repeated at all scales.

ticularly interested in this, preferring to await a nontrivial—that is, reflexive—thesis. Of course the market had begun to act it out before I could formulate such a thesis, but I could still be ahead of the market in formulating it. Such historical, reflexive theses would present themselves only intermittently and there were long fallow periods in between when I might be better off doing nothing.

I doubt whether I would still have a competitive edge in recognizing the larger, historic theses, because market participants have now become aware of the potential held by reflexivity. There has been a noticeable change, for instance, away from fundamentals and toward technical considerations. As the participants' belief in the importance of fundamentals declines, technical analysis becomes more important. This has some implications for the stability of markets, but before I consider them I must introduce a distinction that plays a key role in my conceptual framework.

I want to distinguish between near-equilibrium and far-from-equilibrium conditions. I have borrowed these terms from chaos theory, with which my approach has certain affinities. In near-equilibrium conditions, the market operates with trivial theses, so that a move away from equilibrium is likely to provoke a countermove that takes prices back toward the position from which they started. These fluctuations resemble the ripples sloshing around in a swimming pool.

By contrast, if a reflexive thesis manages to establish itself, it will affect not only prices but the fundamentals, and a reversal will not result in a return to the starting position. It will be more like a tidal wave or an avalanche. Full-fledged boom/bust sequences penetrate into far-from-equilibrium territory. That is what gives them historic significance. Where is the demarcation line?

The threshold of dynamic disequilibrium is crossed when a trend prevailing in the real world becomes dependent on a bias prevailing in the participants' minds, and vice versa. Both trend and bias then develop further than would have been possible in the absence of a double feedback, reflexive connection. For example, in the 1990s the enthusiasm of international investors and bankers for Asian shares and assets produced domestic booms spurred by high valuations and easy credit. These booms accelerated growth in the area and increased valuations, which in turn validated and encouraged further capital inflows from abroad. (But there was a fly in the ointment: The boom could not have developed as far as it did without the informal dollar peg that allowed the countries to sustain a trade deficit longer than they should have. More on that later.)

A prevailing bias is not enough by itself; it must find a way to become validated by establishing or reinforcing a trend in the real world. I realize that the point I am making is tautological: When a double feedback is in operation, we can speak of a dynamic disequilibrium. But the point is worth making: The participants' thinking is always biased, but it does not always translate into a boom/bust sequence. For instance, the conglomerate boom could have been cut short if investors had realized that their concept of per-share earnings growth was flawed as soon as the conglomerate companies started to exploit it. The Asian boom could have been cut short if investors and lenders had realized that although the region's capital inflows and current account deficits were financing "productive investments," these investments would remain "productive" only as long as the capital inflows could be sustained.

This is not the end of the story. What happens when the reflexive connection between fundamentals and valuations is recognized by market participants? That can also become a source of instability. It can lead to an emphasis on so-called technical factors to the neglect of the fundamentals and generate trend-following speculation. How can stability be preserved? Only by continuing to rely on the so-called fundamentals, in spite of the fact that they are contingent on our valuations. This can be achieved by ignorance. If market participants are unaware of reflexivity, markets remain stable as long as some loophole does not allow a boom/bust process to develop. But how can stability be preserved when the market participants become aware of reflexivity? The answer is that it cannot be done by market participants alone; preserving stability must become an objective of public policy.

It can be seen that the concept of reflexivity is itself reflexive. Economic theory has actually promoted the tendency toward equilibrium by ignoring reflexivity and emphasizing the importance of fundamentals. By contrast, my argument leads to the conclusion that markets cannot be left to their own devices. Awareness of reflexivity only serves to increase instability unless the authorities are equally aware and intervene when the instability threatens to get out of hand.

The problem of instability is becoming more acute. The belief in fundamentals is eroding and trend-following behavior is on the rise. It is fostered by the increasing influence of institutional investors whose performance is measured by relative rather than absolute performance and by the large money center banks that act as market makers in currencies and derivatives: They benefit from increased volatility both as market makers and as providers of hedging mechanisms. The role of hedge funds is more ambivalent: As users of leverage, they contribute to volatility, but to the extent that they are motivated by absolute rather than the relative performance they often go countertrend. Because financial markets themselves develop in a historical manner, the danger of increasing instability should not be taken lightly. I address it in the chapters on the global capitalist system, but before I do that we need to look a bit more closely at reflexivity and historical patterns.

CHAPTER 4

Reflexivity in History

Interpret financial markets as a historical process. I believe my interpretation also has some relevance to history at large—by which I mean not only the history of the human race, but all forms of human interaction. People act on the basis of imperfect understanding and their interaction with each other is reflexive.

As I mentioned earlier, we may classify events into two categories: humdrum, everyday events that do not provoke a change in perceptions and unique, historical events that affect the participants' bias and lead to further changes in prevailing conditions. The distinction is tautological but useful. The first kind of event is susceptible to equilibrium analysis, the second is not: It can be understood only as part of a historical process.

In everyday events, neither the participating function nor the cognitive function undergo any significant change. In the case of unique, historic developments, both functions operate simultaneously in such a way that neither the participants' views nor the situation to which they relate remain the same as they were before. That is what justifies describing such developments as historic.

The historical process, as I see it, is open ended. When a situation has thinking participants, the sequence of events does not lead directly from one set of facts to the next; rather it connects facts to perceptions and perceptions to facts in a shoelace pattern. But history is a very peculiar kind of shoelace. The two sides of the shoe are not made of the same material; indeed, only one side is material—the other consists of the ideas of the participants. The two sides do not match and the divergences between them determine the shape of the events that tie them together. The knots that have already been tied have a determinate shape but the future is open ended. This is very different from natural phenomena for which the same universally valid laws can be used to explain the past and predict the future.

It must be acknowledged that this shoelace theory of history is a kind of dialectic between our thoughts and reality. It can be interpreted as a synthesis of Hegel's dialectic of ideas and Marx's dialectical materialism. Hegel propounded the dialectic of an idea that eventually leads to the end of history: freedom. Marx, or more exactly Engels, provided the antithesis by claiming that the conditions and relations of production determine the ideological superstructure. The shoelace theory could be regarded as a synthesis. Instead of either thoughts or material conditions evolving in a dialectic fashion on their own, it is the interplay between the two that produces a dialectic process. The only reason I do not use the word dialectic more prominently is that I do not want to be burdened by the excess baggage that comes with it. After all, Marx propounded a deterministic theory of history that is diametrically opposed to my own position. The interplay between the material and the ideal is interesting exactly because they do *not* correspond to or determine each other. The lack of correspondence renders the participants' bias a causal force in history. The mistakes, misinterpretations, and misconceptions of the participants play the same role in historical events that genetic mutations do in biological events: They make history.

Boom/Bust

I contend that the boom/bust process is just as relevant to history in general as it is to financial markets. Needless to say, it is not the only path that history can take. It is also possible that the prevailing bias and the prevailing trend are initially self-correcting, so that the boom/bust process does not even get started. Alternatively, the bias may be corrected at an early stage. This self-correcting process is less dramatic but more frequent. Most historical developments do not have a regular shape or pattern at all. That is because reality is infinitely complex and any process we may single out for attention interacts with a number of other processes.

The boom/bust process assumes particular significance because it bridges near-equilibrium with far-from-equilibrium conditions. I can demonstrate its presence in history by using a concrete example: the rise and fall of the Soviet system. I was actively involved in the tail end of the process and I was guided by the theory of history I am expounding here. I developed a boom/bust interpretation, which I published in *Opening the Soviet System* in 1990. This is what I said:

> The initial bias and the initial trend led towards a closed society. There was a mutually self-reinforcing relationship between the rigidity of the dogma and the rigidity of prevailing social conditions. The system reached its zenith in the last few years of Stalin's rule. It was all-embracing: a form of government, an economic system,

a territorial empire, and an ideology. The system was comprehensive, isolated from the outside world, and rigid. But the gap between the actual state of affairs and its official interpretation was wide enough to qualify as a case of static disequilibrium.

After Stalin's death there was a brief moment, the moment of truth, when Krushchev revealed some of the truth about Stalin's rule, but eventually the hierarchy reasserted itself. A twilight period began, when dogma was preserved by administrative methods but was no longer reinforced by a belief in its validity. Interestingly, the rigidity of the system increased even further. As long as there had been a live totalitarian at the helm, the Communist party line could be changed at his whim. But now that the regime was run by bureaucrats, that flexibility was lost. At the same time the terror which forced people to accept the communist dogma also abated, and a subtle process of decay set in. Institutions started to jockey for position. Since none of them enjoyed any real autonomy, they had to engage in a form of barter with the other institutions. Gradually an elaborate system of institutional bargaining replaced what was supposed to be central planning. At the same time, an informal economy developed which supplemented and filled in the gaps left by the formal system. This twilight period is what is now called the period of stagnation. The inadequacy of the system became increasingly evident and the pressure for reform mounted.

Reform accelerated the process of disintegration, because it introduced or legitimized alternatives while the system depended on the lack of alternatives for its survival. Economic reform enjoyed an initial period of success in every communist country, with the notable exception of the Soviet Union itself. The Chinese reformers called this phase the Golden Period, when the existing capital stock was redirected to meet consumer needs. But all reform movements are based on a misconception: the system cannot be reformed because it does not permit the economic allocation of capital. When existing capacity has been reoriented, the reform process starts running into difficulties.

It is understandable why this should be so. Communism was meant to be an antidote to capitalism, which had alienated the worker from the means of production. All property was taken over by the state, and the state was an embodiment of the collective interest as defined by the Party. Thus, the Party was put in charge of the allocation of capital. This meant that capital was allocated not on economic grounds, but on the grounds of a political, quasi-religious dogma. The best analogy is with the pyramid building of the pharaohs: the portion of resources devoted to investment was maximized, while the economic benefit derived from it remained at a minimum. Another point of similarity was that investments took the form of monumental projects. We may view the gigantic hydroelectric dams, the steel mills, the marble halls of the Moscow subway, and the skyscrapers of Stalinist architecture as so many pyramids built by a modern pharaoh. Hydroelectric plants do produce energy, and steel mills do turn out steel, but if the steel and energy are used to produce more dams and steel mills, the effect on the economy is not very different from that of building pyramids.

Our theoretical framework tells us that in the far-from-equilibrium conditions of a closed society there must be distortions that would be inconceivable in an open society. What better demonstration could one ask for than the Soviet economy? The communist system attributes no value to capital; more exactly, it does not recognize the concept of property. As a result, economic activity under the Soviet system is simply not economic. To make it so, the Party must be removed from its role as the guardian and allocator of capital. It was on this point that all reform attempts were bound to come to grief.

Interestingly, the failure of economic reform attempts served to accelerate the process of disintegration because it demonstrated the need for political reforms. With the advent of *pere-*

stroika in the Soviet Union, the process of disintegration entered into its terminal phase because the reform was primarily political and, as I have mentioned previously, the Golden Period was missing so that the reform produced little or no economic benefit. As living standards started to decline, public opinion turned against the regime, leading to a catastrophic disintegration which culminated in the total collapse of the Soviet Union.

The pattern is almost identical with the one we can observe in financial markets, with one major difference: in financial markets the boom/bust process seems to manifest itself as a process of acceleration, whereas in the case of the Soviet system the complete cycle comprised two phases, one a process of slowdown culminating in the standstill of the Stalin regime and the other a process of acceleration leading to a catastrophic collapse.*

I then went on to explain that a similar two-phase boom/bust process can be found in financial markets. I cited the case of the U.S. banking system, which became rigidly regulated after it collapsed in 1933, after which it took about thirty-five years to come to life. In the aftermath of the oil crisis and the international lending boom of the 1970s, when the banks served to recycle the surplus of the oil-producing countries, the banking system swung over into dynamic disequilibrium. The point of this far-fetched comparison between the rise and fall of the Soviet system and the fall and rise of the U.S. banking system was to show that far-from-equilibrium conditions can prevail at either extreme of change and changelessness. Closed society is the obverse of revolution and chaos; a reflexive process is at work at both extremes, with the difference being in the time scale. In a closed society, little happens over a long period; in a revolution much happens over a short period. In either case, perceptions are far removed from reality.

*Condensed from Chapter 4 of George Soros, *Opening the Soviet System* (London: Weidenfeld & Nicolson, 1990).

This is a significant insight. Discussing boom/bust processes in the context of financial markets, one is normally led to think in terms of acceleration. But the trend may also find expression in the form of deceleration or lack of change. Once we became aware of this possibility, we could even find an actual example in the stock market: the case of bank stocks from the Great Depression to 1972.* In history the cases of changelessness or static disequilibrium are much more common.

A Conceptual Framework

This insight about disequilibrium conditions is helpful in establishing a conceptual framework that divides historical situations into three categories: static disequilibrium, near equilibrium, and dynamic disequilibrium. The possibility of a static equilibrium has been ruled out by the fact that participants always base their decisions on a biased interpretation of reality. This leaves three possibilities.

One is that the reflexive interplay between the cognitive and participating functions prevents thinking and reality from drifting too far apart. People learn from experience; they act on the basis of biased views, but there is a critical process at work that tends to correct the bias. Perfect knowledge remains unattainable, but there is at least a tendency toward equilibrium. The participating function ensures that the real world, as experienced by the participants, is

---

*I ran into a similar case in Sweden in 1960, and I had the privilege of playing the role of Prince Charming awakening the Sleeping Beauty. The Swedish stock market was totally isolated from the rest of the world; you had to sell Swedish shares held abroad to buy Swedish shares in Sweden. Companies were allowed to retain their earnings without paying taxes by setting up various reserves, but they could not use these reserves to increase their dividends. Shares were valued on the basis of their dividend yields. As a result, there were tremendous divergences in price/earnings ratios and the best companies were tremendously undervalued until Prince Charming came along. Swedish shares held abroad rose to a hefty premium, but due to the restrictions on trading, the interest I awakened could not be satisfied and eventually the market went back to sleep until regulations were changed.

constantly changing yet people are sufficiently well grounded in a set of fundamental values that the participants' bias cannot get too far out of line with real events. That is what I call near equilibrium. This state of affairs is characteristic of an open society such as the modern Western world. Such a society is closely associated with a critical mode of thinking. We may call this the "normal" relationship between thinking and reality, because we are familiar with it from our own experience.

We can also encounter conditions in which the participants' views are quite far removed from the way things really are and the two show no tendency to come closer together—in some circumstances they may be driven even further apart. At one extreme, there are regimes that operate with an ideological bias and they are unwilling to adjust it to changing circumstances. They try to force reality into their conceptual framework even though they cannot possibly succeed. Under the pressure of the prevailing dogma, social conditions may also become quite rigid but reality is liable to remain quite far removed from its authorized interpretation. Indeed, in the absence of a corrective mechanism, the two may drift even further apart because no amount of coercion can prevent changes in the real world. This state of affairs is characteristic of a closed society such as ancient Egypt or the Soviet Union. It may be described as static disequilibrium.

At the other extreme, events may unfold so rapidly that the participants' understanding cannot keep up with them and the situation slips out of control. The divergence between prevailing views and actual conditions may become unsustainable, precipitating a revolution or some other kind of breakdown. Again, there is a wide divergence between thinking and reality, but it is bound to be transitory. The ancien régime that has been swept away will be eventually replaced by a new regime. This can be described as a case of regime change, or dynamic disequilibrium.

The tripartite division I have introduced may be compared with the three states in which water can be found in nature: liquid, solid, and gaseous. The analogy may be far-fetched, but it is intriguing. To make it meaningful, we need to identify the two demarcation lines that separate near-equilibrium from far-from-equilibrium conditions. In the case of water, the demarcation lines are expressed in degrees of temperature. In the case of history, the demarcation lines cannot be so precise and quantitative, but they must provide an observable distinction; otherwise the whole framework becomes a mere flight of the imagination.

Regimes

To establish what Popper would have called the criterion of demarcation, we must first consider what it is that is demarcated. For this purpose, I introduce the concept of a regime. A regime is a set of social conditions that hang together sufficiently so that they coexist in reality, although in accordance with my working hypothesis there is bound to be something deficient or missing in their relationship, so that they carry the seeds of their own destruction. Regime is a nebulous term but nonetheless useful. It can be applied to a wide range of situations. There can be political regimes prevailing in individual countries or individual regimes can be tied together in larger regimes such as the cold war. There can be regimes in the lives of institutions and in the lives of individuals. A marriage can be considered as a regime. Regimes do not have fixed boundaries; they overlap and succeed each other. They are different from machines, which are genuinely closed systems. A regime may be regarded as an attempt to introduce some kind of closure in what is an inherently open system, some set of rules that prevails in a particular relationship over a long enough period of time to be noticeable. Regime has to do with ruling and rules. Regimes have two aspects: the way people think and the way things really are.

The two aspects interact in a reflexive fashion: The mode of thinking influences the actual state of affairs, and vice versa, without a correspondence between the two ever being reached.

Ideal Types

Some forty years ago, in the early 1960s, I constructed theoretical models of society, which I would now call regimes, based on different attitudes toward historical change. I distinguished between a traditional mode of thinking, which ignored the possibility of change and accepted the prevailing state of affairs as the only one possible; a critical mode, which explored the possibilities of change to the full; and a dogmatic mode, which could not tolerate uncertainty. I argued that different forms of social organization correspond to these modes of thinking; I called them organic society, open society, and closed society. Needless to say, the correspondence between modes of thinking and social structures was less than perfect. Both open and closed society left something to be desired in the relationship between reality and thinking that could be found only in the other. Closed society offered the certainty and permanence that was lacking in an open society, and open society offered the freedom that was denied to the individual in a closed society. As a consequence, the two principles of social organization stood in opposition to each other. Open society recognizes our fallibility; closed society denies it. Which one is right, it is impossible to say. One can only judge by the consequences, but given the ubiquity of unintended consequences even that criterion is unreliable. There is a genuine choice involved and I came down firmly on the side of open society.*

*Open and closed society constitute ideal types. Modeling ideal types is a legitimate method for the study of society. It was legitimated by Max Weber and employed by such latter-day practitioners as Ernest Gellner. It has the advantage—or drawback—that it can play not only an informative but also a normative role. Perfect competition as postulated by economic theory is such an ideal type.

Open Society

When I established the Open Society Fund in 1979, its mission, as I formulated it at the time, was to help open up closed societies, help make open societies more viable, and foster a critical mode of thinking. After an abortive start in South Africa, I concentrated on the countries under communist rule, especially my native country, Hungary. My formula was simple: Any activity or association that was not under the supervision or control of the authorities created alternatives and thereby weakened the monopoly of dogma. My foundation in Hungary, established in 1984 as a joint venture with the Hungarian Academy of Science, acted as the sponsor of civil society. Not only did it support civil society, but civil society supported it; as a result it was exempt from many of the unintended adverse consequences foundations usually suffer from. Enticed by its success, I became a philanthropist in spite of my critical attitude toward philanthropy. As the Soviet empire started to crumble, I threw myself into the fray. I realized that in a revolutionary period it is possible to do things that would be inconceivable at other times. I felt that with the help of my boom/bust theory I understood the situation better than most others, I was clear about my goals, and I had the financial means. This put me in a unique position and I spared no effort. I increased the size of my foundations 100-fold in the space of a few years.

Only in the course of the Soviet collapse did I discover a flaw in my conceptual framework. It treated open and closed society as alternatives. The dichotomy might have been appropriate during the cold war when two diametrically opposed principles of social organization were confronting each other in deadly conflict, but it does not fit the conditions that have prevailed since the end of the cold war.

I was forced to realize that the collapse of a closed society does not lead automatically to the establishment of an open society; on the contrary, it may lead to the breakdown of authority and the disintegration of society. A weak state may be as much of a threat to open society as an authoritarian state.* Instead of a dichotomy between open and closed society, open society becomes an idea that is threatened from more than one side.

The emergence of the increasingly global capitalist system in the 1990s confirmed that conclusion. I felt obliged to engage in a painstaking reexamination and the framework I present here is the result of that process. I now envisage open society occupying a precarious middle ground where it is threatened by dogmatic beliefs of all kinds, some that would impose a closed society, others leading to the disintegration of society. Open society represents near-equilibrium conditions; alternatives include not only the static disequilibrium of closed society but also a dynamic disequilibrium. I had been aware of certain deficiencies in open societies that could lead to their breakdown, but I assumed that the breakdown would lead to the formation of a closed society. I did not realize that conditions of dynamic disequilibrium could persist indefinitely, or, more exactly, that a society could hover on the edge of chaos without actually going over. This was a curious oversight on my part, as I was aware of the contention of evolutionary systems theory that life occurs at the edge of chaos. The framework I present here is intended to correct the error of my earlier formulation.

Demarcation Lines

We are now ready to return to the key question I posed earlier: What separates near-equilibrium and far-from-equilibrium conditions? When does a boom/bust sequence or some other disequilibrium process destroy the near-equilibrium conditions of open

*Stephen Holmes, "What Russia Teaches Us Now: How Weak States Threaten Freedom," *The American Prospect* (July-August 1997): 30–39.

society? We have seen that the two-way interaction between thinking and reality can easily lead to excesses in the direction both of
rigidity and of chaos. There must be some anchor that prevents the
participants' thinking from being dragged too far away from reality
for an open society to prevail. What is that anchor?

In answering the question, we must distinguish between expectations and values. After all, decisions are based not only on people's perceptions of reality but also on the values they bring to bear.
In the case of expectations, the anchor is easy to identify: It is reality itself. As long as people realize that there is a difference between
thinking and reality, the facts provide a criterion by which the
validity of people's expectations can be judged. Reflexivity may render events unpredictable, but once they come to pass, they become
uniquely determined, so they can be used to decide whether our
predictions were correct.

In conditions of static disequilibrium, thinking and reality are far
removed from each other and exhibit no tendency to come closer
together. In a closed society, expectations cannot be anchored in
reality, because expectations that deviate from the official dogma
cannot even be voiced. There is a gap between the official version
of reality and the facts; its removal brings immense relief and a
sense of liberation.

In conditions of dynamic disequilibrium, we have the opposite
state of affairs; the situation is changing too rapidly for people's
understanding, causing a gap between thinking and reality to
appear. The interpretation of events cannot keep up with the pace
of events; people become disoriented and events run out of control.
Thus reality can no longer act as an anchor for expectations. That
is what happened during the disintegration of the Soviet system. As
I argue in Chapter 7, I believe the global capitalist system has now
moved into dynamic disequilibrium. But first, we must turn from
expectations to the other possible anchor for open society, namely,
the anchor of ethical and moral values.

The Question of Values

Can we distinguish between the role of values in near-equilibrium and disequilibrium conditions? Here I am on more uncertain grounds, for both subjective and objective reasons, and my argument is more tentative. I have already mentioned the subjective consideration: I have been trained as an economist and I have always struggled to figure out how market values relate to the values that guide decisions in other spheres of existence, social, political, or personal. Often I am genuinely baffled and I suspect I am not alone in that regard. There seems to be a lot of confusion in contemporary society about values in general and the relationship between market values and social values in particular. So the subjective difficulty merges into the objective one. Let me state the problem as I see it, first on the theoretical and then on the practical level.

On the theoretical level, cognition has an objective criterion, namely, reality, by which it can be judged. As we have seen, the criterion is not totally independent but it is independent enough to be called objective: No participant is in a position to impose his or her will on the course of events. By contrast, values cannot be judged by any objective criteria because they are not supposed to correspond to reality: The criteria by which they are to be judged are contained in the values themselves.

Because values are not constrained by reality, they can vary over a much wider range than cognitive views. That is what makes any discussion of values so difficult. Economic theory did well to take them as given. With the help of that methodological device, economic theory established the concept of equilibrium. Although I have been critical of the concept, it has been indispensable for my analysis. I could show how far-from-equilibrium conditions could arise in financial markets only because the concept of equilibrium from which reality could diverge was well developed. No similar concept is available for the nonmarket sector of society.

On the practical level, our contemporary society seems to be suffering from an acute deficiency of social values. Of course, people have bemoaned the decline of morality throughout history, but there is one factor at play that makes the present different from earlier times. It is the spread of market values. Market values have penetrated into areas of society that were previously governed by nonmarket considerations. I have in mind personal relations, politics, and the professions such as law and medicine. Moreover, there has been a subtle and gradual, but nevertheless profound, transformation in the way the market mechanism operates. First, lasting relationships have been replaced by individual transactions. The general store where owner and customer are familiar with each other has yielded to the supermarket and more recently to the Internet. Second, national economies have been superseded by an international economy, but the international community, insofar as it exists, shares few social values.

Transactional Society

The replacement of relationships by transactions is an ongoing, historical process that will never be carried to its logical conclusion but is well advanced—far more advanced than it was in the early 1960s when I arrived in this country and first thought about it. I came from England and I was struck by the difference: Relations in the United States were much easier to establish and to abandon. The trend has progressed a great deal since then. There are still marriages and families, but in investment banking, for instance, transactions have almost completely superseded relationships. This offers the clearest possible example of the changes occurring in many other social institutions.

In the City of London in the 1950s, it was almost impossible to transact any business without having a prior relationship. It was not a question of what you knew but whom you knew. That was the main reason why I left London: Because I was not well connected in London, my chances were much better in New York. In a short time, I established regular trading contacts with leading firms although I was working in a relatively unknown brokerage house. I could never have done that in London. But even in New York, the underwriting of securities was still entirely governed by relationships: Firms participated in syndicates in a certain pecking order and it was a major event when a firm moved up or down a bracket. All this has changed. Each transaction stands on its own and investment bankers compete for each individual piece of business.

The difference between transactions and relationships has been well analyzed by game theory in the form of the so-called prisoners' dilemma. Two crooks have been caught and are interrogated. If one provides evidence against the other, he or she can earn a reduced sentence but the other is more certain to be convicted. Both of them taken together will do better if they remain loyal to each other, but each one of them separately can profit at the other's expense. In the case of an individual transaction, it may be rational to betray; in a lasting relationship it pays to be loyal. The analysis shows how cooperative behavior may develop with the passage of time but it can also be used to show that cooperation and loyalty can be undermined by replacing relationships with transactions.*

All this relates to the original question about the demarcation lines defining social disequilibrium and the anchoring role of values. We are inclined to take social or moral values for granted. We refer to them as intrinsic or fundamental, implying that their validity is somehow independent of prevailing conditions. As I have

---

*Anatol Rapoport and Albert M. Chammah, with the collaboration of Carol J. Orwant, *Prisoner's Dilemma: A Study in Conflict and Cooperation* (Ann Arbor, MI: University of Michigan Press, 1965).

pointed out before, nothing could be further from the truth. Values are reflexive. They are influenced by social conditions and, in turn, they play a role in making social conditions what they are. People may believe that God handed down the Ten Commandments and society will be more just and stable if they do. Conversely, the absence of moral constraints is liable to generate instability.

A transactional society undermines social values and loosens moral constraints. Social values express a concern for others. They imply that the individual belongs to a community, be it a family, a tribe, a nation, or humankind, whose interests must take precedence over the individual's self-interests. But a transactional market economy is anything but a community. Everybody must look out for his or her own interests and moral scruples can become an encumbrance in a dog-eat-dog world. In a purely transactional society, people who are not weighed down by any consideration for others can move around more easily and are likely to come out ahead.

It should be noted, however, that even such a society will not be totally devoid of ethical and moral considerations. The external constraints may be removed but some internal constraints are liable to remain. Even if people have been transformed into single-minded competitors, the transformation has occurred relatively recently. Moreover people are not born that way: They absorb social values as they grow up. So the question of social values remains relevant. A purely transactional society could never exist, yet we are closer to it than at any time in history. As we shall see, this is particularly true on the global scale.

Two Kinds of Values

What can we say about the demarcation line between near-equilibrium and far-from-equilibrium conditions and the role of social values? For present purposes, we may distinguish between two kinds of values: fundamental principles that people espouse irrespective of the consequences, and expediency, whereby people are guided entirely by the anticipated consequences of their actions. People who believe in fundamental values often see them as originating from some source other than their own thinking, so that the validity of the values is not dependent on the person's endorsement. Typically, fundamental values are associated with religious beliefs, although the Enlightenment has turned reason and science into sources of independent authority. Expediency does not have the support of an external authority; on the contrary, it is often in conflict with prevailing social precepts and therefore it tends to be associated with a sense of inferiority or even guilt. Those who act expediently are constantly looking for social support. If a course of action is not approved by those who matter, it is unlikely to be found expedient. (It would be an extreme case when nobody else mattered.) When the untrammeled pursuit of self-interest is widely approved, it becomes expedient.

The dichotomy between fundamental principles and expediency is obviously artificial but that is precisely what makes it useful. The two categories are obviously extreme—there must be something in between. Indeed, between these two extremes of fundamentalism and pure expediency lie the near-equilibrium conditions of open society that I am trying to identify. We need two dividing lines: one that separates near equilibrium from static disequilibrium and another that separates it from dynamic disequilibrium. The first has to do with fundamental principles, the second with expediency.

Fundamental Principles

Open society requires some basic agreement on what is right and what is wrong and people must be ready to do the right thing even if it has unpleasant consequences: rush to the defense of the fatherland or rise to defend liberty. This does not go without saying. In a transactional society where expediency prevails, people are inclined to shirk unpleasant consequences. But an unconditional commitment to fundamental values can also endanger open society if people ignore the fact that actions have unintended consequences. The road to hell is paved with good intentions. We must be willing to adjust our principles in the light of experience. This requires a critical attitude. We must recognize that no one is in possession of the ultimate truth.

Failure to recognize unintended consequences spawns conspiracy theories: When something unpleasant happens, somebody has to be responsible for it. Insistence on absolute values gives rise to what I call the either/or syndrome: If a particular principle turns out to have negative consequences, the ultimate solution must lie in its opposite. This line of argument is quite absurd but it is surprisingly widespread. It is the distinguishing mark of fundamentalist thinking (as distinct from fundamental principles). It can easily lead to extreme positions that are far removed from reality. It is characteristic of both religious and moral fundamentalism.

Before we give up hope of defining a middle ground where open society can coexist with strong fundamental values, we should remember that it is not necessary for all participants to adopt a critical attitude for a critical mode of thinking to prevail. The critical mode is robust enough to accommodate fundamentalist thinking as long as it remains at the fringes. Indeed, the critical mode of thinking has a way of softening up fundamental beliefs so that they take into account the existence of alternatives: Religions have shown a tendency to become more tolerant of other beliefs when their proponents have to compete for people's allegiance. But that is not always the case. Some religious and political movements gain adherents by their extreme intolerance. If they make too much headway, as the Nazis and communists did in the Weimar Republic, open society is endangered, but only when one of them attains a monopolistic position by suppressing the alternatives can we speak of a dogmatic mode of thinking or a closed society.

77

Expediency

The second dividing line—between an open society that is stable and one in dynamic disequilibrium—is more problematic, albeit more relevant to the situation in which we find ourselves. If people abandon their belief in fundamental principles and seek to be guided solely by the results of their actions, society becomes unstable. Why this should be so is not immediately obvious but it is important that it should be understood. Our ability to anticipate the consequences of our actions is deficient; therefore, if we always relied on consequences to form our intentions, our values would constantly be changing. That would not be so bad by itself; what renders the situation unstable is that the results of our actions are not a reliable guide to the validity of the thinking that lies behind these actions.

The reflexive connection between thinking and reality has a way of validating results beyond the point where they are sustainable. For instance, demanding lower taxes may make people feel richer and thereby encourage further reductions in taxes, but this process may continue beyond the point where essential social services and perhaps even society itself begin to be endangered. The reflexive connection may also work in the opposite direction: When an objective is attained it no longer seems as desirable as it was when it was only a distant goal; success turns sour after an initial burst of enthusiasm, giving rise to short-lived fads. For example, one generation's success in achieving material wealth gives its children the luxury of rejecting the work ethic. The financial market is full of examples where trend-following behavior is a source of instability. The same applies to society in general. When fundamental principles are widely ignored in the name of expediency and anything goes, people become disoriented and the yearning for firm rules and strict discipline is reinforced. Stability cannot be maintained unless people adhere to some fundamental principles irrespective of the consequences. When success is the only criterion by which actions are judged, there is nothing to stop the reflexive interaction from drifting too far and moving into far-from-equilibrium territory.

How does a willingness to accept some fundamental values prevent a destabilizing boom/bust social process from getting out of hand? This is where the experience gained in the laboratory of financial markets may come in useful. The answer is, by inhibiting trend-following behavior, which is as much a threat to stability in society as it is in financial markets.

This is an important point but it is perhaps too abstract. It can be made more vivid by looking at some practical examples in the financial markets. I have demonstrated in *The Alchemy of Finance* that currency movements tend to overshoot because of trend-following speculation, and we can observe similar trend-following behavior in stock, commodity, and real estate markets, of which the Dutch tulip mania was the prototype. Such moves could not be carried to excess if market participants were more firmly wedded to valuing the so-called fundamentals. The trouble is that a belief in the so-called fundamentals is, at least in financial markets, demonstrably false. I have shown that what are considered fundamental values or objective criteria are often reflexive and it is the failure to recognize this fact that engenders a boom/bust process. That was the case in the conglomerate boom of the late 1960s, in the international lending boom of the late 1970s, and in the current global financial crisis. So you are damned if you do not believe in the so-called fundamentals and indulge in trend-following behavior but you are also damned if you do believe in the so-called fundamentals because the markets are liable to prove you wrong. Not much hope for stability!

At this point, we must be careful to observe the distinction between the values that guide economic behavior and the values that prevail in society. I have been able to show that boom/bust sequences in financial markets are driven by belief in the so-called fundamentals, which turn out to be demonstrably false. But this has no bearing on fundamental values in general. To equate the so-called fundamentals in financial markets with fundamental values would be tantamount to basing my argument on a pun. There is a sounder basis to be found: It can be shown that in a transactional society fundamental values always rest on shaky grounds. This is less strong than claiming that fundamental values are demonstrably false, but it is strong enough to raise doubts about the stability of open society.

Why, after all, should people be guided by a sense of right and wrong, irrespective of the consequences? Why should they not pursue success by whatever means works best? These are legitimate questions that do not have a simple answer. They may sound shocking to people who have been reared to be morally upright citizens but that means only that these people do not realize that a sense of morality is an acquired sense. It is inculcated in people by society—parents, schools, laws, traditions—and it is needed to sustain society. In a perfectly changeable, transactional society the individual is paramount. From the point of view of the individual it is not necessary to be morally upright to be successful; indeed it can be a hindrance. The more people adopt success as the criterion by which they judge other people, the less they need to be morally upright. To abide by a moral code, you must put the common interest ahead of your individual self-interest. In a society where stable relationships prevail, this is much less of a problem because it is difficult to be successful if you violate the prevailing social norms. But when you can move around freely, social norms become less binding, and when expediency becomes established as the social norm society becomes unstable.

The Precarious Middle Ground

It can be seen that the near-equilibrium conditions of open society are threatened from both sides; open society is precariously perched between the static disequilibrium of closed society and the dynamic disequilibrium of a purely transactional society. This is very different from my original framework, in which I recognized only a dichotomy between open and closed society. Although the dichotomy was appropriate to cold war conditions, the idea of open society occupying a middle ground between fundamentalist ideologies on the one hand and an absence of shared fundamental values on the other seems to fit the present situation much better.

One can, of course, question the value of a universally valid conceptual framework that can be so readily adjusted to changing circumstances, but conceptual frameworks are neither perfect nor timeless. They can, as I pointed out earlier, never amount to more than a fertile fallacy. That does not absolve us, however, from the obligation to correct errors, which is what I have done here. The deficiency of values was already present in my original model of open society but at that time I envisaged the emergence of a closed society as the only alternative to an open society. Contemporary history is teaching us that there is at least one other alternative: instability and chaos leading to a possible breakdown of society. This is particularly true outside the relatively stable societies of Europe and North America.

Consider some concrete contemporary examples. The disintegration of the Soviet Union has created a vacuum of state power and a breakdown of law and order that may be as much a threat to liberty as the Soviet repression used to be.* We have experienced similar breakups and breakdowns of state power in the 1990s in the

*Holmes, "What Russia . . . ," *The American Prospect.*

former Yugoslavia and Albania, in various parts of Africa (Somalia, Rwanda, Burundi, Congo, etc.), and in Asia (Afghanistan, Tajikistan, Cambodia). When we look at the world at large, we find a very unstable situation: We discern the presence of a global economic system but the absence of a global political system. I am sure that in describing instability as *one* other alternative I am oversimplifying again, because instability can take many forms, but we need to simplify to make some sense out of an otherwise confusing world. As long as we are aware of what we are doing, the conceptual framework I am developing here can be useful not only in illuminating the current state of affairs but also in helping to make it more stable.

Open society is always endangered but the threat at this moment in history comes more from instability than from totalitarian rule, more from a deficiency of shared social values than from a repressive ideology. Communism and even socialism have been discredited whereas the belief in laissez faire capitalism has elevated the deficiency of social values into a moral principle. How can open society be defended? Only by people learning (or remembering) to distinguish between what is right and what is expedient and doing what is right even if it is not expedient. This is a tall order. It cannot be justified by a calculation of narrow self-interest. Self-interest would dictate saying, thinking, and doing what is expedient. Indeed, more and more people have gone through the calculation and have come out in favor of expediency. They may continue to profess their devotion to moral principles, but only because it is expedient. Their position has been greatly simplified by the prevailing bias of recognizing self-interest as a moral principle. The bias manifests itself, as discussed in the second half of this book, in market fundamentalism, in geopolitical realism, in a simplistic interpretation of Darwinism, and in several new disciplines such as "law and economics." It has allowed the market mechanism to penetrate into aspects of society that were outside its sway until recently.

Bias and trend are mutually self-reinforcing. No longer is there any need to profess moral principles other than self-interest. Success is admired above all other considerations. Politicians gain recognition for getting elected, not for the principles they represent. Businesspeople are esteemed for their wealth, not for their probity or the contribution of their business to social and economic well-being. What is right has been subordinated to what is effective and this has made it easier to succeed without paying any heed to what is right. Needless to say, I see a grave danger here to the stability of our society.*

---

*President Bill Clinton's persecution and possible indictment appear, in this context, as violent reactions in the opposite direction. In my opinion, both Clinton and Independent Counsel Kenneth W. Starr are in the wrong, but Starr's behavior is a greater danger to the constitution than Clinton's.

CHAPTER 5

Open Society

Open Society as an Ideal

The supreme challenge of our time is to establish a set of fundamental values that applies to a largely transactional, global society. Fundamental principles have been traditionally derived from some external authority such as religion or science. But at the present moment in history, no external authority remains undisputed. The only possible source is internal. A firm foundation on which we can build our principles is the recognition of our own fallibility. Fallibility is a universal human condition; therefore it is applicable to a global society. Fallibility gives rise to reflexivity and reflexivity can create conditions of unstable disequilibrium, or to put it bluntly, of political and economic crisis. It is in our common interest to avoid such conditions. Here is the common ground on which a global society can be built. It means accepting open society as a desirable form of social organization.

Unfortunately people are not even aware of the concept of open society; they are very far from regarding it as an ideal. Yet without a conscious effort to preserve it, open society cannot survive. This contention is, of course, denied in the laissez faire ideology according to which the untrammeled pursuit of self-interest yields the best of all possible worlds. But this ideology is refuted every day by events. It should be obvious by now that financial markets are not self-sustaining and the preservation of the market mechanism ought to take precedence as a common goal over the self-interests of individual market participants. Unless people believe in open society as a desirable form of social organization and are willing to constrain their self-interest to sustain it, open society will not survive.

The open society that people can believe in must be different from the present state of affairs. It has to serve as an ideal. A transactional society suffers from a deficiency of social values. As an ideal, open society would cure that deficiency. But it could not cure all deficiencies; if it did so it would contradict or deny the principle of fallibility on which it is based. So open society has to be a special kind of ideal, a self-consciously imperfect ideal. That is very different from the ideals that usually fire people's imagination. Fallibility implies that perfection is unattainable and that we must content ourselves with the next best thing: an imperfect society that is always open to improvement. That is my definition of open society. Can it gain widespread acceptance?

The Relevance of Universal Ideas

Perhaps the biggest obstacle to the adoption of open society as an ideal is a fairly widespread rejection of universal ideas. I discovered this after I set up my network of foundations and, frankly speaking, I was surprised by it. During the communist regime and afterward in the heady days of revolution, I had no difficulty finding people who were inspired by the principles of an open society even if they did not use the same conceptual framework. I did not bother to explain what I meant by open society: It meant the opposite of the closed society in which they lived and they all knew what that meant. But the attitude of the West disappointed and disconcerted me. At first I thought that people in the open societies of the West were just slow to recognize a historic opportunity; eventually I had to come to the conclusion that they genuinely did not care enough about open society as a universal idea to make much of an effort to help the formerly communist countries. All the talk about freedom and democracy had been just that: propaganda.

After the collapse of the Soviet system, the appeal of open society as an ideal started to fade, even in the formerly closed societies. People got caught up in the struggle for survival and those who continued to be preoccupied with the common good had to ask themselves whether they were clinging to the values of a bygone age—and often they were. People grew suspicious of universal ideas. Communism was a universal idea and look where it had led!

This induced me to reconsider the concept of open society. Yet in the end, I concluded that the concept is more relevant than ever. We cannot do without universal ideas. (The pursuit of self-interest is also a universal idea, even if it is not recognized as such.) Universal ideas can be very dangerous, especially if they are carried to their logical conclusion. By the same token, we cannot give up thinking and the world in which we live is just too complicated to make any sense of it without some guiding principles. This line of thought led me to the concept of fallibility as a universal idea and to the concept of open society, which is based on the recognition of our fallibility. As I mentioned earlier, in my new formulation open society no longer stands in opposition to closed society but occupies a precarious middle ground where it is threatened from all sides by universal ideas that have been carried to their logical conclusions, all kinds of extremism, including market fundamentalism.

If you think that the concept of open society is paradoxical, you are right. The universal idea that universal ideas carried to their logical conclusion are dangerous is another instance of the paradox of the liar. It is the foundation on which the concept of fallibility is built. If we carry the argument to its logical conclusion, we find ourselves confronted by a genuine choice: We can either accept our fallibility or we can deny it. Acceptance leads to the principles of open society.

The Enlightenment

I shall try to derive the principles of open society from the recognition of our fallibility. I am aware of the difficulties. Every philosophical argument is liable to raise endless new questions. If I tried to start from scratch, my task would be well-nigh impossible. Fallibility implies that political and moral principles cannot be derived from prior principles—may Immanuel Kant rest in peace. Fortunately I do not have to start from ground zero. The philosophers of the Enlightenment, Kant foremost among them, tried to deduce universally valid imperatives from the dictates of reason. Their very limited and imperfect success corroborates our fallibility and provides a basis for establishing the principles of open society.

The Enlightenment constituted a giant step forward from the moral and political principles that prevailed previously. Until then, moral and political authority was derived from external sources, both divine and temporal. Allowing reason to decide what is true and false, what is right and wrong, was a tremendous innovation. It marked the beginning of modernity. Whether we recognize it or not, the Enlightenment has provided the foundations for our ideas about politics and economics, indeed, for our entire outlook on the world. The philosophers of the Enlightenment are no longer read—indeed, we may find them unreadable—but their ideas have become ingrained in our way of thinking. The rule of reason, the supremacy of science, the universal brotherhood of man—these were some of their main themes. The political, social, and moral values of the Enlightenment were admirably stated in the Declaration of Independence, and that document continues to be an inspiration for people throughout the world.

The Enlightenment did not spring into existence out of nowhere: It had its roots in Christianity, which in turn built on the monotheistic tradition of the Old Testament and on Greek philosophy. It should be noted that all of these ideas were couched in universal terms, with the exception of the Old Testament, in which a great deal of tribal history is mixed with monotheism. Instead of accepting tradition as the ultimate authority, the Enlightenment subjected tradition to critical examination. The results were exhilarating. The creative energies of the human intellect were unleashed. No wonder that the new approach was carried to excess! In the French Revolution, traditional authority was overturned and reason was anointed as the ultimate arbiter. Reason proved unequal to the task and the fervor of 1789 deteriorated into the terror of 1793. But the basic tenets of the Enlightenment were not repudiated; on the contrary, Napoleon's armies spread the ideas of modernity throughout the European continent.

Modernity's achievements are beyond compare. Scientific method produced amazing discoveries and technology allowed their conversion to productive use. Humankind came to dominate nature. Economic enterprises took advantage of the opportunities, markets served to match supply and demand, and both production and living standards rose to heights that would have been unimaginable in any previous age.

In spite of these impressive achievements, reason could not quite live up to the expectations attached to it, especially in the social and political arena. The gap between intentions and outcomes could not be closed; indeed, the more radical the intentions, the more disappointing the outcomes. This applies, in my opinion, both to communism and to market fundamentalism. I want to highlight one particular case of unintended consequences because it is relevant to the situation in which we find ourselves. When the original political ideas of the Enlightenment were translated into practice, they gave rise to the nation-state. In trying to establish the rule of reason, people rose up against their rulers, and the power they captured was the power of the sovereign. That is how the nation-state, in which sovereignty belongs to the people, was born. Whatever its merits, it is a far cry from its universalist inspiration.

In culture, the debunking of traditional authority gave rise to an intellectual ferment that produced great art and literature, but after a long period of exciting experimentation when all authority had been debunked by the second half of the twentieth century, much of the inspiration seemed to dissipate. The range of possibilities has become too broad to provide the discipline that is required for artistic creation. Some artists and writers manage to establish their own private language but the common ground seems to have disintegrated.

The same kind of malaise seems to affect society at large. The philosophers of the Enlightenment, Kant foremost among them, sought to establish universally valid principles of morality based on the universal attributes of reason. The task Kant set himself was to show that reason provides a better basis for morality than traditional, external authority. But in our modern, transactional society, the reason for having any kind of morality has been brought into question. The need for some kind of moral guidance lingers; indeed, it is perhaps more intensely felt than in the past because it goes unsatisfied. But the principles and precepts that could provide that guidance are in doubt. Why bother about the truth when a proposition does not need to be true to be effective? Why be honest when it is success, not honesty or virtue that gains people's respect? Although social values and moral precepts are in doubt, there can be no doubt about the value of money. That is how money has come to usurp the role of intrinsic values. The ideas of the Enlightenment permeate our view of the world and its noble aspirations continue to shape our expectations, but the prevailing mood is one of disenchantment.

It is high time to subject reason, as construed by the Enlightenment, to the same kind of critical examination as the Enlightenment inflicted on the dominant external authorities, both divine or temporal. We have now lived in the Age of Reason for the past 200 years—long enough to discover that reason has its limitations. We are ready to enter the Age of Fallibility. The results may be equally exhilarating and, having learnt from past experience, we may be able to avoid some of the excesses characteristic of the dawning of a new age.

We need to begin the reconstruction of morality and social values by accepting their reflexive character. Doing so will lead directly to the concept of open society as a desirable form of social organization. As fallibility and reflexivity are universal concepts, they should provide common ground for all the people living in the world. I hope we can avoid some of the pitfalls associated with universal concepts. Of course, open society is not without its shortcomings but its deficiency consists in offering too little rather than too much. More precisely, the concept is too general to provide a recipe for specific decisions. This is self-consistent and leaves ample scope for trial and error. It will be a sound foundation for the kind of global society we need.

Moral Philosophy

Kant derived his categorical imperatives from the existence of a moral agent who is guided by the dictates of reason to the exclusion of self-interest and desire. Such an agent enjoys transcendental freedom and autonomy of the will in contrast with the "heteron-omy" of the agent whose will is subject to external causes.* This agent is able to recognize unconditional moral imperatives, which are objective in the sense that they apply universally to all rational beings. The golden rule that we should do as we would be done to by others is one such categorical imperative. The unconditional authority of the imperatives is derived from the idea of people being rational agents.

The trouble is that the rational agent described by Kant does not exist. It is an illusion created by a process of abstraction. Enlighten-ment philosophers liked to think of themselves as detached and unencumbered but in reality they were deeply rooted in their soci-ety with its Christian morality and ingrained sense of social obliga-tions. They wanted to change their society. For this purpose, they invented the unattached individual endowed with reason who obeyed the dictates of his own conscience, not the dictates of an exter-nal authority. They failed to realize that a truly unattached individ-ual would not be endowed with their sense of duty. Social values may be internalized, but they are not based on the unattached individual endowed with reason; they are rooted in the community to which the individual belongs. Modern neurological research has gone further and identified individuals whose brain has been damaged in a pecu-liar way that left their faculties of detached observation and reason-ing intact but damaged their sense of identity. Their judgment was impaired and their behavior became erratic and irresponsible.

Thus it seems clear that morality is based on a sense of belong-ing to a community, be it family, friends, tribe, nation, or human-ity. But a market economy does not constitute a community, especially when it operates on a global scale; being employed by a corporation is not the same as belonging to a community, especially when management gives precedence to the profit motive over all

*Roger Scruton, *Kant* (Oxford, U.K.: Oxford University Press, 1989).

other considerations and the individual may be fired at the drop of a hat. People in today's transactional society do not behave as if they were governed by categorical imperatives; the prisoners' dilemma seems to throw more light on their behavior.* Kant's metaphysic of morals was appropriate to an age when reason had to contend with external authority but it seems strangely irrelevant today when the external authority is lacking. The very need to distinguish between right and wrong is brought into question. Why bother, as long as a course of action achieves the desired result? Why pursue the truth? Why be honest? Why care about others? Who are the "we" who constitute global society and what are the values that ought to hold us together? These are the questions that need to be answered today.

It would be a mistake, however, to dismiss the moral and political philosophy of the Enlightenment altogether just because it failed to live up to its grandiose ambitions. In the spirit of fallibility, we ought to correct excesses in thinking, not swing to the opposite extreme. A society without social values cannot survive and a global society needs universal values to hold it together. The Enlightenment offered a set of universal values and its memory is still alive even if it seems somewhat faded. Instead of discarding it, we should update it.

The Encumbered Individual

Enlightenment values can be made relevant to the present day by replacing reason with fallibility and substituting the "encumbered individual" for the unencumbered individual of the Enlightenment philosophers. By encumbered individuals, I mean individuals in need of society, individuals who cannot exist in splendid isolation yet

*Rapoport, et al., *Prisoner's Dilemma.*

are deprived of the sense of belonging that was so much a part of people's lives at the time of the Enlightenment that they were not even aware of it. The thinking of encumbered individuals is formed by their social setting, their family and other ties, the culture in which they are reared. They do not occupy a timeless, perspectiveless position. They are not endowed with perfect knowledge and they are not devoid of self-interest. They are ready to fight for survival but they are not self-contained; however well they compete they will not survive because they are not immortal. They need to belong to something bigger and more enduring, although, being fallible, they may not recognize that need. In other words, they are real people, thinking agents whose thinking is fallible, not personifications of abstract reason.

In putting forward the idea of the encumbered individual, I am, of course, engaging in the same kind of abstract thinking as the Enlightenment philosophers. I am proposing another abstraction based on our experience with their formulation. Reality is always more complicated than our interpretation. The range of people living in the world can vary from those who are not far removed from the Enlightenment ideal to those who barely act as individuals, with the distribution curve heavily skewed toward the latter.

The point I want to make is that a globalized society could never satisfy encumbered individuals' need to belong. It could never become a community. It is just too big and variegated for that, with too many different cultures and traditions. Those who want to belong to a community must look for it elsewhere. A global society must always remain something abstract, a universal idea. It must respect the needs of the encumbered individual, it must recognize that those needs are not met, but it must not seek to meet them in full, because no form of social organization could possibly satisfy them once and for all.

A global society must be aware of its own limitations. It is a universal idea and universal ideas can be dangerous if they are carried too far. Specifically, a global state would carry the idea of a global society too far. All that the universal idea could do is to serve as a basis for the rules and institutions that are necessary for the coexistence of the multiplicity of communities that make up a global society. It could not provide the community that would satisfy individuals' need for belonging. Yet the idea of a global society must represent something more than a mere agglomeration of market forces and economic transactions.

The Principles of Open Society

How can the encumbered individual be linked with the open society or, less abstractly, how can a world composed of encumbered individuals cooperate in forming a global open society? Recognition of our fallibility is necessary but not sufficient. An additional link is needed.

Fallibility establishes the constraints that collective decision making must respect in order to protect the freedom of the individual but fallibility must be accompanied by a positive impulse to cooperate. A belief in open society as a desirable form of social organization could provide that impulse. In the present situation, where we are already closely interlinked in a global economy, the impulse must operate on a global level. It is not difficult to identify shared goals. Avoidance of devastating armed conflicts, particularly nuclear war; the protection of the environment; preservation of a global financial and trading system: Few people would disagree with these objectives. The difficulty lies in deciding what needs to be done and in establishing a mechanism for doing it.

Cooperation on a global scale is exceedingly difficult to attain. Life would be much simpler if Friedrich Hayek were right and the common interest could be treated as the unintended by-product of people acting in their own best interest. The same applies to the communist prescription: From each according to his or her means, to each according to his or her needs. Unfortunately neither precept is valid. Life is more complicated. There *are* common interests, including the preservation of free markets, that are not served by free markets. In case of conflict, the common interests must take precedence over individual self-interests. But in the absence of an independent criterion, it is impossible to know what the common interests are. It follows that the common interest ought to be pursued with great circumspection, by a process of trial and error. To claim knowledge of the common interest is just as wrong as to deny its existence.

A participatory democracy and a market economy are essential ingredients of an open society, as is a mechanism for regulating markets, particularly financial markets, as well as some arrangements for preserving peace and law and order on a global scale. Exactly what shape these arrangements should take cannot be derived from first principles. To redesign reality from the top down would violate the principles of open society. That is where fallibility differs from rationality. Fallibility means that nobody has a monopoly on the truth. In fact, the principles of open society are admirably stated in the Declaration of Independence. All we need to do is to replace, in the first sentence, "These truths are held to be self-evident," with "We have chosen to adopt these principles as self-evident truths." This means that we are not obeying the dictates of reason but making a deliberate choice. In truth, the truths of the Declaration of Independence are not self-evident but reflexive in the sense in which all values are reflexive.

There are other reasons why I believe that fallibility and the encumbered individual provide a better basis for establishing a global open society. Pure reason and a moral code based on the value of the individual are inventions of Western culture; they have little resonance in other cultures. For instance, Confucian ethics are based on family and relationships and do not sit well with the universal concepts imported from the West. Fallibility allows for a broad range of cultural divergences. The Western intellectual tradition ought not to be imposed indiscriminately on the rest of the world in the name of universal values. The Western form of representative democracy may not be the only form of government compatible with an open society.

Nevertheless there must be some universal values that are generally accepted. Open society may be pluralistic by conception, but it cannot go so far in the pursuit of pluralism that it fails to distinguish between right and wrong. Toleration and moderation can also be carried to extremes. Exactly what is right can be discovered only by a process of trial and error. The definition is liable to vary with time and place, but there must be a definition at any one time and place. Whereas the Enlightenment held out the prospect of eternal verities, open society recognizes that values are reflexive and subject to change in the course of history. Collective decisions cannot be based on the dictates of reason; yet we cannot do without collective decisions. We need the rule of law exactly because we cannot be sure what is right and wrong. We need institutions that recognize their own fallibility and provide a mechanism for correcting their own mistakes.

A global open society cannot be formed without people subscribing to its basic principles. I do not mean all the people, of course, because many people do not give much thought to such matters and it would be contrary to the principles of open society if those who do were able to come to a universal agreement on the subject, but there must be a preponderance of opinion in its favor for open society to prevail.

Why should we accept open society as an ideal? The answer should be obvious by now. We cannot live as isolated individuals. As market participants, we serve our self-interest, but it does not serve our self-interest to be nothing but market participants. We need to be concerned with the society in which we live, and when it comes to collective decisions we ought to be guided by the interests of society as a whole rather than our narrow self-interest. The aggregation of narrow self-interests through the market mechanism brings unintended adverse consequences. Perhaps the most severe, at the present moment in history, is the instability of financial markets.

PART II

The Present Moment in History

CHAPTER 6

The Global Capitalist System

Now we come to the crux of the matter: How can the abstract theoretical framework that I have elaborated at such length shed some light on the present moment in history?

We live in a global economy that is characterized not only by free trade in goods and services but even more by the free movement of capital. Interest rates, exchange rates, and stock prices in various countries are intimately interrelated and global financial markets exert tremendous influence on economic conditions. Given the decisive role that international financial capital plays in the fortunes of individual countries, it is not inappropriate to speak of a global capitalist system.

The system is very favorable to financial capital, which is free to go where it is best rewarded, which in turn has led to the rapid growth of global financial markets. The result is a gigantic circulatory system, sucking up capital into the financial markets and institutions at the center and then pumping it out to the periphery either directly in the form of credits and portfolio investments or indirectly through multinational corporations. As long as the circulatory system is vigorous, it overwhelms most other influences. Capital brings many benefits, not only an increase in productive capacity but also improvements in the methods of production and other innovations; not only an increase in wealth but also an increase in freedom. Thus countries vie to attract and retain capital and making conditions attractive to capital takes precedence over other social objectives.

But the system is deeply flawed. As long as capitalism remains triumphant, the pursuit of money overrides all other social considerations. Economic and political arrangements are out of kilter. The development of a global economy has not been matched by the development of a global society. The basic unit for political and social life remains the nation-state. The relationship between center and periphery is also profoundly unequal. If and when the global economy falters, political pressures are liable to tear it apart.

My critique of the global capitalist system falls under two main headings. One concerns the defects of the market mechanism. Here I am talking primarily about the instabilities built into international financial markets. The other concerns the deficiencies of what I have to call, for lack of a better name, the nonmarket sector. By this I mean primarily the failure of politics both on the national and on the international level.

In the next three chapters, I deal mainly with the failings of the market mechanism, although I also take into account the absence of appropriate regulatory and political arrangements. After an analytical survey of the main features of the global capitalist system, I propose an interpretation based on my boom/bust analysis. I identify a prevailing bias—market fundamentalism—and a prevailing trend—international competition for capital. The boom/bust analysis will take up this chapter. In Chapter 7, I come to a much more definite conclusion about the future than in the current chapter. What I predict is the imminent disintegration of the global capitalist system.*

An Abstract Empire

The first question that needs to be answered is whether there is such a thing as a global capitalist system. My answer is, yes, but it is not a thing. We have an innate tendency to reify or personify abstract concepts—it is built into our language—and doing so can have unfortunate consequences. Abstract concepts take on a life of their own and it is only too easy to go off on the wrong track and become far removed from reality; yet we cannot avoid thinking in abstract terms, because reality is just too complex to be understood in its entirety. That is why ideas play such an important role in history—more important than we realize. This is particularly true at the present moment in history.

That the global capitalist system is an abstract concept does not make it any less significant. It rules our lives in the way that any regime rules people's lives. The capitalist system can be compared to an empire that is more global in its coverage than any previous empire. It rules an entire civilization and, as in other empires, those who are outside its walls are considered barbarians. It is not a territorial empire because it lacks sovereignty and the trappings of

---

*The trouble with trying to analyze a boom/bust sequence is that it does not stand still. As I mentioned in the introduction, I started to write this book as a sequel to my February 1997 article in *The Atlantic Monthly* titled "The Capitalist Threat." The first draft of this chapter was written in spring 1998. The following chapter incorporates more recent events. When the crisis in Russia reached its terminal phase, I briefly conducted a real-time experiment by keeping a diary from August 9 to August 31. The rest of the boom/bust analysis was completed in September. That explains why the next chapter contains more definite predictions than this one.

sovereignty; indeed, the sovereignty of the states that belong to it is the main limitation on its power and influence. It is almost invisible because it does not have any formal structure. Most of its subjects do not even know that they are subjected to it or, more correct, they recognize that they are subjected to impersonal and sometimes disruptive forces but they do not understand what those forces are.

The empire analogy is justified because the global capitalist system does govern those who belong to it—and it is not easy to opt out. Moreover, it has a center and a periphery just like an empire and the center benefits at the expense of the periphery. Most important, the global capitalist system exhibits some imperialistic tendencies. Far from seeking equilibrium, it is hell-bent on expansion. It cannot rest as long as there are any markets or resources that remain unincorporated. In this respect, it is little different from Alexander the Great or Attila the Hun and its expansionary tendencies may well prove its undoing. When I speak of expansion, I do not mean in geographical terms but in influence over people's lives.

In contrast to the nineteenth century when imperialism found a literal, territorial expression in the form of colonies, the current version of the global capitalist system is almost completely nonterritorial, or even extraterritorial, in character. Territories are governed by states and states often pose obstacles to the expansion of the capitalist system. This is true even of the United States, which is the most capitalistic of countries although isolationism and protectionism are recurrent themes in its political life.

The global capitalist system is purely functional in nature and the function it serves is (not surprisingly) economic: the production, consumption, and exchange of goods and services. It is important to note that the exchange involves not only goods and services but also the factors of production. As Marx and Engels pointed out 150 years ago, the capitalist system turns land, labor, and capital into commodities. As the system expands, the economic function comes to dominate the lives of people and societies. It penetrates into areas that were previously not considered economic, such as culture, politics, and the professions.

Despite its nonterritorial nature, the system does have a center and periphery. The center is the provider of capital; the periphery is the user of capital. The rules of the game are skewed in favor of the center. It could be argued that the center is in New York and London, because that is where the international financial markets are located, or in Washington, Frankfurt, and Tokyo, because that is where the world's money supply is determined; equally, it could be argued that the center is offshore, because that is where the most active and mobile part of the world's financial capital is domiciled.

An Incomplete Regime

The global capitalist system is not new or even novel. Its antecedents go back to the Hanseatic league and Italian city-states, in which different political entities were linked together by commercial and financial ties. Capitalism became dominant in the nineteenth century and remained so until it was disrupted by the First World War. But the global capitalist regime that prevails today has some novel features that set it apart from previous incarnations. The speed of communications is one such feature, although it is questionable how novel that is: The invention of telephony and telegraphy represented at least as great an acceleration in the nineteenth century as the development of computer communications does at present. Some other features that I shall try to identify are more peculiar to the present moment.

Although we can describe global capitalism as a regime, it is an incomplete regime: It governs only the economic function, even if the economic function has come to take precedence over other functions. The current regime has a history but it is not a well defined one. It is difficult even to identify when the regime came into existence. Was it in 1989 after the collapse of the Soviet empire? Around 1980 when Margaret Thatcher and Ronald Reagan came to power? Or at some earlier date? Perhaps it was in the 1970s when the offshore market in Eurodollars developed.

The distinguishing feature of the global capitalist system is the free movement of capital. International trade in goods and services is not enough to create a global economy; the factors of production must also be interchangeable. Land and other natural resources do not move and people move with difficulty; it is the mobility of capital, information, and entrepreneurship that is responsible for economic integration.

Because financial capital is even more mobile than physical investment, it occupies a privileged position: It can avoid countries where it is subjected to onerous taxes or regulations. Once a plant has been built, it is difficult to move it. To be sure, multinational corporations enjoy flexibility in transfer pricing and can exert pressure at the time they make investment decisions, but their flexibility does not compare to the freedom of choice enjoyed by international portfolio investors. The range of available opportunities is also enhanced by being at the center of the global economy rather than at the periphery. All these factors combine to attract capital to the financial center and to allocate it through the financial markets. That is why financial capital plays such a dominant role in the world today and that is why the influence of the financial markets has continually increased within the global capitalist system.

In fact, the free movement of capital is a relatively recent phenomenon. At the end of the Second World War, economies were largely national in character, international trade was at a low ebb, and both direct investments and financial transactions were practically at a standstill. The Bretton Woods institutions—the IMF and the World Bank—were designed to make international trade possible in a world devoid of international capital movements. The World

Bank was designed to make up for the lack of direct investments; the IMF, for the lack of financial credit to offset imbalances in trade. International capital in less developed countries was engaged mainly in the exploitation of natural resources and, far from encouraging international investment, the countries concerned were more likely to expropriate it—for instance, Anglo-Iranian Oil was nationalized in 1951. Nationalization of strategic industries was the order of the day in Europe as well. Most of the investment in less developed countries was in the form of government-to-government aid—for instance Britain's ill-fated groundnut scheme in Africa.

Direct investment picked up first. U.S. firms moved into Europe, then into the rest of the world. Companies originating in other countries caught up later. Many industries, such as autos, chemicals, and computers, came to be dominated by multinational corporations. International financial markets were slower to develop because many currencies were not fully convertible and many countries maintained controls over capital transactions. Capital controls were lifted only gradually. When I started in the business in London in 1953, both financial markets and banks were strictly regulated on a national basis and a fixed exchange rate system prevailed with many restrictions on the movement of capital. There was a market in "switch sterling" and "premium dollars"—special exchange rates applicable to capital accounts. After I moved to the United States in 1956, international trade in securities was gradually liberalized. With the formation of the Common Market, U.S. investors began to buy European securities, but the accounting of the companies concerned and the settlement arrangements left a lot to be desired—conditions were not very different from some of the emerging markets today, except the analysts and traders were less skilled. I was a one-eyed king among the blind. As late as 1963, President Kennedy proposed a so-called interest equalization tax on U.S. investors buying foreign stocks, which was then signed into law in 1964, practically putting me out of business.

The real emergence of global capitalism came in the 1970s. The oil-producing countries banded together in the Organization of Petroleum Exporting Countries (OPEC) and raised the price of oil, first in 1973 from $1.90 per barrel to $ 9.76 per barrel, and then in 1979, in response to political events in Iran and Iraq, from $12.70 to $28.76 per barrel. The oil exporters enjoyed sudden large surpluses while the importing countries had to finance large deficits. It was left to the commercial banks with behind-the-scenes encouragement from Western governments to recycle the funds. Eurodollars were invented and large offshore markets developed. Governments started to make tax and other concessions to international financial capital to entice it back onshore. Ironically, these measures gave off-shore capital more room to maneuver. The international lending boom ended in a bust in 1982, but by that time the freedom of movement for financial capital was well established.

The development of international financial markets received a big boost around 1980 when Margaret Thatcher and Ronald Reagan came to power with a program of removing the state from the economy and allowing the market mechanism to do its work. This meant imposing strict monetary discipline, which had the initial effect of plunging the world into a recession and precipitating the international debt crisis of 1982. It took several years for the world economy to recover—in Latin America they speak of the lost decade—but recover it did. From 1983 on, the global economy has enjoyed a long period of practically uninterrupted expansion. In spite of periodic crises, the development of international capital markets has accelerated to a point where they can be described as truly global. Movements in exchange rates, interest rates, and stock prices in various countries are intimately interconnected. In this respect, the character of the financial markets has changed beyond all recognition during the forty-five years that I have been involved in them.

Capitalism Versus Democracy

The balance of advantage has swung so far in favor of financial capital that it is often said that multinational corporations and international financial markets have somehow supplanted or impinged on the sovereignty of the state. That is not the case. States remain sovereign. They wield legal powers that no individual or corporation can possess. The days of the East India Company and the Hudson Bay Company are gone forever.

Although governments retain the power to interfere in the economy, they have become increasingly subject to the forces of global competition. If a government imposes conditions that are unfavorable to capital, capital will seek to escape. Conversely, if a government keeps down wages and provides incentives for favored businesses it can foster the accumulation of capital. So the global capitalist system consists of many sovereign states, each with its own policies, but each subject to international competition not only for trade but also for capital. This is one of the features that makes the system so complicated: Although we can speak of a global regime in economic and financial matters there is no global regime in politics. Each state has its own regime.

There is a widespread belief that capitalism is somehow associated with democracy in politics. It is a historical fact that the countries that constitute the center of the global capitalist system are democratic but the same is not true of all the capitalist countries that lie on the periphery. In fact, many claim that some kind of dictatorship is needed to get economic development going. Economic development requires the accumulation of capital and that, in turn, requires low wages and high savings rates. This is more easily accomplished under an autocratic government that is capable of imposing its will on the people than a democratic one that is responsive to the wishes of the electorate.

Take Asia, home to the most successful cases of economic development. In the Asian model, the state allies itself with local business interests and helps them to accumulate capital. The strategy requires government leadership in industrial planning, a high degree of financial leverage, and some degree of protection for the domestic economy, as well as the ability to control wages. Such a strategy was pioneered by Japan, which had the benefit of democratic institutions, introduced at the time of the U.S. occupation. Korea tried to imitate Japan quite slavishly but without democratic institutions. Instead, the policy was carried out by a military dictatorship holding sway over a small group of industrial conglomerates (*chaebol*). The checks and balances that prevailed in Japan were missing. There was a similar alliance between the military and the mainly Chinese business class in Indonesia. In Singapore, the state itself became a capitalist by setting up well-managed and highly successful investment funds. In Malaysia, the ruling party balanced favors to business interests with benefits for the ethnic Malay majority. In Thailand, the political arrangements are too difficult for an outsider to understand: Military meddling in business and financial meddling in the elections were two glaring weaknesses of the system. Hong Kong alone was exempt from the intermingling of government and business, due to its colonial status and relatively strict rule of law. Taiwan also stands out for having successfully completed the transition from an oppressive to a democratic political regime.

It is often argued that successful autocratic regimes eventually lead to the development of democratic institutions. The argument has some merit: An emerging middle class is very helpful in the creation of democratic regimes. But it does not follow that economic prosperity necessarily leads to the evolution of democratic freedoms. Rulers are reluctant to relinquish their power; they need to be pushed. For instance, Lee Kwan Yu of Singapore was more strident in propounding the merits of the "Asian way" after decades of prosperity than he was before.

But there is a more fundamental difficulty with the argument that capitalism leads to democracy. Forces within the global capitalist system that might push individual countries in a democratic direction are missing. International banks and multinational corporations often feel more comfortable with a strong, if autocratic, regime. Perhaps the most potent force for democracy is the free flow of information, which makes it difficult for governments to misinform the people. But the freedom of information should not be overestimated. In Malaysia, for instance, the regime has sufficient control over the media to allow Prime Minister Mahathir Mohammed to put his own spin on events with impunity. Information is even more restricted in China, where the government exerts control even over the Internet. In any case, the free flow of information will not necessarily impel people toward democracy, especially when people living in democracies do not believe in democracy as a universal principle.

Truth be told, the connection between capitalism and democracy is tenuous at best. Capitalism and democracy obey different principles. The stakes are different: In capitalism wealth is the object, in democracy it is political authority. The criteria by which the stakes are measured are different: In capitalism the unit of account is money, in democracy it is the citizens' vote. The interests that are supposed to be served are different: In capitalism it is private interests, in democracy it is the public interest. In the United States, this tension between capitalism and democracy is symbolized by the proverbial conflicts between Wall Street and Main Street. In Europe, the extension of the political franchise led to the correction of some of the worst excesses of capitalism: the dire predictions of the *Communist Manifesto* were in fact frustrated by the broadening of democracy.

Today the ability of the state to provide for the welfare of its citizens has been severely impaired by the ability of capital to escape taxation and onerous employment conditions by moving elsewhere. Countries that have overhauled their social security and employment arrangements—the United States and United Kingdom foremost among them—have flourished while others that have sought to preserve them—exemplified by France and Germany—have lagged behind.

The dismantling of the welfare state is a relatively new phenomenon, and its full effect has not yet been felt. Since the end of the Second World War, the state's share of gross national product (GNP) in the industrialized countries taken as a group has almost doubled.* Only after 1980 did the tide turn. Interestingly, the state's share of GNP has not declined perceptibly. What has happened instead is that the taxes on capital and employment have come down while other forms of taxation particularly on consumption have kept increasing. In other words, the burden of taxation has shifted from capital to citizens. That is not exactly what had been promised, but one cannot even speak of unintended consequences because the outcome was exactly as the free-marketeers intended.

The Role of Money

A global economic system that is not matched by a global political system is very difficult to analyze, especially in light of the tortuous relationship between capitalism and democracy. Obviously I have to simplify. But my task is easier than one could expect because there is a unifying principle in the global capitalist system. It is not a principle that is introduced for the sake of simplification; it is truly a dominant principle. That principle is money. Talking about market principles would confuse the issue, because money can be amassed in other ways than by competition. There can be no dispute

*Dani Rodrik, "Has Globalization Gone Too Far?," *Institute of International Economics* (Washington, DC), (1992).

that in the end it all boils down to profits and wealth measured in terms of money.

We can go a long way in understanding the global capitalist system if we understand the role that money plays in it. Money is not an easy concept but we do know a lot about it. The textbooks say it has three major functions: It serves as a unit of account, a medium of exchange, and a store of value. These functions are well understood, although the third function, money as a store of value, is open to dispute. In the classical interpretation, money is a means to an end, not an end in itself; it represents exchange value, not intrinsic value. That is to say, the value of money depends on the value of the goods and services for which it can be exchanged. But what are the intrinsic values that economic activities are supposed to serve? This is a troubling question that has never been satisfactorily answered. Eventually economists decided that they need not resolve the issue; they can take the agents' values as given. Their preferences, whatever they are, can be expressed in the form of indifference curves and indifference curves can be used to determine prices.

The trouble is that, in the real world, values are not given. In an open society, people are free to choose for themselves but they do not necessarily know what they want. In conditions of rapid change when traditions have lost their sway and people are assailed with suggestions from all sides, exchange values may well come to replace intrinsic values. This is particularly true in a capitalist regime that emphasizes competition and measures success in monetary terms. To the extent that other people want money and are willing to do almost anything to get it, money is power, and power can be an end in itself. Those who succeed may not know what to do with their money but at least they can be sure that other people envy their success. This may be enough to keep them going indefinitely despite the lack of any other motivation. The ones who keep going end up wielding the most power and influence in the capitalist system.

I shall defer consideration of the moral question whether money should serve as an intrinsic value till Chapter 9. For present purposes, I take it as a fact that the dominant value in the global capitalist system is the pursuit of money. I can do so because there are economic agents whose sole purpose is to make money and they dominate economic life today as never before. I am speaking of publicly owned corporations. These corporations are managed by professionals who apply management principles whose sole objective is to maximize profits. These principles are applicable interchangeably to all fields of activity and result in corporate managers buying and selling businesses in the same way as portfolio managers buy and sell stocks. The corporations, in turn, are owned mainly by professional portfolio managers whose sole objective in owning the stock is to make money on it.

In the theory of perfect competition, the firm is a profit-maximizing entity, but in practice business has not always been conducted with the sole purpose of maximizing profits. Private owners are often guided by other goals. Even publicly traded corporations often have managers who feel sufficiently well entrenched to indulge motivations other than profit. These motivations may range from their own perks, benefits, and lifestyle to altruistic or nationalistic considerations. The managers of the large German multinationals have traditionally considered themselves beholden to their workers and the general public as well as to their shareholders. The Japanese economy has been characterized by interlocking share holdings, and relationships have often taken precedence over profits. Korea carried the Japanese example to extremes and went for broke in an attempt to capture market share in key industries.

But in today's global capitalist system, there has been a pronounced shift in favor of profit-maximizing behavior and a corresponding heightening of competitive pressures. As markets become global, privately owned companies are at a disadvantage in preserving or gaining market share; companies need to raise capital from outside shareholders to exploit the opportunities presented by globalization. As a result, publicly traded companies have come to dominate the scene and they have become increasingly single-minded in the pursuit of profits.

In the United States, shareholders have become more assertive and the stock market has become more discriminating in favor of managers who are committed to maximizing profits. Success is measured by short-term performance and managers are rewarded by stock options rather than perks. In Europe, companies used to de-emphasize profits, both in their public image and in their public accounts. This was because higher profits tended to generate higher wage demands and it was considered inadvisable to attract attention to the profitability of the enterprise. But the pressure of global competition has served to moderate wage demands and shifted the emphasis to the need to finance expansion. The creation of the European Union as a single market with a single currency has set off a scramble for market share. The price of stock has become much more important, both for raising capital and as a vehicle for acquisitions (or, in the case of a low price, as an enticement for being acquired). Social goals, such as providing employment, have to take second place. Competition has forced consolidation, downsizing, and the transfer of production abroad. These are important factors in creating a persistently high level of unemployment in Europe.

So the hallmark of the current form of global capitalism, the feature that sets it apart from earlier versions, is its pervasive success: the intensification of the profit motive and its penetration into areas that were previously governed by other considerations. Non-monetary values used to play a larger role in people's lives; in particular, culture and the professions were supposed to be governed by cultural and professional values and not construed as business enterprises. To understand how the current global capitalist regime differs from previous regimes, we must recognize the growing role of money as an intrinsic value. It is no exaggeration to say that money rules people's lives to a greater extent than ever before.

Credit as a Source of Instability

Money is closely connected with credit but the role of credit is less well understood than the role of money. This is not surprising because credit is a reflexive phenomenon. Credit is extended against collateral or some other evidence of creditworthiness and the value of the collateral as well as the measurements of creditworthiness are reflexive in character because creditworthiness is in the eye of the creditor. The value of collateral is influenced by the availability of credit. This is particularly true for real estate—a favorite form of collateral. Banks are usually willing to lend against real estate without recourse to the borrower, and the main variable in the value of real estate is the amount the banks are willing to lend against it. Strange as it may seem, the reflexive connection is not recognized in theory and it is often forgotten in practice. Construction is notorious for its boom/bust character and after each bust bank managers become very cautious and resolve never to become so exposed again. But when they are again awash with liquidity and desperate to put money to work, a new cycle begins. The same pattern can be observed in international lending. The creditworthiness of sovereign borrowers is measured by certain ratios—debt to GNP, debt service to exports, and the like. These measures are reflexive because the prosperity of the borrowing country is dependent on its ability to borrow, but the reflexive connection is often ignored. That is what happened in the great international lending boom of the 1970s. After the crisis of 1982, one would have thought that excessive lending would never happen again; yet it did happen again in Mexico in 1994 and yet again, as we shall see, in the Asian crisis of 1997.

Most economic theoreticians do not recognize reflexivity. They seek to establish the conditions of equilibrium and reflexivity is a source of disequilibrium. John Maynard Keynes was very much aware of reflexive phenomena—he described financial markets as a beauty contest where people have to guess how other people guess how other people guess—but even he presented his theory in terms of equilibrium to make it academically acceptable.

A favorite way of avoiding the reflexivity inherent in credit is to concentrate on the money supply instead. The money supply can be quantified so that its measurement presumably reflects credit conditions—in this way the reflexive phenomena connected with the expansion and contraction of credit can be ignored. But a stable money supply does not create a stable economy, as experience with the gold standard has shown. Excesses may be self-correcting, but at what cost? The nineteenth century was punctuated by devastating panics followed by economic depressions. We are currently in the process of reliving that experience.

Keynes discredited monetarism in the 1930s but after his death he fell out of favor because his prescription for curing deflation led to the emergence of inflationary tendencies. (Had Keynes lived, he would have probably changed his prescription.) Instead, the establishment and preservation of monetary stability became the prime objective. This led to the reinvention of monetarist theory by Milton Friedman. Friedman's theory is flawed as it disregards the reflexive element in credit expansion and contraction. In practice monetarism has worked quite well but largely by disregarding the theory. Central banks do not rely exclusively on monetary measurements but take into account a large variety of factors—including the irrational exuberance of markets—in deciding how to maintain monetary stability. The German central bank goes to great lengths to maintain the illusion that it is guided by monetary aggregates. By contrast, the Federal Reserve is more agnostic and openly admits that monetary policy is a matter of judgment. That is how practice has been reconciled with a theory that does not recognize reflexivity. But in the current global financial crisis, both theory and practice are proving inadequate.

Credit plays an important role in economic growth. The ability to borrow greatly enhances the profitability of investments. The anticipated rate of return is usually higher than the riskless rate of interest—otherwise the investment would not be made in the first place—and there is therefore a positive profit margin on borrowing. The more an investment can be leveraged the more attractive it becomes, provided the cost of money remains the same. The cost and availability of credit thus become important elements in influencing the level of economic activity; indeed, they are probably the most important factors in determining the asymmetric shape of the boom/bust cycle. There may be other elements at play, but it is the contraction of credit that renders the bust so much more abrupt than the boom that preceded it. When it comes to the forced liquidation of debts, the sale of collateral depresses collateral values, unleashing a self-reinforcing process that is much more compressed in time than the expansionary phase. This holds true whether the credit was provided by the banks or the financial markets and whether the borrowing was against securities or physical assets.

International credit is particularly unstable because it is not nearly as well regulated as domestic credit in economically advanced countries. Ever since the birth of capitalism, there have been periodic financial crises, often with devastating consequences. To prevent recurrence, both banks and financial markets have been subjected to regulations, but the regulations usually addressed the last crisis and not the next one, so that each new crisis led to another advance in regulations. That is how central banking, banking supervision, and the supervision of financial markets have evolved to their present, highly sophisticated state.

The development was not linear. The crash of 1929 and the subsequent failure of the U.S. banking system led to a very restrictive regulatory environment in the U.S. both for the stock market and for the banks. Since the end of the Second World War, a thawing-out process has occurred, very slowly at first but gradually accelerating. The separation between banks and other financial institutions imposed by the Glass-Steegal Act has not yet been repealed, but the regulation of both banks and financial markets has been greatly relaxed.

Deregulation and the globalization of financial markets have gone hand in hand in a reflexive fashion. Most regulations were national in scope so the globalization of markets meant less regulation and vice versa. But it was not a one-way street. Even as national regulations were relaxed, some international regulations were introduced. The two Bretton Woods institutions, the IMF and the World Bank, adapted to the changing circumstances and became more active as global watchdogs. The monetary authorities of the leading industrial nations established channels for cooperation and some genuinely international regulations were introduced. By far the most important are the capital requirements for commercial banks that were established under the aegis of the Bank for International Settlements (BIS) in Basle in 1988.

In fact, without the intervention of the monetary authorities the international financial system would have collapsed on at least four occasions: 1982, 1987, 1994, and 1997. Nevertheless, international controls remain quite inadequate in comparison with the regulatory environment that prevails in the advanced countries. Moreover, the countries at the center are more likely to respond to crises that affect them directly than to those whose primary victims are at the periphery. It is noteworthy that the U.S. stock market crash of 1987, which was purely domestic in origin, led to regulatory changes, namely, the introduction of so called circuit breakers; disturbances in the international financial markets did not provoke a similar response. Although the introduction of the BIS standards in 1988 was a belated answer to the crisis of 1982, the fact remains that international regulations have not kept pace with the globalization of financial markets.

This inadequacy of international regulations can be attributed partly to the failure to understand the reflexive nature of credit and partly to the prevailing antiregulatory mood, but mainly to the lack of appropriate international institutions. National financial systems are in the charge of central banks and other financial authorities. By and large they do a good job; there has been no breakdown in the financial systems of the major industrial countries for several decades. But who is in charge of the international financial system? The international financial institutions and the national monetary authorities cooperate at times of crisis, but there is no international central bank, no international regulatory authority to compare with the institutions that exist on a national level. Nor is it easy to see how such institutions could be introduced: Both money and credit are intimately connected with issues of national sovereignty and national advantage and nations are disinclined to give up their sovereignty.

Asymmetry, Instability, and Cohesion

By definition, the center is the provider of capital, the periphery the recipient. An abrupt change in the willingness of the center to provide capital to the periphery can cause great disruption in the recipient countries. The nature of the disruption depends on the form in which capital was provided. If it was in the form of debt instruments or bank credits, it can cause bankruptcies and a banking crisis; if it was in stocks, it can precipitate a stock market crash; if it was in the form of direct investments, it cannot be readily withdrawn, so the disruption manifests itself only in the absence of new investments. Usually all forms of capital move in the same direction.

What happens when a country defaults on its debt? The answer is shrouded in mystery because formal defaults are usually avoided. There is a general impression that the country concerned will suffer irreparable damage, but in reality many countries have failed to meet their obligations and ways have been found to accommodate them. Following the international debt crisis of 1982, the Paris Club was set up to deal with official debt and the London Club for commercial debt. In addition, so-called Brady bonds were issued to reduce the principal amount of debt outstanding. In the case of African countries, some debts have been forgiven entirely to give the countries the chance of a new start. Concessions are made only in the context of negotiations; unilateral repudiation of obligations will not be tolerated (at least this was the official view until Russia's repudiation of its domestic debt in August 1998) and help from the international financial institutions is contingent on the orderly settlement of obligations. Although the IMF is not supposed to be partial to the banks, its primary mission is to preserve the international banking system. Moreover, it does not have sufficient resources to act as the lender of last resort; therefore it must mobilize help from the financial markets. Commercial bankers know how to utilize their strategic position. On the few occasions when debt repudiation occurred—for instance in the Russian and Mexican Revolutions—the countries concerned were kept in financial purdah for many years. Countries hooked on foreign credit cannot easily get unhooked.

As a general rule, lenders tend to fare much better in an international debt crisis than debtors. They may have to roll over their loans, extend the dates of maturity, or even grant concessional rates but they do not abandon their claims. Often they can even persuade debtor countries to assume liability for commercial banks that would otherwise be wiped out (which is what happened in Chile in 1982 and in Mexico in 1994 and it is happening again to a limited extent in 1998 in Korea, Indonesia, and Thailand). Of course, the lenders have to set up reserves, but eventually they tend to recover a significant part of the bad debts. Although the debtor countries may not be able to pay off their obligations in full, they will be obliged to pay to the limits of their ability. The burden of doing so will usually weigh them down for many years to come.

This is in sharp contrast with domestic debt crises in advanced countries in which bankruptcy procedures tend to protect the debtors. (U.S. banks lost a lot more money in the savings and loan crisis of 1985–1989 than the international debt crisis of 1982.) The relative immunity of the lenders in the international system creates a dangerous moral hazard: The risks are not large enough to discourage unsound lending practices. This asymmetry is a major source of instability. Every financial crisis is preceded by an unsustainable expansion of credit. If credit is freely available, it is too much to expect the debtors to exercise self-restraint. If the public sector is the borrower, the debt will have to be repaid by future governments—running up debt is a wonderful escape hatch for weak regimes. For instance, the so-called reform communist regime in Hungary tried to buy the allegiance of the people with borrowed money until the crisis of 1982 put an end to it. But it is not just the public sector that lacks restraint, and if the debt is incurred by the private sector the financial authorities might not even be aware of it until it is too late. That was the case in several Asian countries in the crisis of 1997.

Yet the asymmetry is also a source of cohesion. All sorts of financial and political pressures are brought to bear on debtor countries making it very difficult to opt out of the system. The pressures hold the system together even if it is quite painful for some countries to belong to it. For instance, the first democratic elections in Hungary in 1990 would have offered an excellent opportunity to draw a line between past indebtedness and the obligations entered into by the new democratic regime. I tried to prepare such a scheme, but the future prime minister, Joseph Antall, reneged on it because he was far too beholden to Germany, Hungary's largest creditor. Other instances could be cited. The case of Chile in 1982 sticks in my memory. Under the influence of the Chicago school of economists, the banking system had been privatized and the people who had bought the banks had paid for them with money borrowed from the banks themselves. In 1982 when the banks could not meet their international obligations, the state assumed responsibility because the Pinochet regime, lacking legitimacy at home, was eager to maintain its credit standing abroad.

Another asymmetry needs to be noted. Issuing money is a national prerogative and nations whose currency is readily accepted in international financial transactions are much better situated than those that cannot readily borrow in their own currency. This is one of the main advantages of being at the center as opposed to being on the periphery. The benefits of earning seignorage (the interest saved by issuing banknotes rather than treasury bills) are relatively insignificant compared to the advantage of being in charge of one's own monetary policy. Countries on the periphery must take their cue from the center—in the first place the United States. Because the monetary policy of the center countries is guided by domestic considerations, those on the periphery have little control over their destinies. In a sense, the process recalls the problem that sparked the American Revolution: taxation without representation.

The fact that the exchange rates of the three or four major currencies fluctuate against each other can cause further complications. Changes in interest rates and exchange rates hit the dependent countries as exogenous shocks—although in reality they are endogenous to the international financial system. The international debt crisis of 1982 was precipitated by a drastic rise in U.S. interest rates; the Asian crisis of 1997 was touched off by a rise in the U.S. dollar. The intra-European currency crisis of 1992 was caused by a similar asymmetry between Germany and the rest of Europe.

These two asymmetries are the major, but by no means only, sources of instability in the international financial system. Historically, cross-border investments used to be particularly unstable because they used to occur in the advanced stages of bull markets when domestic stocks became overvalued and overexploited and investors became more adventurous. This sudden interest in a foreign market would drive prices in that market through the roof, only to fall equally fast when the domestic bull market came to an end and investors became anxious to bring their money home. This was my initial area of specialization and I lived through several of these episodes. Conditions have since changed. Cross-border investment is no longer an occasional activity but the bread and butter of global financial markets. Although the peculiar rhythm of foreign investing to which I became accustomed during the early years of my career may have gone out of style, it would be foolish to think that stock markets are no longer susceptible to dynamic disequilibrium.

In times of uncertainty, capital tends to return to its place of origin. That is one reason why disturbances in the global capitalist system tend to have a disproportionally larger effect at the periphery than at the center. As the saying goes, when Wall Street catches cold, the rest of the world catches pneumonia. In the case of the Asian crisis, the troubles started at the periphery, but once Wall Street started sniffling, the impulse to withdraw funds from the periphery became overwhelming.

In spite of its asymmetry and instability—or rather because of it—the global capitalist system exhibits considerable cohesion. Being at the periphery has its disadvantages but it is preferable to opting out. For poor countries, attracting outside capital is essential to economic development. To put matters in perspective, the material achievements of the global capitalist system should not be understated. Although the cards are stacked in favor of capital, the countries that have been able to attract capital have not done so badly either. Asia is now in the midst of a severe crisis but the crisis comes after a period of explosive growth. Latin America, after the lost decade of the 1980s and the tequila effect of the Mexican crisis of 1994, has been enjoying a strong inflow of equity capital, particularly in the banking and financial sectors, that was finally beginning to translate into real growth. Even Africa has shown some signs of life. So in addition to its cohesion, the system also shows considerable resilience, counterbalanced on the negative side by its asymmetry and instability.

The Future of the Global Capitalist System

What can we say about the future of the global capitalist system? The past may offer some clues. In some ways, the nineteenth-century version of the global capitalist system was more stable than the current one. It had a single currency, gold; today there are three major currencies crashing against each other like continental plates. There were imperial powers, Britain foremost among them, that derived enough benefits from being at the center of the global capitalist system to justify dispatching gunboats to faraway places to preserve the peace or collect debts; today the United States refuses to act as the police force of the world. Most important, people were more firmly rooted in fundamental values than they are today. Reality was still regarded as something external and thinking was still considered a means of attaining knowledge. Right and wrong, true and false were considered objective criteria on which people could depend. Science offered deterministic explanations and predictions. There were conflicts between the precepts of religion and science but they both covered the same ground: They offered a dependable guide to the world. Together, they created a culture that, in spite of its internal contradictions, dominated the world.

This global capitalist system came to an end with the First World War. It had gone through a number of financial crises prior to the war, some of which were quite severe and caused several years of economic dislocation and decline. Yet it was not the financial crises that destroyed the system but political and military developments.

There was another incarnation of international capitalism in the 1920s, although it was not quite global in scope. It was brought to an end by the crash of 1929 and the subsequent depression. I doubt whether that particular episode of history will recur. Allowing the U.S. banking system to collapse was a policy error that we are not likely to repeat. Nevertheless, I see instability ahead.

Boom/Bust

I am reluctant to apply the boom/bust model to the global capitalist system because I consider the system too open-ended and incomplete to fit the pattern neatly. Yet, almost against my better judgment—I do not want to give the impression that everything should be interpreted as a boom/bust phenomenon—I can identify the makings of a boom/bust pattern: a prevailing trend, namely, international competition for capital, and a prevailing bias, namely, an excessive belief in the market mechanism. In the boom, both bias and trend reinforce each other. In the bust, both of them fall apart. What will bring about the bust? I believe the answer is to be found in the tension between the global scope of the financial markets and the national scope of politics. Earlier I described the global capitalist system as a gigantic circulatory system sucking capital into the center and pushing it out into the periphery. The sovereign states act like valves within the system. While the global financial markets are expanding, the valves open, but if and when the flow of funds is reversed they stand in the way, causing the system to break down.

Market Fundamentalism

The global capitalist system is supported by an ideology rooted in the theory of perfect competition. According to this theory, markets tend toward equilibrium and the equilibrium position represents the most efficient allocation of resources. Any constraints on free competition interfere with the efficiency of the market mechanism;

therefore they should be resisted. In previous discussions, I described this as the laissez faire ideology but market fundamentalism is a better term. This phrase is better because fundamentalism implies a certain kind of belief that is easily carried to extremes. It is a belief in perfection, a belief in absolutes, a belief that every problem must have a solution. It posits an authority that is endowed with perfect knowledge even if that knowledge is not readily accessible to ordinary mortals. God is such an authority and in modern times science has become an acceptable substitute. Marxism claimed to have a scientific basis; so does market fundamentalism. The scientific basis of both ideologies was established in the nineteenth century when science still promised to deliver the ultimate truth. We have learned a great deal since then both about the limitations of scientific method and the imperfections of the market mechanism. Both Marxist and laissez faire ideologies have been thoroughly discredited. The laissez faire ideology was the first to be dismissed, as a consequence of the Great Depression and the rise of Keynesian economics. Marxism lingered on in spite of the excesses of Stalin's rule but, following the collapse of the Soviet system, it is now in almost total eclipse.

In my student days in the early 1950s, laissez faire was even more unacceptable than state intervention in the economy is today. The idea that it would stage a comeback seemed inconceivable. I believe that the revival of market fundamentalism can be explained only by faith in a magic quality ("the invisible hand") that is even more important than the scientific base. Not in vain did President Reagan speak of "the magic of the marketplace."

A key feature of fundamentalist beliefs is that they rely on either/or judgments. If a proposition is wrong, its opposite is claimed to be right. This logical incoherence lies at the heart of market fundamentalism. State intervention in the economy has always produced some negative results. This has been true not only of central planning but also of the welfare state and of Keynesian demand management. From this banal observation, market fundamentalists jump to a totally illogical conclusion: If state intervention is faulty, free markets must be perfect. Therefore the state must not be allowed to intervene in the economy. It hardly needs pointing out that the logic of this argument is faulty.

To be fair, the arguments in favor of unregulated markets are rarely presented in such a crude form. On the contrary, people like Milton Friedman have presented voluminous statistics and the theoreticians of rational expectations have employed arcane mathematics. I am told that some of them have incorporated imperfect and asymmetric information in their models, but their avowed purpose in jumping through hoops has generally been to establish the conditions of perfection, namely, equilibrium. I am reminded of theological discussions in the Middle Ages about the number of angels who can dance on the head of a pin.

Market fundamentalism plays a crucial role in the global capitalist system. It provides the ideology that not only motivates many of the most successful participants but also drives policy. In its absence, we would not be justified in talking about a capitalist regime. Market fundamentalism came to dominate policy around 1980, when Ronald Reagan and Margaret Thatcher came to power more or less simultaneously. The prevailing trend, international competition for capital, started earlier, with the two oil crises in the 1970s and the establishment of an offshore market in Eurocurrencies. Bias and trend have been reinforcing each other ever since. It is a manifold process with various facets that are difficult to disentangle from each other.

The Triumph of Capitalism

Publicly traded companies are increasing in numbers and size and the interests of shareholders loom ever larger. Managers are as much concerned with the market for their shares as with the market for their products. If it comes to a choice, the signals from financial markets take precedence over those from product markets: Managers will readily divest divisions or sell the entire company if this will enhance shareholder value; they maximize profits rather than market share. Managers must either acquire or be acquired in an increasingly integrated global market; either way they need a high price for their stock. Their personal rewards are also increasingly tied to the price of their stock. The change is particularly pronounced in the banking sector, which is undergoing rapid consolidation. Bank shares are selling at several times book value, but managers, mindful of their stock options, continue to repurchase shares, reducing the number of shares outstanding and increasing the market value of the shares.

Merger and acquisition activity is reaching unprecedented levels as industries are consolidating on a global basis. Cross-country transactions become ever more common. The establishment of a single currency in Europe has given Europe-wide consolidation a tremendous push. This realignment of companies is occurring faster than one could have imagined. Global monopolies and oligopolies are beginning to emerge. There are only four major auditing firms left in the world; similar but less pronounced concentration is taking place in other financial functions. Microsoft and Intel are on the verge of worldwide monopolies.

At the same time, the number of shareholders is growing and the relative importance of share ownership in household wealth is increasing at an accelerating rate. This is happening against a background of a sustained and rapid rise in equity prices. Prior to August 1998, the last major break in the bull market that started in the early 1980s was in 1987 and the Standard and Poor (S&P) index has risen by more than 350 percent since then. In Germany, the market has risen by 297 percent since September 1992. The growth in economic activity has been more modest but sustained. The focus on profitability has led to reductions in the number of employees and increases in the output per employee while rapid advances in technology contributed to rising productivity. Globalization and exploitation of cheaper sources of labor have kept the cost of production down and interest rates have, on balance, shown a declining trend since the early 1980s, contributing to the rise in equity prices.

The spread of stock ownership through mutual funds has introduced two potential sources of instability, particularly in the United States. One is the so-called wealth effect. Thirty-eight percent of household wealth and 56 percent of pension funds are invested in stocks. Stock owners have big paper profits, they feel rich, and their propensity to save has been reduced to the vanishing point, as can be seen in Graph 6.1. This graph reveals that personal savings of households as a percent of disposable income has now fallen to 0.1 percent from a peak of 13 percent in 1975. Should there be a sustained decline in the stock market, shareholders' sentiments would be reversed, contributing to a recession and reinforcing the market decline.

Another source of potential instability comes from the mutual funds. Fund managers are judged on the basis of their performance relative to other fund managers, not on the grounds of absolute performance. This may sound like an arcane point but it has far-reaching implications as it practically forces fund managers into trend-following behavior. As long as they keep with the herd, no harm will come to them even if the investors lose money, but if they try to buck the trend and their relative performance suffers even temporarily, they may lose their job. (This is precisely what happened to Jeff Vinik, the manager of Fidelity's largest fund. He has been very successful on his own ever since, earning a performance fee based on absolute performance.) By fall 1998, mutual funds, having become used to a constant inflow of new cash, were carrying the lowest cash reserves ever. Should the trend turn, they will be forced to raise cash, adding to the downward pressure.

However worrisome this is, the main sources of instability are in the international arena. The global capitalist system is currently undergoing the most severe test of its existence: the Asian crisis and its aftermath. Testing constitutes the third stage in the boom/bust pattern. As in every boom/bust cycle, it cannot be predicted with certainty whether a trend will be successfully tested or abruptly reversed. It is more productive to lay out possible scenarios for a successful or an unsuccessful test.

If the global capitalist system survives the present period of testing, this period will be followed by a period of further acceleration that will carry the system into far-from-equilibrium territory if it is not there already. One of the features of this new, more extreme,

Graph 6.1

Personal Savings Rates as Percent of Disposable Income: United States

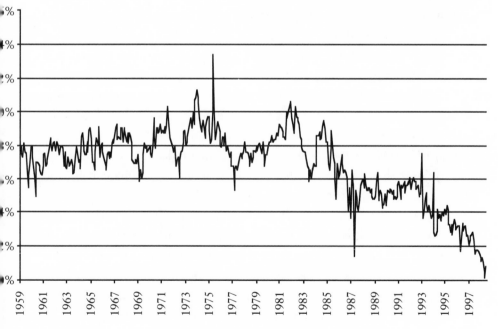

As Reported in January of Each Year

form of global capitalism will be the elimination of one plausible alternative to free market ideology that recently emerged—the so-called Asian, or Confucian, model. As a result of the current crisis, the overseas Chinese and Korean capitalists whose wealth has been severely impaired will have to give up family control. Those who are willing to do so will survive; others will perish. The crisis has also aggravated the situation of heavily indebted companies in all Asian countries. Those with foreign debt have seen their debt to equity ratios deteriorate further; those with domestic debt have been hit by the combination of a rise in interest rates and a decline in earnings. The only way out is to convert debt to equity or to raise additional equity. This cannot be done by the family; usually it cannot even be done locally. There will be no alternative but to sell out to foreigners. The net result will be the end of the Asian model and the beginning of a new era in which the countries concerned will be even more closely integrated into the global capitalist system. International banks and multinational corporations will gain strong footholds. Within local companies, a new generation of family members or professional managers educated abroad will come to the fore. The profit motive will take precedence over Confucian ethics and nationalist pride and the market fundamentalist bias will be further reinforced. Some countries, such as Malaysia, may fall by the wayside if they persist with their xenophobic, anti-market policies, but others will make the grade.

So if the global capitalist system emerges triumphant from the current crisis, it can be anticipated that the world economy will be dominated even more than it is today by publicly owned international corporations. Severe competition will not allow them to pay much heed to social concerns. They will, of course, pay lip service to worthy causes such as the environment, particularly if they have direct dealings with the general public, but they will not be able to afford to maintain employment to the detriment of profits.

On the other hand, it is quite possible that the global capitalist system will not survive the current test. The economic decline has not yet run its course in the periphery countries and it cannot be reversed without a lot of pain. Banks and companies will have to be reorganized; a lot of people have yet to lose their jobs. Political tensions are high or still rising. Political changes brought about by the financial crisis have already led to the demise of the previous corrupt and authoritarian regimes in several countries. Korea was fortunate to elect a new president, Kim Dae Jung, who has been an outspoken critic of the incestuous relationship between government and business all his life. The current prime minister in Thailand is generally admired for his honesty and he is surrounded by a Western-educated, market-oriented cabinet. In Indonesia, Suharto was swept from office by a revolution. In Malaysia, Mahathir is beleaguered. In China, the economic reformers are in charge, but there is a real danger that if economic conditions continue to deteriorate the reformers will lose power. It is often said that revolutions devour their own children. Already anti-American, anti-IMF, antiforeign resentment is building up throughout Asia, including in Japan. Elections in Indonesia could well produce a nationalistic, Islamic government inspired by Mahathir's ideas.

What happens at the center will be decisive. Until recently the trouble at the periphery has been beneficial to the center. It has counteracted incipient inflationary pressures, induced the monetary authorities not to raise interest rates, and allowed stock markets to reach new highs. But the positive effects of the Asian crisis are beginning to wear off and the negative ones are beginning to surface. Profit margins are coming under increasing pressure. Some companies are directly affected by reduced demand or tougher competition from abroad; others in the service industries that are not directly affected by international competition feel the impact of rising labor costs.

The stock market boom has also run its course. Should the market turn down, the wealth effect is liable to translate a market decline into an economic decline. That could, in turn, arouse resistance to imports, which could, in turn, fuel the resentment at the periphery.

Ever since the outbreak of the Asian crisis, capital has been fleeing from the periphery. If the countries on the periphery give up hope that the flow will resume, they may start using their sovereignty to prevent the outflow. That will reinforce the outflow and the system will collapse. The United States is also looking increasingly inward. The refusal of Congress to provide additional funds to the IMF may play the same role today as the Smoot-Hawley tariffs did in the Great Depression.

Which of the two scenarios is likely to prevail? I am inclined to bet on the latter but as a market participant I must maintain an open mind. I have no hesitation, however, in asserting that the global capitalist system will succumb to its defects, if not on this occasion then on the next one—unless we recognize that it is defective and act in time to correct the deficiencies.

I can already discern the makings of the final crisis. It will be political in character. Indigenous political movements are likely to arise that will seek to expropriate the multinational corporations and recapture the "national" wealth. Some of them may succeed in the manner of the Boxer Rebellion or the Zapatista Revolution. Their success may then shake the confidence of financial markets, engendering a self-reinforcing process on the downside. Whether it will happen on this occasion or the next one is an open question.

As long as a boom/bust process survives testing, it emerges reinforced. The more stringent the test, the greater the reinforcement. After each successful test comes a period of acceleration; after a period of acceleration comes the moment of truth. Exactly where we are in this sequence is impossible to determine except in retrospect.

7

The Global Financial Crisis

The Asian Crisis

The financial crisis that originated in Thailand in 1997 is particularly unnerving because of its scope and severity. As I mentioned in the preface, we at Soros Fund Management could see a crisis coming and so could others, but the extent of the dislocation took everyone by surprise. A number of latent and seemingly unrelated imbalances were activated and their interaction touched off a far-from-equilibrium process whose results are entirely out of proportion with the ingredients that went into creating it.

The financial markets played a role that is very different from the one assigned to them by economic theory. Financial markets are supposed to swing like a pendulum: They may fluctuate wildly in response to exogenous shocks, but eventually they are supposed to come to rest at an equilibrium point and that point is supposed to be the same irrespective of the interim fluctuations. Instead, as I told Congress, financial markets behaved more like a wrecking ball, swinging from country to country and knocking over the weaker ones.

It is difficult to escape the conclusion that the international financial system itself constituted the main ingredient in the meltdown process. It certainly played an active role in every country, although the other ingredients varied from country to country. Such a conclusion is difficult to reconcile with the widely held notion that financial markets passively reflect the fundamentals. If my point is valid, then the role that financial markets play in the world ought to be radically reconsidered. To test this thesis about financial markets, let us take an inventory of the other ingredients involved and then take a look at what happened.

The most immediate cause of trouble was a misalignment of currencies. The Southeast Asian countries maintained an informal arrangement that tied their currencies to the U.S. dollar. The apparent stability of the dollar peg encouraged local banks and businesses to borrow in dollars and convert dollars into local currencies without hedging; then the banks lent to or invested in local projects, particularly real estate. This seemed to be a riskless way of making money as long as the informal peg held. But the arrangement came under pressure, partly from the undervaluation of the Chinese currency in 1994, and partly from the appreciation of the U.S. dollar against the yen. The balance of trade of the countries concerned deteriorated, although the trade deficits were at first offset by continuing substantial inflows on capital accounts. Nevertheless, by the beginning of 1997 it was clear to us at Soros Fund Management that the discrepancy between the trade account and the capital account was becoming untenable. We sold short the Thai baht and the Malaysian ringgit early in 1997 with maturities ranging from six months to a year.* Subsequently Prime Minister Mahathir of Malaysia accused me of causing

*We entered into contracts to deliver at future dates Thai baht and Malaysian ringgit that we did not currently hold.

the crisis. The accusation was totally unfounded. We were not sellers of the currency during or several months before the crisis; on the contrary, we were buyers when the currencies began to decline—we were purchasing ringgits to realize the profits on our earlier speculation (much too soon, as it turned out).

If it was clear to us in January 1997 that the situation was untenable, it must have been clear to others. Yet the crisis did not break out until July 1997 when the Thai authorities abandoned the peg and floated the currency. The crisis came later than we had expected because the local monetary authorities kept on supporting their currencies far too long and international banks continued to extend credit although they must have seen the writing on the wall. The delay has undoubtedly contributed to the severity of the crisis. From Thailand, it quickly spread to Malaysia, Indonesia, the Philippines, South Korea, and other countries.

The important point to consider, however, is that some other countries that became engulfed in the Asian crisis did *not* have an informal dollar peg. It is true that the Korean won was overvalued, but that was not the case for the Japanese or Chinese currencies. On the contrary, the competitive advantage enjoyed by China and the significant depreciation of the Japanese yen against the dollar were factors in precipitating the crisis. What, then, did the stricken economies have in common? Some argue that the problem was their common dependence on a distorted or immature form of the capitalist regime now described pejoratively as "crony capitalism" but previously extolled under the name of Confucian capitalism, or the Asian model. There is some truth in this claim, as I explain in the thumbnail sketches that follow. But attributing the crisis to specifically Asian characteristics obviously does not give the full picture, as the crisis has spread to Latin America and Eastern Europe and is now beginning to affect the financial markets and economies of Western Europe and the United States. After a brief discussion of what has been happening in Asia, therefore, I return to the main thrust of my argument—that the global crisis is caused by pathologies inherent in the global financial system itself.

Demise of the Asian Model

There were many structural weaknesses in the Asian economies. Most businesses were family owned and in accordance with Confucian tradition the families wanted to retain control. If they issued shares to the public, they were inclined to disregard the rights of minority shareholders. To the extent that they could not finance their growth out of earnings, they preferred to rely on credit rather than risk losing control. At the same time, government officials used bank credit as a tool of industrial policy; they also used it to reward their family and friends. There was an incestuous relationship between business and government of which this was only one expression. The combination of these factors resulted in very high debt to equity ratios and a financial sector that was neither transparent nor sound. The idea that "bank credit" would discipline company shareholders simply did not apply.*

For instance, the South Korean economy was dominated by family-controlled *chaebol* (conglomerates). The *chaebol* were highly leveraged. The average debt to equity ratio of the thirty largest *chaebol* (indirectly accounting for about 35 percent of Korea's industrial production) was 388 percent in 1996, with individual *chaebol* going up 600 to 700 percent. By the end of March 1998, the average had risen to 593 percent. The owners used their control to cross-guarantee the debt of other members of the group, thereby violating the rights of minority shareholders. To make matters worse, Korean companies operated with very low profit margins:

*Many have argued that bank lending was a key mechanism to exert corporate control in Asia. Joseph E. Stiglitz, "Credit Markets and the Control of Capital," *Journal of Money, Credit and Banking*, Vol. 17, No. 2 (May 1985), Ohio State University Press: 150.

The interest coverage of the thirty largest *chaebol* in 1996 was 1.3 times, and only .94 times by 1997. That means that interest charges were not covered by earnings. Korean banks extended easy credit as part of industrial policy. The government decided to encourage certain industries and the *chaebol* rushed in, fearing to be left out. This led to headlong expansion without regard to profits. In this respect, Korea was consciously imitating the Japan of earlier days, but it turned out to be a crude imitation of a much more subtle model. As I mentioned before, Japan had the benefit of democratic institutions, whereas South Korea had a military dictatorship during much of its postwar history. The consensus-building tradition of Japan and the checks and balances that characterize a democracy were missing.

When nonperforming loans began to accumulate, Korean banks tried to earn their way out of the hole by borrowing even more money abroad and investing it in high-yielding, high-risk instruments in countries like Indonesia, Russia, Ukraine, and Brazil. This was an important factor in the Korean crisis.

Not that Japanese banks have done much better recently. Japan's troubles go back to the Wall Street crash of 1987. The Japanese financial system was tightly controlled by the Ministry of Finance (MOF). Officials at the MOF constituted an intellectual elite, comparable to the Inspecteurs de Finance in France. They understood reflexivity better than any other group I have encountered and they conceived the grandiose idea that Japan could translate its industrial might into financial dominance by supplying liquidity to the world. I remember when the concept was spelled out to me after the crash of 1987 by a MOF official. Unfortunately, the Japanese failed to take into account an important aspect of reflexivity, namely, the unintended consequences. Their decision helped the world to overcome the effects of the crash but it left Japanese financial institutions with many losses abroad and engendered a financial bubble at home that reached its climax in 1991. Due to its tight control over the financial institutions, the MOF was able to deflate the bubble without a crash—the first time in history such a feat was accomplished. But it left a lot of undigested bad assets festering in the balance sheets of the financial institutions. Taxpayers' money could not be used to bail out the banks until the need became irresistible; even then, Japanese custom required that the heads of MOF officials should roll, as eventually they did. No wonder that the MOF resisted the idea as long as it could.

At the outbreak of the Asian crisis, Japan was engaged in a policy of reducing the budget deficit. It was exactly the wrong policy and the Asian crisis came at exactly the wrong time. The Japanese banks, which had big exposures in Thailand, Indonesia, and Korea, started reducing their balance sheets, causing a credit crunch in the midst of overflowing liquidity. The consumers, frightened by the Asian crisis and by some domestic bankruptcies, increased their propensity to save. The low interest rates encouraged capital to be transferred abroad. The yen declined and the economy slipped into recession. Eventually the government was persuaded to cut taxes and to use public money to recapitalize the banks, but it was too little too late. The recession in Japan, the second-largest economy of the world and an important trading partner of the other Asian countries, aggravated the severity of the economic downturn in the rest of Asia.

We can identify many deficiencies in the Asian model of economic development: structural weaknesses in the banking system and in the ownership of enterprises, the incestuous relationship between business and politics, the lack of transparency, and the absence of political freedom. Although these deficiencies were present in many of the affected countries, none of them was present in all. Hong Kong was exempt from most of them. Japan and Taiwan have enjoyed political freedom. Family ownership of major enterprises is not characteristic of Japan. Singapore has a strong banking system. Moreover, the Asian model as such was an extremely successful economic development strategy and was widely admired in business circles. The Asian model produced a dramatic increase in living standards, with these countries averaging 5.5 percent annual per capita income growth over an extended period—faster growth than virtually all emerging market economies. Asian leaders like Lee Kwan Yu of Singapore, Suharto of Indonesia, and Mahathir of Malaysia proudly proclaimed their belief that Asian values were superior to Western values even as the crisis unfolded. They went so far as to challenge the UN Universal Declaration of Human Rights. Lee Kwan Yu considered Western democracies decadent, Mahathir resented the tradition of colonialism, and Suharto extolled the virtues of nepotism. The Association of Southeast Asian Nations (ASEAN) admitted Myanmar as a member of the organization in June 1997, in a direct challenge to Western democracies, which found Myanmar's repressive regime politically and humanely unacceptable.

How did such a successful model of economic development turn so sour so fast? It is impossible to provide an explanation without taking into account the deficiencies of the global capitalist system. The fact that the Asian crisis was not confined to Asia but engulfed also Russia, South Africa, and Brazil, and is likely to affect all emerging markets before it runs its course, reinforces the case that the main source of instability is to be found in the international financial system itself.

The Instability of International Finance

Looking at the system, we must distinguish between direct investors, portfolio investors, banks, and the financial authorities such as the IMF and the central banks. Direct investors did not play a destabilizing role except perhaps as customers of the banks. In the case of portfolio investors, we may single out institutional investors that handle other people's money, hedge funds that employ leverage, and individual investors.

Institutional investors, as discussed in the previous chapter, measure their performance relative to each other, which turns them into a trend-following herd. They allocate their assets between different national markets; as one market rises in value they must increase their allocation or they become underweighted, and vice versa. In addition, mutual funds are likely to attract investors when they perform well and lose them when they incur losses. Mutual funds played no role in precipitating the crash except by overstaying their welcome during the boom that preceded it. But they are playing an important role in making the bust more enduring. Investors are withdrawing from emerging market funds and this turns mutual funds into forced sellers. Hedge fund managers and others who speculate with borrowed money play a similar role. When they are on a winning streak, they can increase their bets; when they lose they are forced to sell to reduce their debt. Options, hedges, and other derivative instruments have a similar self-reinforcing quality about them.

Hedge fund managers and other speculators may trade in currencies directly, without buying or selling securities. So do banks, both for their own account and for their customers. Banks are far more important in currency markets than hedge funds but it must be admitted that hedge funds like mine did play a role in the Asian currency turmoil. Because hedge funds tend to be more concerned with absolute rather than relative performance, they are more likely to be actively involved in precipitating a change in a trend. Of course, this exposes them to criticism when the change is undesirable, but if a trend is unsustainable it is surely better if it is reversed sooner rather than later. For instance, by selling the Thai baht short in January 1997, the Quantum Funds managed by my investment company sent a signal that it may be overvalued. Had the authorities responded, the adjustment would have occurred sooner and it would have been less painful. As it is, the authorities resisted and when the break came it was catastrophic.

The real issue is whether currency speculation is desirable or not. Looking at the evidence, countries with freely convertible currencies have suffered worse dislocations in the current crisis than those that maintained some controls on currency trading. Thailand was more open than Malaysia, and Thailand had a bigger reversal; mainland China was less affected than Hong Kong although Hong Kong has a much sounder banking and financial system. But this evidence is not conclusive. The Korean currency could not be freely traded yet the crisis was as severe as in Southeast Asia and the jury is still out on China. The issue is intimately interconnected with the role of the banks.

Each country has its own banking system and its own regulatory authorities; they interact with each other in intricate ways to form the international banking system. Some large banks at the center of the system are so heavily involved in international transactions that they qualify as international banks. Often they own domestic banks or conduct in-country operations such as consumer credit in multiple countries. Most of the countries involved in the current crisis, however, have had relatively closed banking systems, that is, few in-country banks are foreign owned. Hong Kong and Singapore are exceptions: The major banks there qualify as internationals. Japanese and, more recently, Korean banks have also dabbled in international banking, with disastrous results. Estimates of expected nonperforming loans (that is, loans that cannot be paid back) in Asia alone amount to almost US$2 trillion as shown in Table 7.1.

International and national banks are linked by credit lines that define the limits within which they can enter into various transactions such as currency trades, interest rate swaps, and the like. They may also be connected through longer term credits. Both the credit lines and the loans are fixed in dollars or some other hard currency. In the countries that were pegged either formally or informally to the dollar, the in-country banks and borrowers assumed that the peg would hold. Often they failed to hedge against the currency risk. When the peg broke, they found themselves with large uncovered currency exposures. They scrambled for cover, putting tremendous pressure on the local currencies. The currencies over-

TABLE 7.1

Estimated Nonperforming Loans, Asia and Japan

Country	Expected Peak NPL's	US $ Value
1. Hong Kong	12.0%	15.9
2. India	16.0%	13.0
3. Indonesia	85.0%	34.1
4. Korea	45.0%	167.0
5. Malaysia	40.0%	27.5
6. Philippines	25.0%	7.0
7. Singapore	11.0%	8.5
8. Taiwan	4.5%	16.3
9. Thailand	50.4%	91.7
South East Asia (Total 1-9)		381.0
10. Japan	30.0%	800.0
11. China	25.0%	250.0
GRAND TOTAL		1431.0

Sources: Salomon Brothers, Goldman Sachs, Warburg Dillon Read, and SFM LCC estimates

shot on the downside, causing a sudden deterioration in the balance sheets of the borrowers. For instance, Siam Cement, the largest and strongest company in Thailand, incurred a loss of 52.6 billion Thai baht compared to its beginning equity of 42.3 billion Thai baht and 1996 profits of 6.8 billion Thai baht.* Weaker companies were much worse off. Many of the borrowers had used the loans to finance real estate and real estate values were already in decline when the peg broke. Suddenly there was a credit risk as well as a currency risk and it reduced the willingness of the lenders to extend credit. This, together with foreign investors fleeing from declining markets, set up a self-reinforcing process that resulted in a 42 percent decline in the Thai currency and a 59 percent decline in the Thai stock market, expressed in local currency, between June 1997 and the end of August 1998. The combined result was a 76 percent loss in dollar terms, which compares with an 86 percent loss in Wall Street between 1929 and 1933.

The panic was spread to the neighboring countries by the financial markets—I used the image of a wrecking ball; others have referred to financial contagion as a modern version of the bubonic plague. The imbalances in some of these newly stricken economies were less pronounced but this was no protection. The Malaysian economy was overheating, but the monetary expansion had been mainly internal; the trade deficit was quite modest. The fundamentals in Indonesia seemed quite sound; the main problem was that Indonesia had borrowed heavily from Korean and Japanese banks that had their own problems and were not in a position to renew their loans. When the Hong Kong dollar came under attack, the currency board system caused a rise in local interest rates that in turn depressed the value of real estate and stocks. International banks doing business with Hong Kong banks discovered a credit risk of which they had not been aware. When they entered into

---

*The exchange rate was 24.35 Thai baht to the US dollar before the currency peg was abandoned on July 2, 1997; it was at 45.9 at the end of the year.

back-to-back interest rate swaps,* they had assumed that the amounts were the same on both sides; now they realized that if the exchange rate changed, their Hong Kong counterparty would suddenly owe them more money than they owed to their Hong Kong counterparty. This forced international banks to curtail their credit lines to Hong Kong. Credit risk became an even bigger issue in Korea, where some banks actually defaulted on their guarantees. It was not long before the financial crisis forced Thailand and then Korea and Indonesia to seek the assistance of the IMF.

The Role of the
International Monetary Fund

The IMF found itself confronted with problems it had never had to face before. The Asian crisis was a complex crisis, with a currency component and a credit component. The credit component, in turn, had an international aspect and a domestic aspect, and all the various components were interrelated. What made the Asian crisis different from any the IMF had faced before was that it originated in the private sector; the public sector was in relatively good shape.

The IMF imposed the traditional medicine: raise interest rates and reduce government spending to stabilize the currency and restore the confidence of international investors. It also recognized the structural defects in individual countries and imposed tailor-made conditions, such as the closing of unsound financial institutions. But the IMF programs did not work because they addressed only some aspects of the crisis, but not all. Because the various aspects were interrelated, they could not be cured separately. Specifically, the currencies could not be stabilized until the debt problems were tackled, because debtors

---

*Such a swap occurs when one bank switches between a fixed rate and variable rate loan for its customer against the inverse switch by its correspondent bank abroad.

rushed to cover their exposure when the currency fell and the currency weakness served to increase their exposure in a vicious circle.

Why did the IMF not realize this? Perhaps because it had developed its methodology for dealing with imbalances in the public sector; its understanding of how financial markets operate left much to be desired. This was demonstrated in Indonesia, where the IMF insisted on closing some banks without making adequate provisions for the protection of depositors, provoking a classic run on the banks. The financial panic in turn weakened President Suharto's resolve to abide by the conditions of the IMF rescue program, which he already found distasteful because it encroached on the privileges of his family and friends. The squabble between Suharto and the IMF pushed the Indonesian rupiah into a free fall. The Quantum Funds were badly hurt because we had bought Indonesian rupiah at around 4,000 to the dollar, thinking that the currency had already overshot when it had fallen from 2,430 as of July 1997. It proceeded to fall to more than 16,000 in short order—a chastening experience. I had been fully aware of the corruption of the Suharto regime, and I insisted on selling our share in an Indonesian power plant in which Suharto family members had a financial interest purely because I did not want to be associated with them. Yet here we were, losing money in Indonesia just when the chickens came home to roost.

The IMF has been criticized for setting too many conditions and interfering too much in the internal affairs of the countries that turn to it for assistance. What business is it of the IMF, it is asked, if a regime is corrupt or the banking and industrial structure over-leveraged? All that matters is that a country should be able to meet its obligations. The job of the IMF is to help contain a liquidity crisis; the structural problems are best left to the country concerned. I would argue on the opposite side. Liquidity crises are inextricably interconnected with structural imbalances; they cannot be corrected just by lending a country more money. When both banks and corporations are overindebted (i.e., the debt to equity ratios are too high), an infusion of equity is required. The trouble is that in a crisis situation neither new equity nor further credit is readily available. The only solution is to convert debt to equity. The IMF programs in Asia failed because they did not insist on a debt-to-equity conversion scheme. Far from intruding too much, they were not intrusive enough.

In defense of the IMF, it must be recognized that it may have been impossible to deal with a liquidity crisis and introduce a debt-to-equity conversion scheme at the same time. The international creditors would have balked and without their cooperation no rescue program can succeed. On the other hand, the failure to tackle the debt problem resulted in currency overshoots and punitive interest rates that rendered the borrowers insolvent and plunged the countries concerned into deep depression. Obviously there is a systemic problem here, and the IMF is part of the problem, not part of the solution.

The IMF is now in a crisis of its own. Market confidence has been an essential ingredient in its past success and it has now lost credibility. It has also run out of resources. The failure of the U.S. Congress to provide additional funds has greatly reduced its capacity to deal with problems as they arise. This is a point to which I shall return in the next chapter.

A Brief Overview

In fall 1997, the Indonesian debacle put the Korean and Japanese banks on the defensive and undermined the confidence of international lenders in the Korean banking system. From Korea, the wrecking ball swung to Russia and Brazil, grazing Eastern Europe and demolishing Ukraine on the way. Korean banks had invested in Russia and Brazil, and Brazilians had invested in Russia. Both the Koreans and the Brazilians had to liquidate their holdings and both Brazil and Russia had to raise interest rates high enough to protect their currencies against the selling. Brazil used the crisis to enact long-overdue structural reforms, which helped to contain the situation, but only for a few months.

The international crisis reached a climax at the end of December 1997 when, in spite of an IMF program, foreign banks refused to roll over their loans to Korean banks. The central banks had to intervene and strong-arm the commercial banks under their jurisdiction to renew their loans. A second rescue package was put together. Soon afterward the crisis started to ease. Federal Reserve Chairman Alan Greenspan made it clear that the Asian troubles ruled out any possibility of an interest rate increase and bond and stock markets took heart. The wrecking ball stopped swinging without having penetrated Latin America, with the exception of an initial hit in Brazil. Both Korea and Thailand benefited from the election of new governments dedicated to reform. Only Indonesia continued to deteriorate, but eventually Suharto was removed from power. Bargain hunters returned; currencies strengthened; and, by the end of March, Asian stock markets, including Indonesia's, recovered between a third and a half of their losses, measured in local currencies. This is a characteristic rebound after a major market break.

It was a false dawn. The financial collapse was followed by economic decline. Domestic demand came to a standstill and imports shrank, but exports did not expand, because a high proportion of the exports were directed toward countries that were also affected. In addition, exports were concentrated in a limited number of commodities where the increased selling pressure drove down prices. Semiconductors, in which Korea; Taiwan; and, to a lesser extent, Japan vied for the world market, were particularly hard hit. The economic decline quickly spread to countries that originally had not been involved. Japan slipped into a recession and the economic situation in China became increasingly problematic. Hong Kong came under renewed pressure. The fall in commodity prices, especially oil, hurt Russia and other commodity-producing countries.

The situation in Korea is particularly instructive. Following the liquidity crunch at year-end 1997, the external situation started to improve almost immediately. Consumer demand came to a standstill, imports plummeted, and the trade balance swung into surplus. External indebtedness in relation to GNP had not been too high to start with (only 25 percent as reported in 1997, but it rose to 50 percent when the true figures were revealed in 1998) and the emergence of a big trade surplus rendered it quite respectable. The five big *chaebol* (which directly account for 15 percent of industrial production and indirectly for much more) made a determined effort to meet their international obligations, and the external crisis soon abated. The internal situation, by contrast, continues to deteriorate. Most companies operate at a loss and their balance sheets go from bad to worse. This includes the big five. The recapitalization of the banks is moving very slowly and in spite of a reduction in interest rates the economy continues to languish. Unemployment and labor tensions are on the rise.

The problem in Japan is also entirely internal. Given the tremendous currency reserves and a large and growing trade surplus, it ought to be entirely within the power of the Japanese government to recapitalize the banking system and stimulate the economy. Unfortunately its policies are misconceived. Banks have to fail before public money is made available. Bankers will do everything in their power to delay the evil day when they have to recognize their losses. The result is a credit crunch that has pushed the economy into recession, putting immense pressure on the other Asian countries.

China faces some of the same difficulties as South Korea. It has a banking system that has been guided by political rather than commercial considerations and the accumulation of bad debts is even worse than in Korea. It has an export-driven economy that lost some of its competitive advantage when its competitors devalued. There had been a tremendous boom in commercial property development—at the outbreak of the Asian crisis half the cranes in the world were working in Shanghai. The influx of foreign investment—with 70 percent of the total coming from overseas Chinese—came to a full stop.

The big difference, the saving grace of China, has been that its currency is not convertible; otherwise it surely would have been exposed to the wrecking ball in spite of its enormous official currency reserves. There are foreign currency loans outstanding whose magnitude, as in other Asian countries, is not reliably reported, and foreign investors, particularly the overseas Chinese, would probably have taken flight, or at least hedged their investments in the forward market, if they had an opportunity to do so. As it is, capital controls bought the government time.

The Chinese government has been trying to use that time to stimulate domestic demand. The Communist Party lost the "mandate of heaven" in the Tiananmen Square massacre, so it must provide prosperity on earth in order to be tolerated. This means a growth rate close to 8 percent. But the engines of growth, exports and the inflow of foreign investment, have now been switched off. Domestic demand must take their place. The government is resorting to good old Keynesian remedies: fostering large infrastructure projects and trying to stimulate housing construction. It is determined to avoid devaluing the currency for a number of reasons. It wants to enhance its stature in the world, build a stronger relationship with the United States, and attain membership in the World Trade Organization; it is also afraid of provoking protectionist countermeasures in the United States if it devalued. Devaluation would also undermine the Hong Kong currency board, and the current Chinese government is passionately committed to the idea of "one country, two economic systems" because it wants mainland China to become more like Hong Kong. Hong Kong has been used as the vehicle for privatizing state-owned companies, the so-called red chips. But the Hong Kong market is under severe pressure, and instead of floating new companies the Monetary Authority has been obliged to purchase shares to stabilize the market. The Chinese government was hoping to achieve the same effect as a devaluation by imposing import restrictions and providing export subsidies, but there is a lively trade in clandestine imports, particularly by enterprises associated with the People's Army, which undercuts the demand for domestic products. It remains to be seen whether current policies will work. The banking system and the balance sheets of the state-owned enterprises continue to deteriorate. The trade surplus is illusory because of all the smuggling. The official reserves are barely maintained because of the hidden flight of capital. Steps to encourage private ownership of homes have had the perverse effect of encouraging savings. The banking system uses the savings to preserve moribund state-owned enterprises and this only goes to increase the state's indebtedness to its citizens without stimulating the economy. Radical structural reforms are needed but they had to be put on hold because they may provoke social unrest. In my previous book,* I predicted that the communist regime in China will be destroyed by a capitalist crisis. It may be actually happening, although the crisis originated in the surrounding countries.

Russia

Russia was also a victim of the Asian crisis but it is such a strange case that it deserves special consideration. I have been personally more deeply involved in Russia than in other countries. Russia had swung from one extreme of a rigid closed society to the other extreme of lawless capitalism. The violence of the dislocation could have been moderated by the free world if it had understood what was going on and if it had had a commitment to the ideal of an open society, but that is water over the dam. The most comprehensive, closed social

*Soros on Soros: Staying Ahead of the Curve (New York: John Wiley & Sons, 1995).

system ever invented by humanity disintegrated and no other system took its place. Eventually order began to emerge out of chaos but, regrettably, it bore little resemblance to the idea of an open society.

Mikhail Gorbachev unleashed a process of revolutionary regime change and he managed to stay ahead of it—often by leapfrogging over the state/party apparatus just as it was closing in on him—but he balked at two issues: the privatization of land and the dissolution of the Soviet Union. When he fell from power and the Soviet Union disintegrated, Boris Yeltsin became president of Russia and he was willing to go much further. First he backed Yegor Gaidar as deputy prime minister in charge of the economy, who tried to apply monetary policy to an economy that did not obey monetary signals. When Gaidar failed, an uneasy balancing act followed in which Anatoly Chubais was allowed to push his priority, the transfer of property from state to private hands. He believed that once state property had private owners, the owners would start protecting their property and the process of disintegration would be arrested.

Out of these efforts, the rudiments of a new economic order began to emerge. It was a form of capitalism but it was a very peculiar form and it came into existence in a different sequence from the one that could have been expected under normal conditions. The first privatization was the privatization of public safety and in some ways it was the most successful: Various private armies and mafias took charge. State-owned enterprises adjusted to changed conditions by insiders forming private companies, mainly in Cyprus, which entered into contracts with the enterprises. The factories themselves operated at a loss, did not pay taxes, and fell into arrears in paying wages and settling interenterprise debts. The cash from the operations went to Cyprus. The rudiments of a banking system were formed, partly by state-owned banks, partly by newly emerging capitalist groups, the so-called oligarchs. Some banks made fortunes by handling the accounts of various state agencies, including the Treasury. Then, in connection with the voucher privatization scheme, a market for stocks was born before the stock registrars and the clearing mechanism were properly in place and long before the companies whose stocks were traded started to behave like companies. Insiders generally came to control the companies and outside shareholders had great difficulty in exercising their rights. Incumbent managers were practically obliged to siphon off both earnings and assets to their private benefit, partly to pay for the shares they bought, partly to avoid taxes. No proceeds from the voucher privatization scheme accrued to the companies. Only after managers had consolidated their control and recognized the need for raising additional capital could they start generating earnings within the companies. Only a few companies reached this stage.

These arrangements could be justly described as robber capitalism, because the most effective way to accumulate private capital from a starting point close to zero was to appropriate the assets of the state. There were, of course, some exceptions. The state itself had little value, although the plotters who tried to oust Gorbachev in 1991 did not realize it. When sufficient private property was accumulated, however, the state also acquired value, because it was the source of legitimacy. In 1996, the seven largest capitalists, who also controlled the media, decided to cooperate to ensure the reelection of President Yeltsin. It was a remarkable feat of political engineering. Subsequently the newly established oligarchy proceeded to divide up the remaining assets of the state among themselves. In spring 1997, Yeltsin decided to bring into the government Boris Nemtsov, the reformist governor of Nizhny Novgorod, who was untainted by the reelection campaign. A number of steps were taken to pave the way from robber capitalism to the rule of law. The budget deficit and money supply were kept within bounds and back taxes began to be collected. Inflation and interest rates declined. Shareholder rights were better respected and the stock market boomed. Foreign money poured into both stocks and debt instruments.

I had set up a foundation in Russia as early as 1987 to foster the transition to an open society. I organized an international working group to create an "open sector" within the command economy in 1988–1989, but it soon became clear that the system was beyond redemption. I assisted the so-called 500-day program and brought Grigory Yavlinsky, who conceived the program, and his team to the IMF–World Bank meeting in Washington in 1990 to drum up international support, but to no avail. I set up the International Science Foundation with a grant of $100 million to demonstrate that foreign assistance can be effective. We distributed $20 million to the 40,000 top scientists: $500 was then sufficient to subsist on for a year. The rest went to provide electronic communications and scientific literature and support research programs selected by international peer review. Meanwhile, the foundation I established in 1987 engaged in a truly wide range of activities, of which the most important was educational reform, printing new textbooks free of Marxist ideology, and introducing the Internet.

I abstained from investing in Russia, partly to avoid any conflict of interest problems but mainly because I did not like what I saw. I did not interfere with my fund managers who wanted to invest and I also approved participating in a Russian-run investment fund on equal terms with other Western investors. When Nemtsov was brought into the government, however, I decided to participate in the auction of Svyazinvest, the state telephone holding company. The privatization of Svyazinvest resulted in the first genuine auction in which the state was not shortchanged. Unfortunately it precipitated a knockdown, drag-out fight among the oligarchs, some of whom were eager to make the transition to legitimate capitalism while others resisted it because they were incapable of operating in a legitimate manner. One of the oligarchs, Boris Berezovsky, threatened to pull down the tent around him if he was not given the spoils that he had been promised. The vicious quarrel damaged Chubais, who had acted as campaign manager for Yeltsin and had received illegal payments from the oligarchs, which were now disclosed. This happened just at the moment when the Asian crisis made its effects felt. Korean and Brazilian banks that had invested heavily in the Russian market had to liquidate their positions. Some leading Moscow banks were also exposed because they had large speculative bond positions and were also carrying uncovered forward contracts in the ruble. There were some precarious moments in December 1997, but they passed. Interest rates were sharply raised and government spending reduced, but the Duma balked at passing the laws necessary for structural reform. Yeltsin dismissed Victor Chernomyrdyn as prime minister and forced the Duma to accept Sergei Kiriyenko, a young technocrat selected by Gaidar and Chubais, as replacement. For a brief moment, Russia had a reformist government, the best it has seen since the breakup of the Soviet Union, and the IMF came through with a loan of $18.5 billion, of which $4.5 billion was disbursed. But it was not enough.

At this point, I shall turn to a real-time experiment that I started just before the final meltdown. I reproduce faithfully the notes I wrote during a two-week period while the crisis unfolded.

A Real-Time Experiment

Sunday, August 9, 1998

Ruble (spot)	=	6.29
Ruble Forwards*	=	45%
GKO[†]	=	94.52%
Prins[‡]	=	21.79%
S&P	=	1,089.45
U.S. 30-year Treasury Bond	=	5.63%

*Implicit interest rates on one month nondeliverable forward contracts for rubles traded in dollars.
[†]Yield on ruble-denominated Russian government treasury bills.
[‡]Yield on dollar-denominated Russian government bonds.

I had not been following developments in Russia closely until the last two or three days—I was too busy writing this book. I was aware that the situation remained desperate even after the IMF agreed to an $18 billion bailout package. Interest rates on Russian government debt remained at astronomical levels—between 70% and 90% for one-year ruble-denominated treasury bills (GKOs). The syndicate which had bought 25.1% of Svyazinvest—the Russian telephone holding company—and of which we were the largest foreign participants, was approached by the Russian government to provide a temporary bridge loan leading to the sale of the next tranche of 24.9% in Svyazinvest. It was in our interest to make the sale a success but I did not like the idea of throwing good money after bad—that is why I decided to focus on the situation.

It soon became obvious that the refinancing of the government debt presented a seemingly insuperable problem. The IMF program had assumed that the domestic holders of the debt would roll over (reinvest) their holdings when they matured; the only question was at what price. If the government was successful in collecting taxes, interest rates would eventually come down to tolerable levels, say 25%, and the crisis would be over. What this line of reasoning left out was that much of the debt was held by domestic holders who were not in a position to roll over their maturing GKOs at any price. Corporations were being forced to pay taxes, and what they paid in taxes could not be reinvested in GKOs. More importantly, the banking sector, with the exception of Sberbank, the state-owned savings bank, had bought GKOs with borrowed money. Due to the decline in the Russian stock and bond markets most of these banks were insolvent and even those which were solvent were unable to renew their credit lines. As a result, not only were they not buyers, some of their existing holdings had to be liquidated in order to meet margin calls. Much of the credit had come from foreign banks, some of whom tried to liquidate their own positions as well. Waves of selling depressed the dollar-denominated Russian debt to record low levels. There was a full-blown banking crisis in progress.

A banking crisis is usually contained by the central bank intervening and providing liquidity, for instance, by lending money against collateral at concessionary rates; but in this case the central bank was prevented from doing so by the terms of the IMF agreement. That is what made the situation seemingly insoluble.

On Friday, August 7, I telephoned Anatoly Chubais, who was on vacation, and Yegor Gaidar, who was minding the store. I told them that in my view the situation was terminal: the government would be unable to roll over its debt after September even if the second tranche of the IMF loan was released. To aggravate the situation, the Ukrainian government was on the verge of defaulting on a $450 million loan arranged by Nomura Securities coming due next Tuesday. In these circumstances I could not justify participating in a bridge loan: the risk of default was too great. I saw only one way out: to put together a large enough syndicate to cover the Russian government's needs until the end of the year. It would have to be a public and private partnership. The Svyazinvest group could participate with, say, $500 million, but the private sector on its own could not come up with enough money. I asked how much would be needed. Gaidar told me, $7 billion. This assumed that Sberbank, the only bank that has large deposits from the public, would be able to roll over its holdings. For the time being the public was not withdrawing deposits from the banks on a significant scale. "That means the syndicate would have to be formed with $10 billion," I said, "so as to reestablish public confidence." Half would have to come from foreign government sources, such as the Exchange Stabilization Fund (which is under the control of the U.S. Treasury) and the other half from the private sector. The syndicate would come into operation when the second tranche of the IMF loan is released in September. It would underwrite one-year GKOs starting at, say, 35% p.a., gradually dropping to say 25%. (The current rate is around 90%.) The program would be announced in advance; that would attract some public buying: it would make sense to invest at 35% when a credible program is in effect to reduce the rate to 25% by the end of the year. If successful, only a small portion of the $10 billion would be actally used. Both the public and private component would be difficult to put together, but I was willing to try. Gaidar was understandably enthusiastic.

I called David Lipton, Undersecretary in charge of International Affairs at the U.S. Treasury. He was fully aware of the problem but they had not even thought of using the Exchange Stabilization Fund. The sentiment in Congress was strongly opposed to any kind of bailout. I said I was aware of it but I saw no alternative. There was a panic and it was in our national interest to support a reform-minded government in Russia. If there was private participation it ought to make a bailout politically more palatable. Still, it would require the Russians to make a strong case on Capitol Hill. It would be also very difficult to line up the private participants because they consisted of investment banks and speculative investors like us and they could not be so easily mobilized by the authorities as the large commercial banks.

Just to explore all alternatives, I called Gaidar again and asked him whether it would be possible to impose a charge on those GKO holders who want to take cash on redemption. He said that would destroy the credit standing of the GKOs. He was right of course.

As of the present moment, I believe that without my scheme the government will default with cataclysmic consequences; even with the scheme, most of the Russian banks will be wiped out but it would be a mistake even to try to salvage them.

Tuesday night, August 11

Ruble (spot)	=	6.30
Ruble Forwards	=	91%
GKO	=	147%
Prins	=	23.92%
S&P	=	1,068.98
U.S. 30-year Treasury Bond	=	5.60%

I talked briefly with Lipton on Monday. The U.S. administration had reached no conclusion yet. He promised to call again. On Tuesday there was a collapse in the Russian financial market. Trading on the stock market was temporarily suspended. Government bonds sank to new lows. Even the international markets were affected. The scheme I have proposed is no longer feasible. Only a larger rescue package of minimum $15 billion could stabilize the market and no private investor could be expected to put up money. Lipton left for Moscow without calling me. I heard through the grapevine that he was exasperated going without anything to offer. I decided to write the following letter to the *Financial Times:*

Sir, The meltdown in Russian financial markets has reached the terminal phase. Bankers and brokers who had borrowed against securities could not meet margin calls and forced selling swamped both the stock and the bond markets. The stock market had to be temporarily closed because trades could not be settled; prices of government bonds and Treasury bills fell precipitously. Although the selling was temporarily absorbed, there is a danger that the population will start again to withdraw funds from savings accounts. Immediate action is required.

The trouble is that the action that is necessary to deal with a banking crisis is diametrically opposed to the action that has been agreed with the International Monetary Fund to deal with the budget crisis. The IMF programme imposes tight monetary and fiscal policy; the banking crisis requires the injection of liquidity. The two requirements cannot be reconciled without further international assistance. The IMF programme had assumed that there would be buyers for government bonds at a price: as the government proceeded to collect taxes and slash expenditures interest rates would come down and the crisis would abate. The assumption was false because much of the outstanding debt was held on margin and credit lines could not be renewed. There is a financing gap that needs to be closed. The gap will become bigger if the general public starts withdrawing deposits.

The best solution would be to introduce a currency board after a modest devaluation of 15 to 25 per cent. The devaluation is necessary to correct for the decline in oil prices and to reduce the amount of reserves needed for the currency board. It would also penalize the holders of rouble-denominated government debt, rebutting charges of a bail-out.

About $50bn of reserves would be required: $23bn to cover MI [narrow money supply] and $27bn to cover the shortfall on domestic debt refunding for the next year. Russia has reserves of $18bn; the IMF has promised $17bn. The Group of Seven [G7] needs to put up another $15bn to make a currency board feasible. There would be no bail-out of the banking system. With the exception of a few institutions that hold public deposits, banks can be allowed to fend for themselves. Government bond prices would immediately recover and the sounder financial institutions would survive. Some $40bn is held by Russians in foreign currencies. With a currency board they may be tempted to buy rouble-denominated government bonds at attractive yields. If they do, the G7 standby credit would not need to be used. The reduction in interest rates would help the government to meet its fiscal targets.

If the G7 were willing to put up $15bn right away, the situation could be stabilised even without a currency board, although it might take longer and the damage would be greater. It would also be difficult to accomplish a limited currency adjustment without a currency board because the pressure for further devaluation would become irresistible, as it did in Mexico in December 1994.

If action is delayed, the cost of a rescue will continue to mount. The cost would have been only $7bn a week ago. Unfortunately, international financial authorities do not appreciate the urgency of the situation. The alternatives are default or hyper-inflation. Either would have devastating financial and political consequences.

Thursday, August 13

Ruble (spot)	=	6.35
Ruble Forwards	=	162%
GKO	=	149%
Prins	=	23.76%
S&P	=	1,074.91
U.S. 30-year Treasury Bond	=	5.65%

After I had written my letter to the *Financial Times*, the Deputy Governor of the Russian central bank imposed some restrictions on the convertibility of the ruble. It had a devastating effect on the Russian market: Stocks opened 15% lower and did not rally very much. My letter received a lot of attention but the emphasis was on my advocating devaluation, not on my proposal for a currency board. It became one of the factors in what has come to be called Black Thursday. That is not at all what I intended. I felt obliged to put out another statement as follows:

The turmoil in Russian financial markets is not due to anything I said or did. We have no short position in the ruble and have no intention of shorting the currency. In fact, our portfolio would be hurt by any devaluation.

The purpose of my letter to the *Financial Times* was to issue a wake-up call to the G7 governments. While the Russian government is doing everything in its power to cope with the situation, it cannot succeed without further assistance from abroad.

Friday, August 14

Ruble (spot)	=	6.35
Ruble Forwards	=	162.7%
GKO	=	172%
Prins	=	23.01%
S&P	=	1,062.75
U.S. 30-year Treasury Bond	=	5.54%

I talked to Treasury Secretary Rubin and stressed the urgency of the situation. He was fully aware but his concern was not shared by the other G7 governments, which were largely beyond reach on holidays. I was contacted by Senator Mitch McConnell and I urged him to call Rubin to assure him of Republican support in what would be a very risky operation. Late in the day I was approached on behalf of Kiriyenko. He is still looking for a $500 million bridge loan but that is no longer realistic. I offered to fly to Moscow to discuss the larger issues if it would help.

Sunday night, August 16

Ruble (spot)	=	6.35
Ruble Forwards	=	162.7%
GKO	=	172%
Prins	=	23.01%
S&P	=	1,062.75
U.S. 30-year Treasury Bond	=	5.54%

I spent most of the weekend on Russia. I gave an interview on Echo Moskva radio station explaining my position, and my statement was read on Russian TV. I hope that I managed to correct the false impression that I was advocating devaluation or could benefit from it in some way. Spoke to Gaidar several times. Prepared an article advocating the currency board solution and sent it to him for approval. Just now (6:30 a.m. Monday, Moscow time) he told me that he had spoken to Larry Summers [deputy secretary of the Treasury] and there was no help available; they will have to act unilaterally. I said my article was no longer relevant but he urged me to publish it anyhow. I won't.

Tuesday, August 18

Ruble (spot)	=	6.80
Ruble Forwards	=	305%
GKO*	=	
Prins	=	29.41%
S&P	=	1,101.20
U.S. 30-year Treasury Bond	=	5.56%

On Monday, all hell broke loose. Russia imposed a moratorium and widened the trading band on the ruble, effectively devaluing it by up to 35%. What is worse, Russian banks are not allowed to honor their foreign obligations. This created havoc among their foreign counterparties, who dumped Russian securities at any price. David Lipton called me for a technical explanation and suggested I write them a memo.

On re-reading it I find it rather garbled. The point I was trying to make is that it is still not too late to look for a constructive resolution of the crisis in Russia. The G7 should offer to put up the hard

*Trading in GKOs was suspended as of August 17, so no figures are available in this category for the remainder of the tables.

currency which is needed to set up a currency board *provided* the Duma passes the laws which are needed to meet the IMF conditions. There are two possibilities: the Duma could agree to it or it could reject the offer. In the first case, the value of the ruble would be reestablished, the ruble debt could be restructured in an orderly fashion, and the structural reforms (putting companies that don't pay taxes into bankruptcy, etc.) could be implemented. Most Russian banks would go broke and the international banks and funds that had contracts with those banks would suffer losses; but Russian government obligations would regain some value, the better banks would survive, and the meltdown would be arrested. In the second case, the meltdown would continue but the onus would fall on the Duma. Yeltsin could dissolve the Duma, call elections, and implement the reforms. If they are successful, they would be endorsed by the electorate. Even if Yeltsin failed to rise to the occasion or the reforms were less than successful, we would have done what we could and we would keep the flame of reform alive in Russia. It is a high risk strategy but doing nothing poses an even bigger risk.

Saturday, August 22

Ruble (spot)	=	7.15
Ruble Forwards	=	443%
GKO	=	
Prins	=	36.05%
S&P	=	1,081.18
U.S. 30-year Treasury Bond	=	5.43%

International markets were badly affected by the Russian crisis in the last two days. For instance, the German stock market dropped 6% on Friday. I find it surprising that it took so long for the penny to drop. My partner assures me that the U.S. stock market made a very good temporary bottom on Friday and we were buyers of stocks and sellers of put options. By the way, we did not trade any Russian securities during the entire period of this real-time experiment.

I tried to push my idea with everyone who would listen during the week but to no avail. It could have helped the political situation in Russia. As it is, the Duma will not pass the laws and the IMF will not disburse the second tranche of the package. With no more money coming from abroad in the foreseeable future, Yeltsin will have to scuttle the present government and find a new source of support at home. But where? The oligarchs are fatally weakened. Gazprom and some of the oil companies remain. Is it back to Chernomyrdin? He is certainly aspiring. But no regime can succeed, because the political will to remedy the structural defects is lacking. The downside is open ended.

Sunday, August 23

Ruble (spot)	=	7.15
Ruble Forwards	=	443%
GKO	=	
Prins	=	36.05%
S&P	=	1,081.18
U.S. 30-year Treasury Bond	=	5.43%

Yeltsin dismissed the government and appointed Chernomyrdyn. Now I can't predict it anymore.

Wednesday, August 26

Ruble (spot)	=	10.00
Ruble Forwards	=	458%
GKO	=	
Prins	=	42.83%
S&P	=	1,084.19
U.S. 30-year Treasury Bond	=	5.42%

There is no limit to how far a meltdown can go. The disintegration of the Russian banking system is occurring in a disorderly fashion. Banks have suspended payments and the public has panicked. The terms of the GKO conversion offer were announced and at first they were quite well received but the ruble has gone into a free fall, making the offer practically worthless. The international financial system is experiencing a few disruptions. There may be $75–100 billion of currency contracts outstanding and it is unclear which of them will be honored. A credit agency has downgraded Germany's largest commercial bank. A faint element of credit risk has been introduced into international inter-bank swap transactions. It is likely to be temporary but it may reveal other weaknesses because of the high degree of leverage employed. European and U.S. stock markets have shuddered but are likely to regain their composure. The meltdown in Russia is terminal with incalculable political and social consequences.

. . .

I shall stop the real-time experiment at this point because I am no longer an active participant. The events provide a practical and rather scary illustration of many of the points I am trying to make in a more abstract way in the book. What I find so scary is that there was an excellent team at the U.S. Treasury and Russia had the best government of its short post-Soviet history; nevertheless the meltdown could not be prevented. My own role is also a source of concern.

I was fully aware that the robber-capitalist system was unsound and unsustainable and I was quite vocal about it; nevertheless I allowed myself to be sucked into the Svyazinvest deal. I had good reasons, but the fact remains that the deal did not work. It was the worst investment of my professional career. When I traveled around Russia in October 1997, I was struck by the irresponsibility of foreign investors, lending large amounts of money to Russian municipalities that did not put it to good use. Yet I did not run for the hills. My letter to the *Financial Times* also had unintended negative consequences. I have no regrets with regard to my attempts to help Russia move toward an open society: They did not succeed but at least I tried. I have grave regrets as an investor. It goes to show how difficult it is to reconcile the two roles.

Predicting the Future

I now revert to the larger, global boom/bust process. I shall stop the clock and treat the events ahead of us as the future, although they will continue to unfold while the book is in preparation. In a way, I am starting another real-time experiment. I shall use my theory of history to try and predict what is ahead; the events as they unfold will serve as a test of the validity of my predictions. The test will not be scientific because I shall have to modify my boom/bust pattern to fit the present situation. As I said before, trying to predict the future is more like alchemy than science.

Until recently, I thought that we were in Phase 3 of a boom/bust pattern, namely, a severe test. If the global capitalist system passed the test, it would enter a period of acceleration that would carry it into far-from-equilibrium territory. If it failed the test, it would face the moment of truth. As recently as August 16, I thought that the meltdown in Russia constituted the moment of truth. But this interpretation does not fit the current situation. It would imply a twilight period ahead, to be followed by a crossover point and catastrophic acceleration on the downside. We seem to be much further along the road than I thought. I now believe that the meltdown in Russia represents the crossover point where a trend that has already changed direction is reinforced by the reversal of the prevailing bias to cause a catastrophic collapse. We could interpret the time since the Thai crisis as the twilight period during which people carried on business as usual with the uneasy feeling that something was going awfully wrong. But when was the moment of truth? Moreover, the new interpretation would imply an imminent collapse in the financial markets at the center, which could turn out to be wrong.

On September 1 the stock markets made a temporary bottom on heavy volume and retested it on lower volume at the end of the week. I believe it was a false bottom; we are in a bear market and stock prices will eventually go much lower. But the bust may be much more protracted than the boom/bust model I have been working with would indicate. I feel the need for a somewhat different pattern and I prefer to say so explicitly rather than to quietly rewrite what I had written before. (In fact, I am pleased that events do not fit neatly the boom/bust model I had developed, because I was worried that I was forcing history into a pattern of my own invention.) Rather than tinkering with the old model, I shall design a new one specially for the occasion. This is in keeping with the reservations I held when I started applying a boom/bust analysis to the global capitalist system. The system has a center and a periphery. This could explain why the process of disintegration should take much longer and occur at different times in different parts of the system. Here, then, is my new hypothesis about the dynamic structure of the present crisis:

The global capitalist system was severely tested in the Mexican crisis of 1994–1995, but it survived the so-called tequila effect and came back stronger than ever. That is when the period of acceleration occurred and the boom became increasingly unsound. The fact that the holders of Mexican treasury bills emerged from the crisis unscathed, set a bad example for speculators in Russian treasury bills. The turning point came with the Thai crisis of July 1997. It reversed the direction of the flow of funds. I realized that the music had stopped, particularly with regard to Russia, and I said so at the time, but I seriously underestimated the severity of the problem. I foresaw an open-ended test similar to the Mexican crisis of 1994–1995 rather than the finality of the reversal.

At first, the reversal benefited the financial markets at the center for the reasons I already explained and the buoyancy of the center also brought hope to the periphery. The Asian stock markets retraced almost exactly half their losses in local currency terms before retreating again. This might be interpreted as the twilight period. Eventually the financial markets at the center also succumbed to the bust. At first the erosion was gradual and the flow of funds into mutual funds remained positive, but the meltdown in Russia precipitated a selling climax that had some, but not all, of the earmarks of a market bottom. I believe that it is a false bottom, just as the bottom made by the Asian stock markets at the beginning of 1998 turned out to be false. I expect a retracement of up to 50 percent but I cannot rule out the possibility of a further decline before the rebound. Eventually the markets should go much lower, leading to a global recession. The disintegration of the global capitalist system will prevent a recovery, turning the recession into a depression.

I have three main reasons why I believe that the bottom has not been reached. One is that the Russian meltdown has revealed previously ignored flaws in the international banking system. Banks engage in swaps, forward transactions, and derivative trades among each other and with their clients. These transactions do not show up in the balance sheets of the banks.

When Russian banks defaulted on their obligations, Western banks remained on the hook both on their own account and on behalf of clients. Hedge funds and other speculative accounts also sustained large losses. Banks are now frantically trying to limit their exposure, deleverage, and reduce risk. Their own stocks have plummeted and a global credit crunch is in the making.*

---

*Since then, Long-Term Capital Management collapsed with disastrous consequences.

Second, the pain at the periphery has now become so intense that individual countries have begun to opt out of the global capitalist system or simply fall by the wayside. First Indonesia, then Russia, suffered a pretty complete breakdown. What happened in Malaysia and, to a lesser extent, in Hong Kong is in some ways even more ominous. The collapse in Indonesia and Russia was unintended, but Malaysia shut itself off from international capital markets deliberately. Its action has brought temporary relief to the Malaysian economy and allowed its rulers to maintain themselves in power but, by reinforcing a general flight of capital from the periphery, it has put additional pressure on those countries that are trying to keep their markets open. If the capital flight makes Malaysia look good in comparison with its neighbors, the policy may easily find imitators.

The third major factor working for the disintegration of the global capitalist system is the evident inability of the international monetary authorities to hold it together. IMF programs do not seem to be working and the IMF has run out of money. The response of the G7 governments to the Russian crisis was woefully inadequate, and the loss of control was quite scary. Financial markets are rather peculiar in this respect: They resent any kind of government interference but they hold a belief deep down that if conditions get really rough the authorities will step in. This belief has now been shaken.*

The reflexive interaction among these three factors leads me to conclude that we have passed the crossover point and the trend reversal is reinforced by a reversal of the prevailing bias. How events will unfold depends largely on the response of the banking system, the investing public, and the authorities at the center. The range of probabilities lies between a cascading decline of the stock markets and a more drawn-out process of deterioration.

*These points figured in my congressional testimony on September 15, 1998.

I think the latter alternative more likely. The shock to the international financial system is likely to wear off; the forced liquidation of positions will be absorbed. One of the main sources of tension, the strength of the dollar and the weakness of the yen, has already been corrected. Another trouble spot, Hong Kong, seems to have found a way to regain control over its destiny. Russia has been written off. An interest rate cut is in prospect. Stocks have fallen enough that many of them appear attractive. The public has learned that it pays to buy dips in an everlasting bull market and it will take time before it discovers that the bull market does not last forever. Thus it will take time for the three main negative forces to make their effect felt.

But the false dawn will be followed by a prolonged bear market, just as in the 1930s and in Asia currently. The public will stop buying dips and start moving out of stocks into money market funds or treasury bills. The wealth effect will take its toll and consumer demand will decline. Investment demand will also decline, for a number of reasons: Profits are under pressure, imports are rising and exports falling, and the supply of capital for the less well established enterprises and for real estate deals has dried up. Reductions in interest rates will cushion the market decline and the economy would eventually recover if the global capitalist system held together. But the chances of it falling apart have greatly increased. If and when the U.S. domestic economy slows down, the willingness to tolerate a large trade deficit will decrease and free trade may be endangered.

Earlier I thought that the Asian crisis would lead to the ultimate triumph of capitalism: Multinational corporations would replace the overseas Chinese families and the Asian model would be assimilated into the global capitalist model. That could still happen, but it is now more likely that countries at the periphery will increasingly opt out of the system as their prospects for attracting capital from the center fade away. Banks and portfolio investors have suffered severe losses and there are more to come. Russia is likely to default on its dollar obligations. Losses in Indonesia will also have to be recognized. Banks are punished by their shareholders for their exposure to the periphery: They will not want to increase their commitments. Only international governmental action could pump money into the periphery, but there is no sign of international cooperation.

The sequence of events I describe differs from the original boom/bust model mainly in the length and complexity of its bust portion. The boom portion was characterized by the usual self-reinforcing interaction between bias and trend. The boom was successfully tested in the Mexican crisis of 1994–1995, followed by a period of acceleration. It is the bust portion that is unusual because it is divided into two phases. In the first phase, the stock markets of the center continued to boom, benefiting from the absence of monetary tightening and the reverse flow of funds. In the second phase, both center and periphery are in full contraction and they reinforce each other in a downward direction. Busts are usually quite compressed; this one is quite drawn out and occurs at different times in different parts of the system. When it occurred in the periphery, it was quite compact—we do not yet know what shape it will take at the center. The length of the bust bears testimony to the complexity of the global capitalist system.

It was obvious that the disequilibrium between center and periphery in the first phase of the bust could not be sustained. Either the center would decline before the periphery recovered or the other way round. The first alternative was more probable but not certain. The Russian meltdown decided the issue. Just as in the case of Thailand, the impact of Russia was greater than most people expected, myself included. I took a cataclysmic-enough view of events in Russia but I did not understand the implications for swaps and derivatives and the interbank market until they actually occurred.

It will be recalled that my original boom/bust model has eight stages. Stage 4 is the moment of truth and Stage 5 is the twilight period. It is not clear how these stages fit into the special model I have built for the global capitalist system. One could argue that the time between the Thai crisis in July 1997 and the Russian meltdown in August 1998 was the twilight period. But when was the moment of truth? It may be best not to press the point. Models ought not to be taken too literally: There is nothing determinate about the course of history. Each sequence is unique. The Soviet system had a moment of truth when Khrushchev made his speech to the Twentieth Congress of the Communist Party; perhaps the capitalist system does not have one. We may have a different phenomenon: the false dawn that lulls our sense of danger and allows the next so-called external shock to exert its toll.

The breakdown of the global capitalist system could be prevented by the intervention of the international financial authorities at any time. The prospects are dim because the G7 has just failed to intervene in Russia, but the consequences of that failure may serve as a wake-up call. Perhaps the Russian meltdown will turn out to be the moment of truth after all. There is an urgent need to rethink and reform the global capitalist system. As the Russian example has shown, the problems will become progressively more intractable the longer they are allowed to fester.

CHAPTER 8

How to Prevent Collapse

A s in every financial crisis, there is some soul searching, but
the scope of the current public debate is far too narrow.
It is focused on the need to improve banking supervision and to ensure adequate and accurate data on each
country. Transparency and information are the keywords. It is hotly
debated whether the IMF should make its views on the state of
affairs in individual countries public or not.* There is also some discussion whether hedge funds should be regulated and short-term
capital flows discouraged, but that is about as far as it goes. The
prevailing doctrine on how financial markets operate has not
changed. It is assumed that with perfect information markets can
take care of themselves; therefore the main task is to make the nec-

*For my views, please see Chapter 1.

essary information available and to avoid any interference with the market mechanism. Imposing market discipline remains the goal.

We need to broaden the debate. It is time to recognize that financial markets are inherently unstable. Imposing market discipline means imposing instability, and how much instability can society take? Market discipline needs to be supplemented by another discipline: Maintaining stability in financial markets ought to be an explicit objective of public policy.

To put it bluntly, the choice confronting us is whether we will regulate global financial markets internationally or leave it to each individual state to protect its own interests as best it can. The latter course will surely lead to the breakdown of the gigantic circulatory system, which goes under the name of global capitalism. Sovereign states can act as valves within the system. They may not resist the inflow of capital but they will surely resist the outflow, once they consider it permanent.

Emergency Measures

The most urgent need is to arrest the reverse flow of capital. That would ensure the continued allegiance of the periphery to the global capitalist system, which would in turn reassure the financial markets at the center and moderate the ensuing recession. It is appropriate to lower interest rates in the United States, but that is no longer sufficient to staunch the outflow from the periphery. Liquidity must be pumped more directly into the periphery. It needs to be done very urgently because Brazil is still suffering from the flight of both external and domestic capital and cannot live with sky-high interest rates much longer. Interest rates inside Korea and Thailand have declined, but the risk premium on the external debt of *all* periphery countries remains prohibitive.

In an article published in the *Financial Times* on December 31,

1997,* I proposed establishing an International Credit Insurance Corporation. The proposal was premature because the reverse flow of capital had not yet become a firmly established trend. It will be recalled that the Korean liquidity crisis at the end of 1997 was followed by a false dawn that lasted till April 1998. My proposal fell flat but its time has come.

President Clinton and Treasury Secretary Robert E. Rubin spoke about the need to establish a fund that would enable periphery countries that are following sound economic policies to regain access to the international capital markets. They mentioned a figure of $150 billion and, although they did not say so publicly, I believe that they had in mind financing it with a new issue of Special Drawing Rights (SDRs).† Although their proposal did not receive much support at the annual meeting of the IMF in October 1998 I believe it is exactly what is needed. Loan guarantees could be made available to countries like Korea, Thailand, and Brazil and they would have an immediate calming effect on international financial markets. By injecting liquidity at the periphery, the United States proposal could obviate the need to reduce interest rates at the center, bringing the global economy into better balance.

As we have seen, the IMF programs in Thailand and Korea have failed to produce the desired results because they did not include a debt-to-equity conversion scheme. The external balance of these countries has been reestablished at the cost of a severe contraction of domestic demand, but the balance sheets of both banks and companies continues to deteriorate. As things stand now, these countries are doomed to languish in depression for an extended period. A debt-to-equity conversion scheme could clear the decks and allow the domestic economy to recover, but it would force the international

---

*"Avoiding a breakdown: Asia's crisis demands a rethink of international regulation," *Financial Times* (London), December 31, 1997.
†Special Drawing Rights are best viewed as artificial money put at the disposal of the IMF by its members.

creditors to accept and write off losses. They would be unwilling and unable to extend credit, making it impossible to implement such a scheme without finding an alternate source of international credit. That is where the international credit guarantee scheme would come into play. It would significantly reduce the cost of borrowing and enable the countries concerned to finance a higher level of domestic demand than they are able to sustain currently. This would be helpful not only to the countries concerned but also to the world economy. It would provide a reward for belonging to the global capitalist system and discourage defections along the Malaysian lines.

The case of Brazil is more complicated. After the U.S. Congress has reluctantly approved the capital increase, the IMF will be in a position to put together a rescue package for Brazil. The package would have to be quite large to reassure markets: $30 billion from official sources is mentioned as a starting figure to be complemented by a pledge from commercial banks to maintain their credit lines. Needless to say, Brazil would have to undertake aggressive measures to reduce the fiscal deficit. Even so, there is a real danger that the program may fail. While the package would take care of Brazil's foreign refinancing needs, it would not assure that domestic interest rates can be reduced significantly without rekindling capital flight. At current interest rates of 40 percent the refinancing of domestic debt would add about 6 percent to the budget deficit, which would outweigh any possible belt tightening. What makes the situation so complicated is that the loan guarantee scheme is not meant to be used for the refinancing of domestic debt. Nevertheless, the fact that it would be available for international borrowing would have an indirect affect on domestic interest rates and may make the difference between failure and success.

At present, European central bankers are adamantly opposed to the issue of SDRs because of its inflationary implications. But SDRs reserved for loan guarantees would not create additional money; if ever they were issued they would merely fill a hole that had been created by a default. Truth be told, the opposition to SDRs is based on doctrinaire grounds; but after the German elections, left-of-center governments are now in power throughout Europe and they are likely to prove more amenable to a loan guarantee scheme especially when the recovery of important export markets hinges on it. Japan is likely to be supportive as long as the scheme covers Asia as well as Latin America. In this way the IMF would gain experience in issuing loan guarantees and eventually the method could be institutionalized. I believe it could provide the cornerstone for the "new architecture" everybody is talking about.

Longer Range Reforms

The inadequacies of the current architecture became glaringly obvious during the global financial crisis that was unleashed in Thailand. One deficiency was the lack of adequate international supervisory and regulatory authority. The Bank for International Settlements instituted capital adequacy ratios for international commercial banks but supervision was left to the central banks of individual countries. Their performance left much to be desired. Just to cite one example, the Korean central bank required all loans over one year of maturity to be registered. As a result, most borrowing was for less than one year, and the central bank had no idea of the amounts involved. According to BIS standards, international banks doing business with Korea were exempted from setting up special reserves because Korea was a member of the Organization for Economic Cooperation and Development (OECD). This encouraged the banks to lend to Korea. The fact that most of the loans matured in less than one year made the crisis, when it erupted, more intractable.

In the case of Indonesia the behavior of the central bank was much more suspicious. There was an item in the balance sheet, for instance, showing a large "advance to the private sector" that offset much of the assistance received from Singapore. It was suspected that the advance went to Suharto family members who took the dollars out of Indonesia. As the crisis advanced a mysterious fire erupted in the building where the documents were kept.

The IMF does not have much say in the internal affairs of its member countries except in times of crisis when a member country turns to the IMF for assistance. It may visit and consult but it has neither the mandate nor the tools to interfere in normal times. Its mission is crisis management, not prevention, and on this occasion it did not acquit itself with distinction. I have examined the flaws in the IMF prescriptions in the previous chapter; here we need to consider the role that the IMF has played in the unsound expansion of international credit. It leads us to the second major defect in the current architecture, the so-called moral hazard argument.

IMF programs have served to bail out the lenders and thereby encouraged them to act irresponsibly; this is a major source of instability in the international financial system. As I explained earlier, there is an asymmetry in the way the IMF has treated lenders and borrowers. It imposed conditions on the borrowers but not on lenders; the money it lent and the conditions it imposed enabled the debtor countries to meet their obligations better than they would have been able to do otherwise. In this indirect way the IMF was assisting the international banks and other creditors.

The asymmetry developed during the international debt crisis of the 1980s and became quite blatant in the Mexican crisis of 1994/1995. In that crisis the foreign holders of *tesobonos* (Mexican dollar denominated treasury bills) came out whole although the yield on the *tesobonos* at the time they were purchased implied a high degree of risk. When Mexico could not pay, the U.S. Treasury and the IMF stepped in and took the investors off the hook. A similar situation arose in Russia recently but the U.S. Treasury was inhibited from mounting an effective rescue operation by the fear that it would be accused of bailing out the speculators. As I argued in my real-time experiment, the United States made a mistake in refusing to act *after* the speculators had been punished. I am pleased to note that the IMF is a fast learner. In its $2.2 billion program in Ukraine, it is imposing a new condition: 80 percent of Ukrainian treasury bills have to be "voluntarily" rescheduled into longer-term, lower-yielding instruments before the program can go forward. This would inflict big losses on speculators and imprudent bank lenders and it is a long way from the Mexican bailout of 1995.

There are several interrelated reasons why the asymmetry in the IMF's treatment of debtors and creditors has developed. The primary mission of the IMF is to preserve the international financial system. Imposing penalties on the lenders at a time of crisis might do too much damage to Western banks and run the risk of systemic collapse. Secondly, the IMF needs the cooperation of the commercial lenders to make its programs successful and the banks know how to exploit their position. The international monetary authorities do not have sufficient resources to act as lenders of last resort. Once a crisis has erupted the IMF can deal with it only by restoring market confidence. In the Asian crisis some of the initial IMF programs flopped precisely because they failed to convince the markets. Finally, the IMF is controlled by the countries at the center of the capitalist system; it would go against the national interests of the controlling shareholders if the IMF penalized the lenders. Yet that is exactly what is needed to make the system more stable. The IMF ought to make its intervention conditional on the lenders shouldering their share of losses. The IMF imposes conditions on a country in trouble: It should also impose conditions on the creditors, particularly when the trouble is caused by the private sector (as in the case of the Asian countries). In practice this would mean that the IMF would not only tolerate but encourage voluntary corporate reorganizations. Bankruptcy proceedings would be brought more in line with domestic practice in advanced countries, forcing the banks to take losses.

The asymmetry in the current functioning of the IMF cannot be corrected, in my opinion, without introducing a loan guarantee scheme or some other method of stimulating international lending and investment. The asymmetry (a.k.a. moral hazard) gave rise to an unsound international investment boom; in its absence, it will be very difficult to generate sufficient international investment flows. The rapid recovery of emerging markets after the Mexican crisis of 1994 is highly misleading. As we have seen, the bailout of foreign holders of Mexican *tesobonos* constituted the ultimate confirmation of the asymmetry; no wonder that the flow of capital became stronger and more indiscriminate than ever. Under the new dispensation, foreign investors in Mexican *tesobonos* would have seen their holdings converted into long-term Mexican government bonds. Had that happened, they would have been much more cautious about investing in Russia or Ukraine.

Ideally, the IMF ought to have waited for the global financial crisis to subside before introducing any changes in its method of operation. But this option has been foreclosed by events. Investors and lenders have been severely punished and they are fleeing the periphery in droves, creating an emergency situation. There is nothing to be lost and much to be gained by changing the way the IMF operates right away.

With or without debt-to-equity conversion, it is unlikely that the flow of funds toward the periphery countries can be restarted without providing some inducements for lenders scarred by their recent and impending losses. The credit guarantee insurance scheme will therefore need to be developed into a permanent part of the IMF. This would provide a much improved architecture for the global financial system. Providing both carrots and sticks would help to avoid both feast and famine in international capital flows. The new institution, which would presumably remain part of the IMF, would explicitly guarantee international loans and credits up to defined limits. The borrowing countries would be obliged to provide data on all borrowings, public or private, insured or not. This would enable the authority to set a ceiling on the amounts it was willing to insure. Up to those amounts, the countries concerned would be able to access international capital markets at prime rates plus a modest fee. Beyond these limits, the creditors would be at risk. Providing both carrots and sticks would help to avoid both feast and famine in international capital flows. The ceilings would be set taking into account the macroeconomic and structural policies pursued by individual countries as well as overall economic conditions in the world. The new institution would function, in effect, as a kind of international central bank. It would seek to avoid excesses in either direction and it would have a powerful tool in its hand.*

The thorniest problem is how the credit guarantees allocated to an individual country would be distributed among that country's borrowers. To allow the state to exercise the right would be an invitation for abuse. The guarantees ought to be channeled through authorized banks that would compete with each other. The banks would have to be closely supervised and prohibited from engaging in other lines of business that could give rise to unsound credits and conflicts of interest. The banks would have to be reasonably well capitalized in order to provide a cushion against losses on individual credits. In short, the banks would have to be as closely regulated as U.S. banks were after the breakdown of the U.S. banking system in the banking panic of 1933. It would take time to reorganize the banking system and to introduce the appropriate regulations, but the mere announcement of the scheme would have a calming effect on financial markets and allow time for a more thorough elaboration.

Some will wonder whether it is possible to accomplish such a complicated task. The answer is that the new institution is bound to make mistakes, but the markets will provide valuable feedback

---

*My arguments in this context are not that new. Originally the founders of the Bretton Woods institutions envisioned the role of the World Bank as a "guarantor" of securities issued by developing nations or for developing country issuers. See, Edward S. Mason and Robert E. Asher, *The World Bank Since Bretton Woods* (Washington, DC: The Brookings Institution, 1973).

and the mistakes can be corrected. After all, that is how all central banks operate and on the whole they do a pretty good job.

It is much more questionable whether such a scheme is politically feasible. There is already a lot of opposition to the IMF from market fundamentalists who are against any kind of market intervention, especially by an international organization. If the banks and financial market participants who currently benefit from the asymmetry cease to support it, it is doubtful whether the IMF can survive even in its present inadequate form. It will require a change of mentality to get governments, parliaments, and market participants to recognize that they have a stake in the survival of the system. The question is whether this change of mentality will occur before or after the collapse of the system.

Currency Regimes

Whatever currency regime prevails, it is bound to be flawed. Freely fluctuating currency rates are inherently unstable because of trend-following speculation; moreover the instability is cumulative because trend-following speculation tends to grow in importance over time. On the other hand, fixed exchange rate regimes are dangerous because breakdowns can be catastrophic. The Asian crisis is a case in point. I often compare currency arrangements with matrimonial arrangements: Whatever regime prevails, its opposite looks more attractive.

So what is to be done? Keeping exchange rates flexible would be the safest, but it would make it difficult for the periphery countries to attract capital. Combined with a credit insurance scheme, it could be a sound arrangement. Another alternative is to construct a fixed exchange rate system that does not break down.

A major experiment is currently under way in Europe: the creation of a single currency. It is based on the belief, which I share, that in the long run you cannot have a common market without a common currency. I believe, however, that the design of the euro is flawed because in the long run you cannot have a common currency without a common fiscal policy, including some kind of centralized tax collection or tax redistribution. But the introduction of the common currency was a political decision; the flaws can also be corrected by political decisions.

Another way to create an almost-unbreakable fixed exchange rate regime is to introduce a currency board. This is an automatic mechanism that issues and withdraws local currency if the equivalent amount of reserve currency is deposited with or removed from the currency board. The U.S. dollar serves as the reserve currency in Hong Kong and Argentina, the French franc in the former French colonies in Africa, and the German mark in Estonia and Bulgaria. The currency board idea is gaining support because it has worked better than less formal pegs. I am skeptical, although I advocated it in Russia as a last resort. The social costs of maintaining a currency board can become prohibitive because there is no limit on how high interest rates may go during a crisis. Recent experience has shown that even the firmest of currency boards is not immune from attack. Hong Kong was willing to pay the price and it had the backing of the Chinese government, but Hong Kong is a special case: It is first and foremost a financial center, which could, in principle, survive indefinitely with an overvalued currency. (Switzerland has done so.) The currency board regime also worked in Argentina during the tequila crisis of 1995 but it is not foolproof; specifically, Argentina could become permanently overvalued if its main trading partner, Brazil, devalued, and the currency board would offer no avenue of escape. The same is true of Hong Kong if China devalued.*

---

*The biggest difficulty with a currency board is how to end it when it no longer works. To give it credibility, a currency board is usually enacted by law, and it takes a long time to change laws. What happens during the time the change is under consideration? It is an invitation for a run on the currency. Of course there is a solution: to abrogate the currency board from one day to the next by breaking the law. Doing so, however, is liable to make all currency boards less credible.

With the introduction of the euro, there will be three main currency blocks. Japan faces special problems and the yen is in a state of dynamic disequilibrium so it may be set aside for the moment. This leaves two major currency blocks, with sterling floating uneasily between the euro and the dollar unless Britain decides to join the euro. In the past, the major currency blocks clashed and crashed against each other, causing major dislocations in the stock and bond markets. The rise in the value of the dollar was the immediate cause of the Asian crisis. Going further back, currency turbulence touched off the Wall Street crash of 1987. The precipitous rise in the yen in April 1995 was also very disturbing, although it did not cause a crash. The need for policy coordination has now been recognized and institutional arrangements have been put into place, but the belief in the efficacy of coordinated intervention has eroded since the heady days of the Plaza Agreement of 1985, when the G-5 agreed to cooperate in managing exchange rates.

It is time to revisit the issue. The emergence of two main currency blocks will create a new situation. Rivalry might be disastrous, whereas cooperation may be easier to arrange between two partners than it would be among many. Perhaps the two main currencies could even be linked with each other in a formal way. Linkage would remove one of the main sources of instability in the global capitalist system, but it would create new problems of policy coordination.

Could coordination work? Because I am skeptical about the euro, I must be even more skeptical about a global currency. But there may be ways short of total integration. For instance, there could be almost unlimited swap agreements in which each side would guarantee the other against a change in the rate of exchange. I am particularly taken by the "hard ecu" idea put forward by Sir Michael Butler, a former British treasury official, as an alternative to the single European currency. He proposed establishing a currency basket that would be harder than any of its components.

Should any member country devalue, it would have to make up the deficiency it creates in the basket that makes up the currency unit. Perhaps the two major currencies could be linked together in some such fashion. (There is a problem with Britain joining the euro because sterling dances to a different tune from the continental currencies and moves more in line with the dollar; it might be safer to engineer a three-way link.)

Derivatives, Swaps, and Spreads

Derivatives are constructed on the basis of the theory of efficient markets. The fact that they have become so widely used would seem to imply that the theory of efficient markets is valid. I disagree, but I have to be careful how I state my disagreement because, as I mentioned before, I have not studied the theory of efficient markets in any great detail or spent much time on how derivatives are constructed. Beta, gamma, delta are, for the most part, just Greek letters to me.

As I understand it, volatility can be measured and it is possible to buy insurance against volatility by paying a premium for options. Those who assume the risk by selling options can either offset the risk against their existing positions or they can reinsure themselves by engaging in so-called delta hedging. This is a complex strategy but it boils down to a rather crude method of limiting risk. It involves the seller of the option buying back a certain portion of the underlying security as the price moves against him or her. Delta hedgers are usually professional market makers who derive their profits from the spread between bid and asked prices and limit their risks by delta hedging.

Properly executed, this strategy should yield profits over the long-run, but delta hedging creates automatic trend-following behavior. As the market moves in a certain direction the delta hedger automatically moves in the same direction, buying when the price goes up, selling when it is going down. In this way, the market makers transfer their risk to the market. As a general rule, the market can absorb the risk because different participants move in different directions. Once in a blue moon, the risks pile up on one side of the market and delta hedging can touch off a discontinuity in price movements. On these occasions, efficient market theory breaks down. The occasions are rare enough not to discourage an otherwise profitable business, but when they occur they can have a devastating impact on the market.

Risk management, as it is practiced in the proprietary trading departments of commercial and investment banks, works the same way as delta hedging: By setting limits to the amount of loss a trader can incur it forces the trader to reduce trading positions when they move against him or her. This is, in effect, a self-imposed stop loss order, which reinforces the trend that caused the loss in the first place. The consequences became evident when Long-Term Capital Management got into difficulties.

Trend-following behavior in general and delta hedging in particular tends to increase the volatility of the market but the market makers benefit from volatility because they can charge a higher premium on options and the buyers of the options cannot complain because the higher premium is justified by the higher volatility. There may be hidden costs to the public but they are well hidden. As former Federal Reserve Chairman Paul Volcker has said, everybody complains about volatility in currency markets but nobody will do anything about it because the public cannot complain and the market makers in derivatives make a profit coming and going— by creating volatility and by selling insurance against it.

Derivatives have become increasingly sophisticated and some of them carry a higher risk of causing a discontinuity than others. The 1987 stock market crash was aggravated by the widespread use of a delta hedging technique marketed under the name of portfolio insurance. Those who bought the insurance became more heavily invested in the market than they would have been otherwise. When a market decline activated the insurance, the sudden volume of selling created a discontinuity. To prevent a recurrence, the regulators introduced so-called circuit breakers—temporary suspensions of the market—which destroy the assumption of continuity on which such delta hedging programs are based.

Similarly dangerous derivative instruments are in widespread use in currency markets but nothing has been done to discourage them. For instance, "knockout" options are canceled when a certain price limit is reached, leaving the buyer of the option without insurance. Knockout options used to be very popular among Japanese exporters because they are much cheaper than regular options. When they were all knocked out at the same time in 1995, a stampede ensued that drove the yen from about ¥100 to the dollar to below 80 within a few weeks. Unbalanced option positions have caused other large and seemingly unjustified currency movements at times. The situation cries out for regulation, or at least supervision, but again, as Volcker explained, there has been no constituency clamoring for it.

Generally speaking, there are no margin requirements for derivatives, swaps, and forward transactions except when they are executed on registered exchanges. Banks and investment banks acting as market makers can carry these items as off–balance sheet items. These instruments have developed in an age when people believed in efficient markets, rational expectations, and the self-correcting capacity of financial markets. By contrast, margin requirements on stock purchases are left over from a bygone age. If my contention is correct and some of the recently invented financial instruments and trading techniques are based on a fundamentally flawed theory of financial markets, the absence of margin requirements may pose a serious systemic risk.

On a more fundamental level, we ought to reconsider our attitude toward financial innovations. Innovation is regarded as one of the main benefits of free markets, but because financial markets are inherently unstable financial innovations may be creating instability. We ought to view financial innovations differently from the way we view better mousetraps and other inventions. This will require quite an adjustment, because the best brains in the world have been attracted to the financial markets and the combination of computer capacity with efficient market theory has produced an explosive growth in new financial instruments and new types of arbitrage. The dangers that they may pose to the financial system have been ignored because markets are supposed to be self-correcting, but that is an illusion. The innovative instruments and techniques are not properly understood either by the regulators or the practitioners; therefore they pose a threat to stability.

Perhaps derivatives and other synthetic financial instruments ought to be licensed in the way new issues of securities have to be registered with the Securities and Exchange Commission. It goes against the grain that the creative energies of innovators should be subjected to constraints administered by plodding bureaucrats but that is what I suggest. Innovations bring intellectual excitement and profit to the innovators, but maintaining stability or, more exactly, preventing excesses ought to take precedence.

The Russian meltdown has revealed some of the systemic risks. The failure of Long-Term Capital Management, a hedge fund that pioneered the use of risk management techniques based on efficient market theory demonstrates the failure of the theory. The fact that a rescue effort had to be orchestrated by the Federal Reserve indicates that a systemic risk was involved. Long-Term Capital Management carried a balance sheet of over $100 billion on an equity base of less than $5 billion. In addition, it had off–balance sheet liabilities in excess of $1 trillion. The dislocations caused by the Russian meltdown eroded the equity base until it was down to $600 million at the time of the rescue. If Long-Term Capital Management had been allowed to fail, the counterparties would have sustained losses running into billions, especially as they carried similar positions for their own account. As it is, the counterparties banded together under the prodding of the Federal Reserve and put additional capital into the failing company to permit a more gradual unwinding. The Federal Reserve did what it is supposed to do: prevent systemic failure. When the emergency has passed, the system needs to be reformed. The reform could be superficial, as it was after the 1987 stock market crash with the introduction of so-called circuit breakers, or it could be more fundamental. I hardly need to repeat that I favor a more fundamental rethinking because I believe that our current views about financial markets are based on a false theory.

Hedge Funds

Following the bailout of Long-Term Capital Management there is much talk about regulating hedge funds. I believe the discussion is misdirected. Hedge funds are not the only ones to use leverage; the proprietary trading desks of commercial and investment banks are the main players in derivatives and swaps. Most hedge funds are not engaged in those markets. Soros Fund Management, for instance, is not in that line of business at all. We use derivatives sparingly and operate with much less leverage. Long-Term Capital Management was in some ways exceptional: It was, in effect, the proprietary trading desk of an investment bank, Salomon Brothers, transplanted into an independent entity. Having proved successful, it was beginning to spawn imitators. Even so, hedge funds as a group did not equal in size the proprietary trading desks of banks and brokers and it was the threat that Long-Term Capital Management posed to those institutions that prompted the Federal Reserve Bank of New York to intervene. The correct remedy is to impose margin requirements and so-called haircuts on derivative and swap transactions and other off-balance sheet items. These regulations should apply to the banks and their customers, the hedge funds, alike.

I am not defending hedge funds. I believe hedge funds should be regulated like all other investment funds. They are difficult to regulate because many of them operate offshore, but if the regulatory authorities cooperate, this should not present any insuperable difficulties. The important point is that the regulations should apply to all entities equally.

Capital Controls

It has become an article of faith that capital controls should be abolished and the financial markets of individual countries, including banking, opened up to international competition. The IMF has even proposed amending its charter to make these goals more explicit. Yet the experience of the Asian crisis ought to make us pause. The countries that kept their financial markets closed weathered the storm better than those that were open. India was less affected than the Southeast Asian countries; China was better insulated than Korea.

Having open capital markets is highly desirable not only for economic but also for political reasons. Capital controls are an invitation for evasion, corruption, and the abuse of power. A closed economy is a threat to liberty. Mahathir of Malaysia followed up the closing of capital markets with a political crackdown.

Unfortunately international financial markets are unstable. Keeping domestic financial markets totally exposed to the vagaries of international financial markets could cause greater instability than a country that has become dependent on foreign capital can endure. Some form of capital controls may therefore be preferable to instability even if it would not constitute good policy in an ideal world. The challenge is to keep international financial markets stable enough to make capital control unnecessary. A credit guarantee scheme could help to accomplish that goal.

Allowing foreign banks into domestic markets is an altogether different matter. They are likely to cream off the wholesale market where they enjoy competitive advantages and leave the less profitable retail business under served. They are also likely to prove much more fickle than domestic banks. This holds true for the center as well as the periphery. The first to pull credit lines in the United States after the Russian meltdown were the European banks. Latin America benefited greatly from the entry of Spanish banks since 1995, but it remains to be seen how much capital the Spanish banks will devote to Latin America when their shareholders punish them for their Latin American exposure. There is much to be said for developing a domestic source of capital as Chile has done by establishing private pension funds.

On their own, short-term capital movements probably do more harm than good. As the Asian crisis has demonstrated, it is very risky for a recipient country to allow short-term capital inflows to be used for long-term purposes. The proper policy is to sterilize the inflow. This is usually done by accumulating reserves, but that is costly and it tends to attract further inflows. Chile invented a better way: It has imposed reserve requirements on short-term capital inflows. Ironically, it is now in the process of dismantling this system to attract capital.

The main justification for keeping capital markets open is to facilitate the free flow of capital into long-term instruments such as stocks and bonds. When the direction of the flow is reversed the justification disappears. Sovereign states can act as valves: allowing the inflow but resisting the outflow. It is imperative that countries on the periphery be encouraged not simply to turn their backs on the global system in the Malaysian manner; to ensure this the IMF and other institutions may have to recognize the case for some regulations on capital flows. There are subtle ways in which currency speculation can be discouraged that fall well short of capital controls. Banks can be required to report on the currency positions they hold both for their own and for their clients' accounts and, if necessary, limits can be imposed on the size of such positions. These techniques can be quite effective. For instance, at the time of the European currency turmoil in 1992 we at Soros Fund Management found it practically impossible to go short of the Irish punt, although we were certain that it would be devalued. The constraint on national central banks is that they can exercise control only over their own banks; but once the principle that some controls are legitimate is established, there could be a lot more cooperation between national central banks. It should be possible to curb speculation without incurring all the harmful side effects of capital controls.

This is about as far as I want to go in prescribing solutions. Perhaps I have already gone too far. All I wanted to do was to stimulate a discussion out of which the appropriate reforms may emerge. There are no permanent and comprehensive solutions; we must always remain on the alert for further problems. One thing is certain: Financial markets are inherently unstable; they need supervision and regulation. The only question is whether we have the wisdom to strengthen our international financial authorities or do we leave it to individual countries to fend for themselves. In the latter case we ought not be surprised by the spread of capital controls.

Who are the "we"? Where is the global society to match the global economy? These are questions I will address in the next chapter.

CHAPTER 9

Toward an Open Society

In the previous chapters, I examined the deficiencies of the market mechanism and made some suggestions on how they could be corrected. Now I come to a more difficult task: to discuss the inadequacies of the nonmarket sector of society. These are more pervasive than the markets failures I have identified. They include the insufficient weight given to social values, the substitution of money for intrinsic values, the deficiencies of representative democracy in some parts of the world and its absence in other parts, and the lack of international cooperation. This list is not meant to be complete, but it constitutes a challenging-enough agenda.

Market Values Versus Social Values

I have had great difficulties throughout this book in discussing the relationship between market values and social values. The problem is not in establishing that there is a difference between the two; it is in discussing the content and character of social values. Market fundamentalists try to disregard social values by arguing that whatever those values are they find expression in market behavior. For instance, if people want to take care of others or protect the environment they can express their sentiments by spending money on these ends and their altruism becomes just as much part of the GNP as their conspicuous consumption. To show that this argument is false, I do not need to resort to abstract reasoning, of which we have had too much already; I can draw on my personal experience.

As an anonymous participant in financial markets, I never had to weigh the social consequences of my actions. I was aware that in some circumstances the consequences might be harmful but I felt justified in ignoring them on the grounds that I was playing by the rules. The game was very competitive and if I imposed additional constraints on myself I would end up as a loser. Moreover, I realized that my moral scruples would make no difference to the real world, given the conditions of effective or near-perfect competition that prevail in financial markets; if I abstained somebody else would take my place. In deciding which stocks or currencies to buy or sell, I was guided by only one consideration: to maximize my profits by weighing the risks against the rewards. My decisions related to events that had social consequences: When I bought shares in Lockheed and Northrop after the managements were indicted for bribery I helped to sustain the price of the stock. When I sold sterling short in 1992, the Bank of England was on the other side of my transactions and I was taking money out of the pockets of British taxpayers. But if I had tried to take the social consequences into account, it would have thrown off my risk/reward calculations and my chances of being successful would have been reduced. Fortunately I did not need to bother about the social consequences because they would have occurred anyway: Financial markets have a sufficiently large number of participants so that no single participant can have an appreciable effect on the outcome. Bringing my social conscience into the decision-making process would not make any difference in the real world. Britain would have devalued anyway. If I were not single-minded in the pursuit of profit, it would affect only my own results.

I recognized that this argument was valid only for the financial markets. If I had to deal with people instead of markets, I could not have avoided moral choices and I could not have been so successful in making money. I blessed the luck that led me to the financial markets and allowed me not to dirty my hands.* The fact remains that anonymous market participants are largely exempt from moral choices as long as they play by the rules. In this sense, financial markets are not immoral; they are amoral.

This characteristic of markets makes it all the more important that the rules that govern markets should be properly formulated. The anonymous participant can ignore moral, political, and social considerations, but if we look at financial markets from the standpoint of society we cannot leave such considerations out of account. As we have seen, financial markets can act as a wrecking ball knocking over economies. Although we are justified in playing by the rules, we ought also to be concerned with the rules by which we play. Rules are made by the authorities, but in a democratic society the authorities are chosen by the players. Collective action can also be brought to bear more directly. For instance, the boycott of South African investments turned out to be successful in promoting a change of regime in South Africa. But the South African case was an exception, because it involved collective action. Normally social values do not find expression in the market behavior of individual participants and therefore they need to find some other form of expression.

---

*My position changed when I became a public figure. Suddenly I *could* influence markets. This raised moral issues from which I was previously exempt, but I do not want to discuss them here because it would distract attention from the argument.

Market participation and rule making are two different functions. It would be a mistake to equate the market values that guide individual participants with the social values that ought to guide the setting of rules. Unfortunately the distinction is rarely observed. Collective decision making in contemporary democracies is largely a power play between competing interests. People try to bend the rules to their own advantage. When they engage in lobbying, for instance, the exemption from moral considerations should no longer apply.

Social values come into play not only in making rules for market participation (e.g., rules against insider trading) but also in serving communal needs such as public safety or education or protecting the environment. Many of these needs can be satisfied commercially. We can have toll roads, private education, and commercially run prisons; we can trade pollution rights. Where to draw the line between public and private and, having drawn the line, how to regulate the private provision of public services remain collective decisions.

All this is plain enough; the real difficulties begin once the distinction between market values and social values has been recognized. How do they relate to each other? Clearly market values reflect the interests of the individual market participant whereas social values have to do with the interests of society as perceived by its members. Market values can be measured in monetary terms but social values are more problematic. They are difficult to observe and even more difficult to measure. To measure profits, all we need to do is to look at the bottom line. But how can we measure the social consequences of a course of action? Actions have unintended consequences that are scattered among all the lines that stand above the bottom line. They cannot be reduced to a common denominator because they affect different people differently. As a philanthropist, I am acutely aware of all the unintended consequences that lie in wait and I try to weigh them. I have the advantage of being my own master. In politics, the decisions have to be taken collectively, making it much harder to evaluate the results. With different people advocating different courses of action, the connection between intentions and consequences becomes very tenuous indeed. No wonder that the political process functions less efficiently than the market mechanism.

The deficiencies of the political process have become much more acute since the economy has become truly global and the market mechanism has penetrated into aspects of society that were previously exempt from it. It is easy to see why this should be so. As I discussed earlier, social values express a concern for others. They imply a community to which we belong. If we were truly independent and unattached, there would be no compelling reason to be concerned with others except our own inclinations; the external pressures that come from the community to which we belong would be missing. But a market economy does not function as a community and a global economy is even less so. As a consequence, the external pressures have been to a large extent relaxed. The internal disposition to belong may remain—it may be argued that it is innate in human nature—but in a transactional market, as distinct from a market built on relationships, morality can become an encumbrance. In a highly competitive environment, people weighed down by a concern for others are liable to do less well than those who are free of all moral scruples. In this way, social values undergo what may be described as a process of adverse natural selection. The unscrupulous come out on top. This is one of the most disturbing aspects of the global capitalist system.

But the argument runs into a logical difficulty. If people decide to neglect their social obligations, who can say that they have neglected them? On what basis can the prevailing social values be deemed deficient when those are the values that actually prevail? Where is the standard by which social values can be judged? There is no objective criterion for social values as there is for natural science.

I shall try to overcome the difficulty by comparing the political process with the market mechanism. I have been successful in demonstrating the deficiencies of financial markets because I had a standard, namely, equilibrium, to which I could compare them. I shall try to do the same for the political process by comparing it with the market mechanism.

I seek to make two related points. One is that the spread of monetary values and their influence on politics renders the political process less effective in serving the common interest than it used to be when social values, or "civic virtue," weighed more heavily on people's minds. The other is that the political process is less effective than the market mechanism in correcting its own excesses. These two considerations reinforce each other in a reflexive fashion: Market fundamentalism undermines the democratic political process and the inefficiency of the political process is a powerful argument in favor of market fundamentalism. The institutions of representative democracy that for so long have functioned well in the United States, much of Europe, and elsewhere, have become endangered, and civic virtue, once lost, is difficult to recapture.

Representative Democracy

Democracy is supposed to provide a mechanism for making collective decisions that serve the best interests of the community. It is meant to achieve the same objective for collective decision making as the market mechanism does for individual decision making. Citizens elect representatives who gather in assemblies to make collective decisions by voting. This is the principle of representative democracy. It presupposes a certain kind of relationship between the citizens and their representatives. The candidates stand up and tell the citizens what they stand for, and the citizens then choose the person whose ideas are the closest to their own. That is the sort of representative Thomas Jefferson was in the good old days, except that he stayed at home during the campaign. The process is based on the assumption of honesty in the same way as the concept of perfect competition is based on the assumption of perfect knowledge. The assumption is of course unrealistic. Candidates discovered a long time ago that they have a better chance of getting elected if they tell the electorate what it wants to hear rather than what they really think. The flaw is not fatal because the system has allowed for it. If candidates fail to live up to their promises, they can be thrown out of office. In this case, conditions remain near equilibrium. The voters do not always get the representatives they desire, but they can correct their mistakes in the next round of elections.

Conditions may, however, veer quite far from equilibrium by a reflexive process. Candidates develop techniques for exploiting the gap between promises and actions. They conduct public opinion surveys and focus group meetings to discover what the electorate wants to hear and fashion their messages to match the electorate's desires. The process produces a correspondence between the candidates' statements and the voters' desires, but the correspondence is brought about in the wrong way by making the candidates' promises correspond to the voters' expectations rather than by producing a candidate whose ideas correspond to the voters' ideas. The voters never get the representatives they desire; they are disappointed and lose faith in the process.

The voters are not blameless. They are supposed to be looking for representatives who will have the best interests of the community at heart, but they put their own narrow self-interests ahead of the interests of the community. The candidates in turn attempt to appeal to voters' individual self-interests. Because the candidates cannot satisfy all interests, particularly if they are in conflict with each other, they are practically forced into striking bargains with particular interests. The process deteriorates further when the voters cease to care whether their candidates cheat and lie as long as they represent the voters' personal interests. The corruption is complete when money comes in to play. Certainly in the United States, only candidates who strike bargains with particular interests can get enough money to get elected. Far-from-equilibrium conditions are reached when the electorate no longer expects candidates to be honest but judges them purely on their ability to get elected. The dynamic disequilibrium is further reinforced by the role that television ads play in elections. Commercials substitute for honest statements of beliefs and further enhance the importance of money because they have to be paid for. Those are the conditions that prevail today.

Compare these conditions with the conglomerate boom I described earlier. Conglomerate managements exploited a flaw in the valuations that investors applied to earnings. They discovered that they could increase their earnings per share by promising to increase their earnings per share through acquisitions. This is similar to telling the voters what they want to hear. Both are examples of dynamic disequilibrium. But what a difference! The conglomerate boom was corrected by a bust. It was also a more-or-less isolated incident, although similar incidents continue to occur. Still, markets have a way of correcting their excesses; bull markets are followed by bear markets. Representative democracy seems to be less successful in this respect. It is true that governments and legislators are regularly replaced by the electorate; that is how the system is designed. But democracy seems incapable of correcting its own excesses; on the contrary, it seems to be progressing ever deeper into far-from-equilibrium territory. This analysis is borne out by the increasing disaffection of the electorates.

Such disaffection has happened before. Between the two world wars, it led to the breakdown of democracy and the rise of fascism in several European countries. This time the dissatisfaction is manifesting in a different way. Democracy is not seriously threatened in any of the countries at the center of the global capitalist system and it is actually on the rise at the periphery. But the political process has been increasingly discredited. People put their faith in the market mechanism instead, giving rise to market fundamentalism. The failure of politics becomes the strongest argument in favor of giving markets free rein. Market fundamentalism has in turn facilitated the rise of the global capitalist system, which has in turn reduced the ability of the state to provide social security to its citizens, thereby providing another demonstration of the failure of politics, at least as far as the citizens in need of social security are concerned. Cause and effect cannot be separated in a reflexive process. The comparison with the conglomerate boom helps to show how far politics have drifted from equilibrium. Equilibrium means, in this context, that the political process satisfies the expectations of the electorate.

Just one word of warning about this argument. I stress the ability of markets to correct their excesses just at the moment when financial markets may have lost that ability. Investors have lost their faith in the fundamentals. They have come to realize that the game is about making money, not about underlying values. Many of the old yardsticks have fallen by the wayside and those who continue to abide by them have lost out in comparison with those who believe in the dawning of a new age. But the conclusion that we are in far-from-equilibrium territory would only be strengthened if markets have also lost their anchor.

What is true of politics is equally true of social values. In many ways, social values are inferior to market values. They cannot be quantified—they cannot even be identified. They cannot be reduced to a common denominator, money. Nevertheless, a well-defined community has well-defined values; its members may abide by them or transgress against them, be sustained by them or oppressed by them, but at least they know what those values are. We do not live in that kind of community. We have difficulties in deciding between right and wrong. The amorality of markets has undermined morality even in those areas where society cannot do without it. There is no consensus on moral values. Monetary values are much less confusing. Not only can they be measured, but we can feel reassured that they are appreciated by the people around us. They offer a certainty that social values lack.

Social values may be more nebulous than market values but society cannot exist without them. Market values have been promoted into the position of social values but they cannot fill that function. They are designed for individual decision making in a competitive setting and they are ill suited for collective decision making in a situation that requires cooperation as well as competition.

A confusion of functions has been allowed to occur that has undermined the collective decision-making process. Market values cannot take the place of public spirit or, to use an old-fashioned word, civic virtue. Whenever politics and business interests intersect, there is a danger that political influence will be used for business purposes. It is a well-established tradition that elected representatives should look out for the interests of their electorate. But where to draw the line between what is legitimate and what is not? The prominence given to business interests—and the self-interest of politicians—has pushed the line beyond the point that most voters consider acceptable; hence the disillusionment and disaffection. It can be observed both in domestic and international politics. In international affairs, it is further compounded by the fact that in democracies foreign policy tends to be dictated by domestic political considerations. The tendency is particularly strong in the United States with its ethnic voting blocs, but the French government, for instance, has an even stronger tradition of pushing business interests through political means. The president of an Eastern European country I know was shocked when in a meeting with President Jacques Chirac the French president spent most of their time together pushing him to favor a French buyer in a privatization sale. I shall not even mention arms sales.

There has always been corruption, but in the past people were ashamed of it and tried to hide it. Now that the profit motive has been promoted into a moral principle, politicians in some countries feel ashamed when they fail to take advantage of their position. I could observe this first hand in countries where I have foundations.

Ukraine, in particular, has given corruption a bad name. I also made a study of African countries and I found that people in resource-rich and resource-poor countries are equally poor; the only difference is that the governments of the resource-rich countries are much more corrupt.

And yet, to discard collective decision making just because it is inefficient and corrupt is comparable to abandoning the market mechanism just because it is unstable and unjust. The impulse in both cases comes from the same source—an inability to accept that all human constructs are imperfect and in need of improvement.

The prevailing theories about both the market mechanism and representative democracy were formed under the influence of the Enlightenment and without even acknowledging it they treat reality as if it were independent of the participants' thinking. Financial markets are supposed to discount a future that is independent of present valuations. Elected representatives are supposed to represent certain values that they hold independently of their desire to be elected. That is not how the world works. Neither the market mechanism nor representative democracy fulfill the expectations attached to them. But that is no reason to abandon them. Instead we need to acknowledge that perfection is unattainable and work on correcting the deficiencies of the existing arrangements.

Market fundamentalists dislike collective decision making in any shape or form because it lacks the automatic error-correcting mechanism of a market that supposedly tends toward equilibrium. They argue that the public interest is best served indirectly, by allowing people to pursue their own interests. They put their faith in the "invisible hand" of the market mechanism. But this faith is misplaced for two reasons. First, the common interest does not find expression in market behavior. Corporations do not aim at creating employment; they employ people (as few and as cheaply as possible) to make profits. Health care companies are not in business to save lives; they provide health care to make profits. Oil companies do not seek to protect the environment except to meet regulations or to protect their public image. Full employment, affordable medicine, and a healthy environment may, under certain circumstances, turn out to be the by-products of market processes, but such welcome social outcomes cannot be guaranteed by the profit principle alone. The invisible hand cannot adjudicate over interests that do not come under its jurisdiction.

Second, financial markets are unstable. I fully appreciate the merits of financial markets as a feedback mechanism that not only allows but forces the participants to correct their mistakes, but I would add that sometimes financial markets themselves break down. The market mechanism also needs to be corrected by a process of trial and error. Central banks are particularly well suited for the job because they interact with financial markets and receive feedback information that allows them to correct their own mistakes.

I share the prevailing aversion toward politics. I am a creature of the markets and I enjoy the freedom and the opportunities that they offer. As a market participant, I can make my own decisions and I can learn from my own mistakes. I do not need to convince others to get something done and the results are not obfuscated by the collective decision-making process. Strange as it may sound, participating in financial markets gratifies my quest for the truth. I have a personal bias against politics and other forms of collective decision making. Nevertheless I recognize that we cannot do without them.

Reinventing Intrinsic Values

So far I have been talking about social values, but there is something wrong with individual values as well. As discussed in Chapter 6, monetary values have usurped the role of intrinsic values and markets have come to dominate areas of society where they do not properly belong. I have in mind the professions such as law and medicine, politics, education, science, the arts, and even personal relations. Achievements or qualities that ought to be valued for their own sake are converted into monetary terms; they are judged by the amount of money they fetch rather than their intrinsic merits.

Money has certain attributes that intrinsic values lack: It has a common denominator, it can be quantified, and it is appreciated by practically everyone. These are the attributes that qualify money as a medium of exchange, but not necessarily as the ultimate goal. Most of the benefits attached to money accrue from spending it; in this respect money serves as a means to an end. Only in one respect does money serve as the ultimate goal: when the goal is to accumulate wealth.

Far be it from me to belittle the benefits of wealth; but to make the accumulation of wealth the ultimate goal disregards many other aspects of existence that also deserve consideration, particularly from those who have satisfied their material needs for survival. I cannot specify what those other aspects of existence are; it is in the nature of intrinsic values that they cannot be reduced to a common denominator and they are not equally appreciated by everyone. Thinking people are entitled to decide for themselves—it is a privilege they enjoy once they have met the requirements of survival. But instead of enjoying the privilege, we have gone out of our way to abdicate from it by giving such prominence to the accumulation of wealth. When everybody is striving for more money, competition becomes so intense that even the most successful are reduced to the position of having to fight for survival. People reproach Bill Gates, the chairman of Microsoft, for not giving away more of his wealth; they do not realize that the industry he is engaged in is so fast moving and competitive that he cannot afford to think about philanthropy.* The autonomy and discretion enjoyed by the privileged in the past has been lost. I believe we are all poorer for it.

*Now that he is engaged in an antitrust suit, being philanthropic will become part of his business strategy.

There ought to be more to life than survival. But the survival of the fittest has become the goal of our civilization.

Does the concept of open society imply a different set of values? I believe it does but I must be careful how I present the case. Open society certainly requires the correction of errors and excesses but it also recognizes the absence of an objective criterion by which they can be judged. I can argue that the promotion of the profit motive into an ethical principle is an aberration but I cannot set myself up as the ultimate arbiter who adjudicates in the name of open society. What I can say with confidence is that the substitution of monetary values for all other values is pushing society toward a dangerous disequilibrium and suppressing human aspirations that deserve to be considered as seriously as the growth of GNP.

Let me state the argument. Profit-maximizing behavior follows the dictates of expediency and ignores the demands of morality. Financial markets are not immoral; they are amoral. By contrast, collective decision making cannot function properly without drawing a distinction between right and wrong. We do not *know* what is right. If we did, we would not need a democratic government; we could live happily under the rule of a philosopher king as Plato proposed. But we must have a sense of what is right and what is wrong, an inner light that guides our behavior as citizens and politicians. Without it, representative democracy cannot work. The profit motive dims the inner light. The principle of expediency takes precedence over moral principles. In a highly competitive, transactional market, concern for the interests of others can turn into a handicap. Our founding fathers took a modicum of civic virtue for granted, but they did not reckon with the rise of highly competitive, transactional markets. The ascendancy of the profit motive over civic virtue undermines the political process. That would not matter if we could rely on the market mechanism to the extent that market fundamentalists claim. But as I have shown earlier, that is not the case.

There is also another argument to be considered. Whether people will be satisfied with an open society will depend a great deal on the results that an open society can produce. The strongest argument in favor of open society is that it offers infinite scope for improvement. Being reflexive, open society needs to be reinforced by the results. The results in turn depend on what is considered satisfactory. Progress is a subjective idea, as much dependent on people's values as on the material conditions of life. We are accustomed to measuring progress by GNP, but this is tantamount to accepting money as the intrinsic value. The GNP measures monetary exchange; the more social interactions take the form of monetary exchange, the greater the GNP. For instance, the spread of AIDS, other things being equal, would add to the GNP because of the cost of treatment. This is an aberration. Intrinsic values cannot be measured in monetary terms. We need some other measure of happiness, even if it cannot be quantified. In my opinion, the autonomy that citizens enjoy would be a better measure, because there ought to be more to life than survival. Using this yardstick, it is not clear whether the world is progressing or regressing.

The global capitalist system is based on competition. To relax in the fight for survival and concern oneself with the finer things in life can be very dangerous. Some people and some societies have tried it and they had to pay a heavy penalty. For instance, people in England tend to be attached to their homes; this puts them at a competitive disadvantage in the job market. People on the Continent have cherished social security; they had to pay for it with high unemployment.

Yet I believe that change is possible. It must start from the top, as in most cases of revolutionary regime change. Only those who are successful in the competition are in a position to institute changes in the terms on which the competition is carried on. Those who are less successful can opt out, but their leaving will not change the rules of the game. Citizens in successful democracies do, however, enjoy some discretion in improving the quality of their own political life. Suppose that people came to recognize that global competition has become too fierce and there is greater need for cooperation; suppose further that they learned to distinguish between individual decision making and collective decision making. The representatives they elected would then advocate different policies and they would be held to different standards of behavior. They would have some discretion to bring about change within their own country. They could not change the way the global capitalist system works without cooperating with other countries, but at least they could establish a greater willingness to cooperate. The change would have to begin with a change of attitudes, which would be gradually translated into a change of policies.

This is, of course, a very roundabout way to effect change and it does not seem very realistic given the prevailing trend. The forces of global competition have been released only recently—for present purposes I would put the date around 1980—and they have not yet made their full effect felt. Every country is under pressure to become more competitive and many of the social security arrangements that had been established under different circumstances have become unsustainable. The process of dismantling them is not yet complete. Those that spearheaded the move—the United Kingdom and the United States—are now reaping the benefits while the those that resisted it are burdened by high unemployment. Conditions are not ripe for a change of direction. But events are unfolding at a rapid pace.

I hope that the argument of this book will contribute to the reversal of the present trend, although I must admit that in some ways I may not be a good role model. I enjoy widespread respect and recognition not because of my philanthropy or my philosophy but on account of my ability to make money in the financial markets. I wonder if you would be reading this book if I had not gained a reputation as a financial wizard.

Originally I became engaged in the financial markets as a way of earning a living, but in the last decade I have deliberately used my financial reputation as a platform for launching my ideas. The main idea I should like to convey to the reader is that we must learn to distinguish between individual decision making as expressed in market behavior and collective decision making as expressed in social behavior in general and politics in particular. In both cases, we are guided by self-interest; but in collective decision making we must put the common interest ahead of our individual self-interest. I admit that the distinction is not widely observed. Many people, probably the majority, follow their narrow self-interest even in collective decision making. It is tempting to throw up our hands and join the crowd, but it would be wrong, because it would hurt the common interest. If we really believe in a common interest, we must recognize it on our part even if others do not recognize it on their part. What distinguishes intrinsic values is that they are worthwhile irrespective of whether they prevail or not. There is a cleavage between intrinsic values and market values. Markets are competitive and the goal is to win. Intrinsic values are deserving in their own right. I have never forgotten the words of Sergei Kovaliev, the Russian dissident and human rights activist, who told me proudly that he has been fighting losing battles all his life. I have not quite lived up to his standards but I do practice what I preach. I try to be a winner as a market participant and I try to serve the common interest as a citizen and a human being. Sometimes it is difficult to keep the two roles separate, as we have seen in the case of my involvement in Russia, but the principle is clear.

There will always be people who put their personal interests ahead of the common interest. This is called the free rider problem and it bedevils all cooperative endeavors. But it makes all the difference in the world if we recognize it as a problem or accept it as a fact. In the first case we would disapprove of free riders even if we cannot banish them; in the second, we would tolerate them and might even join them. Free riders could be discouraged by general opprobrium. Encumbered individuals, to use my earlier phrase, care a great deal what others think of them. They might be single-minded in the pursuit of money, but if others valued civic virtue they would at least pretend that they were public spirited. This would be a great improvement over the current state of affairs.

Of course, interpersonal criticism could never work as well in politics and social life as it does in natural science so we should not form unrealistic expectations that would lead to disappointment. Science has an independent, external criterion to work with, which enables the truth to prevail even if it does not conform to common sense. Social life lacks such a criterion. As we have seen, if people are guided entirely by the results of their actions they can stray very far from the common interest. The only criterion available is inter-nal: The intrinsic values held by the citizens. It is not a reliable basis for an interpersonal process of critical evaluation because it is only too easy to dissemble. As we have seen, social science works less well than natural science because the question of motives enters into the discussion. Marxists, for instance, used to deflect any crit-icism of their dogma by accusing their opponents of representing hostile class interests. So the critical process is less effective when it deals with motives rather than facts. Nevertheless, politics does work better when citizens are guided by a sense of right and wrong rather than sheer expediency.

I have seen it happen in my native country, Hungary, but it took a revolution. I left the country with bitter memories: The popula-tion had not done much to help their Jewish fellow-citizens when they were being exterminated during the Nazi occupation. When I returned two decades later I found a different atmosphere. It was the legacy of the 1956 revolution. People were acutely aware of the political oppression. A few became dissidents; the majority found ways to accommodate themselves, but they were aware that they were making compromises and they admired those who did not. Interestingly, the clear sense of right and wrong that prevailed at the time when I set up my foundation has faded since the dissolution of the communist regime. Could it be preserved or revived in a democracy? I believe so, but the impulse must come from individuals who act on the basis of their values irrespective of what others do. Nevertheless, *some* people must be willing to stand up for their principles and others must respect them for it. That would be sufficient to improve the social and political climate.

CHAPTER 10

The International Context

So far I have dealt with the shortcomings of representative democracy. But as we have seen, the connection between democracy and market economy is rather tenuous. The global capitalist system is associated with a variety of political regimes. There is no global society to correspond to the global economy and there is certainly no global democracy. International relations are based on the principle of national sovereignty. Sovereign nations are guided by their national interests. The interests of the states do not necessarily coincide with the interests of their own citizens, and states are even less likely to be concerned with the citizens of other states. There are practically no safeguards built into the present arrangements to protect the interests of the people. The United Nations has adopted the Universal Declaration of Human Rights, but it has no enforcement mechanism. There are some international treaties and some international institutions, but their influence is confined to the narrow sphere that the sovereign nations have assigned to them. What goes on within the borders of individual states is largely exempt from international supervision.

All this might not endanger the global capitalist system if states were democratic and markets self-regulating. But that is not the case. How severe the threat is deserves closer consideration. We shall examine the prevailing attitude toward international relations first and the actual state of affairs afterward.

Geopolitical Realism

International relations are not well understood. They do not have a scientific discipline like economics to rely on, although there is a doctrine called geopolitical realism for which scientific status is claimed. Just like the theory of perfect competition, geopolitics has its roots in the nineteenth century, when science was expected to provide deterministic explanations and predictions. According to geopolitics, the behavior of states is largely determined by their geographical, political, and economic endowments. Henry Kissinger, the apostle of geopolitics, contends that the roots of geopolitical realism go back even further, to Cardinal Richelieu, who proclaimed that, States have no principles, only interests.* This doctrine has some similarity to the doctrine of laissez faire in that both treat self-interest as the only realistic basis for explaining or predicting the behavior of a subject. For laissez faire, the subject is the individual market participant; for geopolitics, the state. Closely allied to both is the vulgar version of Darwinism according to which the survival of the fittest is the rule of nature. The common denominator of the three doctrines is that they are based on the principle of egoism: In the case of geopolitics,

---

*Henry Kissinger, *Diplomacy* (New York: Simon & Schuster, 1995).

this means the national interest, which does not necessarily coincide with the interests of the people who belong to the state. The idea that the state ought to represent the interests of its citizens is beyond its frame of reference. Geopolitical realism may be regarded as a translation of the doctrine of laissez faire into international relations with the difference that the actors are states, not individuals or business units.

This perspective can yield some strange results. Geopolitical realism could not cope, for instance, with the popular opposition to the war in Vietnam. More recently, it could not deal with the disintegration of states such as the Soviet Union or Yugoslavia. A state is a state is a state. We are taught to think of them as pawns on a chessboard. What goes on inside the pawns is not the business of geopolitics.

Interestingly, economic theory suffers from a similar weakness. Geopolitics is based on the state; economics is based on the isolated individual, *Homo economicus*. Neither is strong enough to sustain the weight of the theory that is built on it. The economic beings are supposed to possess perfect knowledge both of their own needs and of the opportunities open to them and to be able to make rational choices based on that information. We have seen that these assumptions are unrealistic; we have also seen how economic theory has wiggled out of the difficulty by taking both preferences and opportunities as given. But we are left with the impression that people are guided by their self-interest as isolated individuals. In reality, people are social animals: The survival of the fittest must involve cooperation as well as competition. There is a common flaw in market fundamentalism, geopolitical realism, and vulgar social Darwinism: the disregard of altruism and cooperation.

No World Order

Turning from ideology to reality, let us look at the actual state of affairs in international relations. The distinguishing feature of the current state of affairs is that it cannot be described as a regime. There is no global political system to correspond to the global capitalist system; moreover, there is no consensus that a global political system is either feasible or desirable. This is a relatively recent state of affairs. Until the collapse of the Soviet empire, one could speak of a regime in international relations. It was called the cold war and it was remarkably stable: Two superpowers representing two different forms of social organization were locked in deadly conflict. Each wanted to destroy the other and both prepared for it by engaging in an arms race. As a consequence, each became strong enough to wreak havoc on the other if attacked. This prevented the outbreak of an outright war, although it did not prevent skirmishes at the margin and jockeying for position.

A balance of powers, such as the cold war, is generally recognized as one way to preserve peace and stability in the world; the hegemony of an imperial power is another; and an international organization capable of effective peacemaking could be a third. At present we have none of the above.

The United States remains the sole surviving superpower, but it has no clear view of its role in the world. During the cold war, the United States was also the leader of the free world and the two roles reinforced each other. With the disintegration of the Soviet empire, this cozy identity of being both superpower and leader of the free world has also disintegrated. The United States could remain the leader of the free world, but to do so it ought to have cooperated with other democratically minded countries, first to help lay the foundations for democracy in the formerly communist countries and then to strengthen the international institutions necessary to maintain what I call a global open society. On two previous occasions when the United States emerged as the leader of the free world—at the end of the First and the Second World Wars—it did exactly that: It sponsored first the League of Nations, then the United Nations. In the first case, Congress refused to ratify the League of Nations; in the second, the cold war rendered the United Nations largely ineffectual.

I was certainly hoping that the United States would take the lead in international cooperation when the Soviet empire started to disintegrate. I set up a network of Open Society Foundations in the formerly communist countries to blaze the trail that I hoped the open societies of the West would follow. In spring 1989, I gave a speech at an East-West conference in Potsdam, which was then still in East Germany, in which I advocated a new kind of Marshall Plan, but my proposal was greeted with outright laughter. In the interest of historical accuracy, I must note that the laughter was initiated by William Waldegrave, Margaret Thatcher's deputy minister for foreign affairs. Subsequently I sought to contact Margaret Thatcher with a "Thatcher Plan" and President Bush prior to the summit meeting with Gorbachev in Malta in September 1989 with a similar idea, but to no avail. In frustration I dashed off what I called an instant book, which contained many of the ideas I repeat here.

The opportunity to reactivate the United Nations was certainly available. When Gorbachev embarked on glasnost and perestroika, one of his first acts was to pay up the Soviet arrears to the United Nations. Then he came to the General Assembly and made an impassioned plea for international cooperation. The West suspected a ruse and wanted to test his sincerity. When he met the test, new tests were designed. By the time he made all the concessions demanded of him, conditions in the Soviet Union deteriorated so much that the Western leadership could conclude that it was too late to extend the assistance that Gorbachev had hoped for. Still, neither Gorbachev nor Yeltsin posed any serious difficulties for the proper functioning of the Security Council for about five or six years. The opportunity to make the Security Council function the way it was originally intended was dissipated, first by an unfortunate incident in Somalia and then by the conflict in Bosnia. The Somalian experience established the principle that U.S. soldiers will not serve under UN command—although they were not under UN command when the incident occurred. It also taught the U.S. government that the public has a very low tolerance for body bags. Nevertheless the Bosnian crisis could have been easily contained if the Western permanent members of the Security Council had agreed among themselves. The task could have been assigned to the North Atlantic Treaty Organization (NATO), as it was in the end, and the tragedy could have been avoided. In 1992, Russia would have posed no objections. But, cowed by the Somalian experience, the United States exerted no leadership, and Europe did not either, and the fighting dragged on until finally the United States took a firmer line. The Dayton agreement left an unfortunate legacy in U.S. foreign policy in blaming Europe for its inability to take a unified stand on security issues. The attitude of the United States toward the United Nations has also deteriorated to a point where the United States is unwilling to pay its dues. After the debacle in Rwanda, it is no exaggeration to say that the United Nations is less effective than it was during the cold war.

The period since the end of the cold war has been anything but peaceful. Rumours concerning the end of history have been greatly exaggerated. There has been only one war involving the United States—the Persian Gulf War—but there have been many local conflicts and in the absence of effective peacemaking some of them proved quite devastating. If we look at a single continent, Africa, the conflicts have been so numerous that I could not even start to enumerate them. I admit that these conflicts do not endanger the global capitalist system, but the same cannot be said of the nuclear arms race between India and Pakistan or of the tensions in the Middle East. It seems that local conflicts have become more rather than less difficult to contain. They need to grow into full-blown crises before they receive attention and even then the political will to deal with them is difficult to muster.

Crisis Prevention

I have now seen enough political and financial crises to know that crisis prevention cannot start early enough. In the early stages, intervention is relatively painless and inexpensive; later on both the damage and the cost escalate exponentially. Fifteen billion dollars earmarked for the payment of pensions and unemployment benefits in Russia in 1992 would have changed the course of history; subsequently the international financial institutions spent much more with much less effect. Or take the case of Yugoslavia: If the Western democracies had objected to Slobodan Milosevic abolishing the autonomy of Kosovo in 1989, both the Bosnian war and the current fighting in Kosovo could have been avoided. At that time, it would have taken only diplomatic and financial pressure to prevent Milosevic from consolidating his power; later on military intervention was needed.

I pride myself that by establishing a network of Open Society Foundations I am in effect practicing crisis prevention. The foundations engage in a wide variety of seemingly disparate activities. Their goal is to support civil society and help build the rule of law and a democratic state with an independent business sector. Each foundation is run by a board of local citizens who decide what the local priorities are. Crisis prevention is successful when no crisis arises. The amount of money we spend is substantially less than what is needed after a crisis erupts. I gave $50 million to the United Nations High Commissioner for Refugees (UNHCR) in December 1992 for humanitarian aid to the inhabitants of Sarajevo and the money was exceptionally well spent. Under the leadership of a particularly gifted relief organizer, Fred Cuny, who subsequently died in Chechnya, an alternative water supply was established, an electric generator was installed in the hospital, people were given seeds to grow vegetables on small plots and balconies, and so on. Nevertheless I considered my gift an admission of defeat: It would have been much better if the crisis could have been prevented and the money could have been spent in countries that were not being destroyed.

The success of crisis prevention is difficult to assess, as only the failures register. Nevertheless I have no doubt that the foundations have made a significant contribution in laying the groundwork for what I call an open society. Interestingly, their efficacy tends to be the greatest the more adverse the conditions under which they operate. For instance, in Yugoslavia the foundation survived an attempt by the government to close it down and it is practically the only source of support for people who have not abandoned the hope for democracy. It has a branch in Kosovo that allows the voice of civil society to be heard even in the midst of fighting; undoubtedly it will be able to play a constructive role when the fighting stops. That is what happened in Bosnia: While the fighting pitted Serbs, Moslems, and Croats against each other, the foundation never abandoned the idea of an open society where all citizens are treated equally. It now operates in Republica Srpska, as well as in the Bosnian and Croatian parts of the country and is governed by a board drawn from all nationalities. In Belarus, a dictatorial president has forced the foundation to close down. It continues to operate from abroad and it is more effective than ever.

I do not expect other people to devote themselves to a cause to the extent I have done—and I must point out that I did it only after I was successful in making money. Nevertheless I cannot avoid asking myself whether it would be possible to engage in conflict prevention along the lines I have followed in my foundations, but on a larger scale, as a matter of public policy. I know it would make the world a better place. I am reluctant to raise the question publicly because it exposes me to the charge of being a naive idealist. Idealist I may be, but naive I am not. I realize that the idea of helping others for the sake of an abstract idea is totally out of line with prevailing attitudes. But I also realize that there is something wrong with prevailing attitudes and I have spent most of this book trying to identify what it is.

Historically, the United States has always been torn between geopolitical realism and the universal principles enunciated in the Declaration of Independence. The United States is quite exceptional in this respect (American exceptionalism is acknowledged even by Henry Kissinger). European powers, with their long colonial history, are much less troubled by the suffering of other people (although it is worth recalling Gladstone's fulminations against the Balkan massacres because he is echoed today in the public reaction to gory pictures on CNN). By the time the public is aroused, it is far too late. It is therefore quite legitimate to ask whether it would be possible to devise ways to respond earlier. Several obstacles stand in the way. Nobody earns any brownie points for solving crises that have not erupted, and finding solutions is more difficult than identifying problems. But the biggest obstacle is that we lack an agreement on the basic principles that ought to guide cooperative action, particularly in the international arena.

I believe the principles of open society could serve that purpose. I can speak from personal experience because I was guided by those principles and they have served me well. I made many mistakes, but they also helped me to identify and correct them. Unfortunately those principles are not even understood, let alone accepted. I must therefore rephrase the question I have posed: Could the principles of open society provide the shared values that would hold our global society together better than it hangs together today?

Open Society as a Shared Value

Both politics and international relations are based on the sovereignty of the state. International relations basically govern the relations between states. Within states, the sovereign power belongs to the state except to the extent that the state has abdicated or delegated sovereignty by international treaty. The arrangements governing relations between states are far from adequate, but there is a much greater deficiency with regard to conditions within states. Any international intervention in those conditions constitutes external interference with the sovereignty of the state. Because crisis prevention requires some degree of external interference, present arrangements stand in the way of effective crisis prevention. At the same time, international capital is free to move around and states are practically at its mercy. This creates an imbalance between the political and the economic spheres and leaves international capital largely beyond any political or social control. That is why I regard the global capitalist system as a distorted form of open society.

Open society stands for a certain kind of relationship between state and society that has important implications for international relations as well. The basic principle is that society and state are not identical; the state should serve society, not rule it. People have some needs that they cannot meet on their own; the state is there to meet those needs. The state should not be in charge of all collective decisions: Some needs are better served by voluntary associations, others by municipal authorities, and yet others by international arrangements. Civil society, state, and local government each have their appropriate spheres of influence; what is appropriate should be decided by the people, not by the state. How the decisions are reached should be governed by a constitution. The constitution defines how laws are made, changed, administered, and enforced. The state should not be beyond the reach of the law.

Not all states meet these conditions. By their nature, states are more suited for rule than for service. Originally, states were ruled by a sovereign, although the power of sovereigns was not always absolute. The state is an archaic instrument that has been adapted to the demands of open society. Sometimes the evolution took a different direction: In the Soviet Union, the party-state apparatus sought to exercise more comprehensive control over society than any absolute ruler. That is what made the distinction between open and closed society so relevant at the time.

We find that states are more likely to abuse their power in relation to their own citizens than in relation to other states because in dealing with other states they are subject to more constraints. People living under oppressive regimes need assistance from the outside. Often it is their only lifeline. But what interest do people living outside have in coming to their aid? That is the point on which our social values are in urgent need of reconstruction. By and large, people living in representative democracies do support the principles of open society within their own countries; they defend their own freedom when it is endangered. But there is not enough support for open society as a universal principle. Many people who are vocal in defending their own freedom see a contradiction in principles when asked to interfere in the affairs of a faraway country. What is worse, they have a point. Actions have unintended consequences and well-intentioned interventions in the name of some abstract principles could end up doing more harm than good. That was the point that was brought home to television viewers when the body of a U.S. airman was dragged through the streets of Mogadishu.

As I said earlier, the supreme challenge of our time is to establish a universally valid code of conduct for our global society. The concept of open society can frame the problem but it cannot actually solve it. In an open society there are no final solutions. It follows from our fallibility that a code of conduct cannot be derived from first principles. Nevertheless, we need a code of conduct, particularly for international relations. International relations cannot be confined to relations between states, because, as we have seen, the interests of the state do not coincide with the interests of people. That is why we need some universally valid rules for the relationship between state and society that safeguard the rights of the individual. We have the rudiments of such rules in some pious declarations but they are far too general and there is no enforcement mechanism behind them. Moreover, it is dangerous to leave the enforcement to states because, as noted above, states have no principles, only interests. Society must be mobilized to impose principles on the behavior of states and the principles that need to be imposed are the principles of open society.

Democratic states are organized according to the principles of open society—at least in principle. A code of conduct is established in the form of laws, which can be revised and refined in the light of experience. The state is under the control of society and not above the law. What is lacking is the rule of international law. How can it be accomplished? Only through the cooperation of democratic states that are controlled by their societies. They would have to yield some of their sovereignty to establish the rule of international law and find some ways to induce other states to do the same. This sounds good in principle, but we must beware of the unintended consequences. Intervening in the internal affairs of another state is fraught with danger, but not intervening may do even more harm.

CHAPTER 11

The Open Society Agenda

Where do we go from here? To prepare a blueprint of global governance would run counter to the principles of open society; it would also be an exercise in futility. We must start with what exists and decide what it is that needs to be changed. We must also be able to mobilize the necessary support. Karl Popper called this piecemeal social engineering. I am not entirely happy with the term because there are times when piecemeal changes are not sufficient. The collapse of the Soviet system was such a moment. Suggestions for piecemeal reform were inadequate. It was a time for "big bangs" like the currency reform in Poland and mass privatization in Czechoslovakia and Russia. The fact that radical reforms are often radically misconceived does not obviate the need for radical reforms.

We are now at another such moment in history. The global capitalist system has been rocked by a series of financial crises and it is literally disintegrating. At the time I started writing this book, I did not think it would happen so soon. Although I may be in a minority, I believe significant changes are called for. Even so, I am opposed to revolutionary changes, because of the dangers of unintended consequences. We must start with what we have and try to improve it. I dealt with the international financial system in Chapter 8; here I want to address the international political system, or rather the lack of it.

The European Union

We are witnessing a gigantic experiment in social engineering: the creation of the European Union. It is worth taking a closer look. The process has come face to face with the issue we have identified as the crucial issue of our time: how to overcome the obstacles posed by national sovereignty to the pursuit of the common interest. The issue is not confronted directly; if it were, the process could not have gone as far as it has. Rather it is approached indirectly, by identifying a concrete objective and gathering sufficient support behind it. It started with the Coal and Steel Community and it has reached as far as the common currency. Each step forward has some flaw in it, which can be corrected only by taking another step forward. The process is fraught with uncertainty and it is impossible to say how far it may go. Each step is resisted and much of the resistance is based on the expectation that it will lead to further steps in the same direction. The expectation is justified. The creation of a common currency, for instance, is unsound without a common fiscal policy. Whether it will be possible to gather sufficient political support for introducing a common fiscal policy remains to be seen.

The process is running into difficulties. It has been driven by a political elite and it is losing the support of the masses. The idea of a united Europe was immensely enticing, especially while the memory of the last war was fresh in people's minds and Europe was exposed to the Soviet menace. The reality of the European Union as it functions today is much less attractive. Politically it is still a union of states that have delegated some of their sovereignty to the union. In the economic sphere, where the delegation has occurred, the union works reasonably well, but in the political sphere there has been practically no delegation. The European Commission is subject to the authority of the Council of Ministers, who are guided more by national interests than by the common interest. Decisions take on the character of an international treaty: difficult to reach and even more difficult to alter. The members of the commission are appointed on the basis of national quotas and the work of the commission suffers from all the faults of a bureaucracy that has to serve not just one master but fifteen. What the people see is a top-heavy bureaucratic organization that works in convoluted ways shrouded in secrecy and not responsible to the public. To change this perception, the administration ought to be made more directly responsible to the people, either through the national parliaments or the European Parliament, but people are not demanding it because they are turned off. National governments have the bad habit of blaming Brussels for anything that people resent and the European Parliament is generally held in very low esteem.

The disenchantment finds expression in a growing minority that rejects the idea of Europe and espouses nationalistic and xenophobic tendencies. It is to be hoped that the political elite will be able to mobilize public opinion once again, but this time the move must be directed against the political elite itself. The people must assert direct political control over the government of the European Union. Such a move would have to confront the issue of national sovereignty more directly than ever before and its success is far from assured. Failure may lead to the disintegration of the European Union, because integration is a dynamic process: If it does not move forward it is liable to move backward. When I said the process is fraught with uncertainty, I really meant it.

(For what it is worth, I believe the best way forward may be to make the government of the union, i.e., the European Commission, responsible not to the European Parliament but to a body drawn from the national parliaments. Such a body would give people a more direct say and be a less direct attack on national sovereignty. It should also enjoy the support of the national parliaments, which would otherwise be threatened by an increased role for the European Parliament. Altogether this arrangement has a better chance of success than changing the powers—and the image—of the European Parliament.)

The European Union has been singularly unsuccessful in the area of foreign policy. The second pillar of the Maastricht Treaty was devoted to a common foreign policy but it did not infringe on the sovereignty of the member countries. The results were to be expected: No common policy emerged. Foreign policy remained subordinated to the interests of individual countries. The common policy was discredited in the very act of negotiating the Maastricht Treaty. As part of the horse trading leading up to the treaty, the former foreign minister of Germany, Hans-Dietrich Genscher, obtained European recognition for an independent Croatia and Slovenia, thereby precipitating the war in Bosnia.

The present situation is highly unsatisfactory but it would be unrealistic to expect the provisions of the Maastricht Treaty to be changed. Moreover, it would be difficult to justify a delegation of powers to the European Union in matters of foreign policy, because the member states do have national interests, particularly in the area of trade and investment. There are many issues of common interest, but they usually extend beyond the member states of the European Union. The Balkans, the Middle East, North Africa, and the former Soviet Union are areas of interest not only to Europe but to the United States and the rest of the world. I believe a broader approach is needed and it ought to be based on a broader alliance centered on the United States.

The United States

The United States, as the sole remaining superpower, ought to resume its role as the leader of the free world. It cannot go it alone. Although it enjoys greater technological superiority than at any time in history, it is not willing to pay the price that being the world's policeman would involve in human lives. And the world does need a policeman. The well-known aversion of the U.S. public to body bags has greatly reduced the awe in which it is held by rogue regimes. You cannot be a policeman without running some risks.

The United States is well justified in refusing to be the sole policeman: It does not derive sufficient benefits from being at the center of the global capitalist system to preserve peace in the world single-handedly. There are others who benefit from peace—both at the center and the periphery—who ought to pull their weight. That requires cooperation—and that is where the United States is balking. It is a shocking thing, but the United States has become the most retrograde country in the world with regard to preserving all the trappings of sovereignty.

There are repressive regimes in the world that maintain an iron grip on their subjects, but when they project their power abroad they are acutely aware that they could step on the toes of a slumbering giant. The United States is anything but repressive at home but it has no constraints in flaunting its power internationally. It does act occasionally as an aggressor when it sees no danger of body bags—bombing a pharmaceutical factory in Sudan was an example. Even more to the point, it is aggressive in refusing to cooperate. It refuses to pay its dues to the United Nations; it hesitates to replenish the IMF; and it imposes sanctions unilaterally at the drop of a hat or, more exactly, at the instigation of domestic constituencies. The United States was one of only seven countries that voted against the International Criminal Court, because the U.S. military objected to its personnel coming under international jurisdiction. The others were China, Iraq, Israel, Libya, Qatar, and Yemen. Not very distinguished company! The Pentagon went so far as to instruct U.S. military attachés based in U.S. embassies around the world to enlist the military leaders of their host governments to lobby against the International Criminal Court. This was a particularly questionable tactic in countries where civilian authority over the armed forces is not firmly established.

The United States has also slipped into the habit of allowing domestic considerations to dictate foreign policy—witness the trade embargo on Cuba, which is designed to please influential Cuban voters in Florida, or NATO expansion, which was designed to please Polish voters in Chicago during the 1996 elections. Long gone are the days of bipartisan foreign policy that prevailed during much of the cold war. It would require a radical change of attitude for the United States to become again the leader of the free world.

Nevertheless I believe that the conditions for a change of attitudes are favorable. The United States has a historical commitment to the ideals of open society, starting with the Declaration of Independence. According to public opinion surveys, the United Nations, despite its current paralysis, is still more popular with the public than Congress or the President. All that needs to be done is to recapture the latent support for an open society.

At present an uneasy alliance prevails in politics between market fundamentalists and religious fundamentalists. They are united in their opposition to big government but they have quite different objectives in mind. Market fundamentalists object to government intervention in the economy; religious fundamentalists oppose the liberal standards imposed by the state. Market fundamentalists are against international cooperation for the same reason that they dis-like big government: They want to give business a free hand. Reli-gious fundamentalists are against it for the opposite reason: They resent the threat global markets pose to their intrinsic values. It is amazing how the two disparate groups have been able to reconcile their differences. I expect that they will find it increasingly difficult to do so the more progress they make in achieving their objectives. I could imagine a reconfiguration of the domestic political scene with bipartisan support for a global open society, but it would require the market fundamentalists to recognize the errors of their ways.

The United Nations

The program for a more cooperative foreign policy needs to be sketched out in a little more detail. We need a worldwide alliance of democratic countries that cooperates in promoting the principles of open society. They could establish standards for the relationship between state and society that would cover such areas as freedom of information, freedom of association, due process, transparency in state procurements, and the like. Members of the alliance would pledge themselves to abide by those standards. The alliance would also admit candidate members who do not meet those standards at present but subscribe to them as a desirable goal. It is to be hoped that members and candidate members of the open society coalition would constitute a majority of the United Nations. If so, the United Nations could be reformed, because it could be run by majority rule. The United Nations would work more like a parliament and it could become much more effective than it is at present.*

---

*It is imperative that not every state that applies should be admitted and those that fail to live up to their obligations should be excluded. Lack of discrimination in membership require-ments has impaired the value of such otherwise worthy entities as the Council of Europe and the Organization for Security and Cooperation in Europe (OSCE).

It is important to understand what the United Nations can and cannot do. It is fundamentally flawed, like every human construct, but as international institutions go it actually has great potential. It has four major components: the Security Council, the General Assembly, the Secretariat, and a number of specialized agencies such as the United Nations Development Program (UNDP), the United Nations Industrial Development Organization (UNIDO), and the United Nations Educational, Scientific, and Cultural Organization (UNESCO), and so on, only a few of which are functioning effectively. Appointments are made on the basis of national patronage and not on the basis of merit. It is difficult to fire officials and even more difficult to wind up organizations when they no longer have a mission. It is these features that have given the United Nations a bad name.

Bureaucracies are always more interested in self-preservation than in carrying out their mission. When a bureaucracy is responsible not to one master but to the entire membership of the United Nations it is beyond control. It must be recognized that an association of states, each of which is guided by its own interests, is ill-suited to carry out any executive functions in service of the common good. To the extent that there are executive functions to be carried out, they ought to be entrusted to appointed officials who are held responsible for their actions. They could report, depending on the function, to the Secretary General or to a board of directors appointed by the General Assembly or, as in the case of Bretton Woods institutions, by those who provide the funding.

The Security Council is a well-conceived structure and it could be effective in imposing peace if the permanent members agreed among themselves. The end of the cold war provided an opportunity for the Security Council to function as it was originally designed but, in the case of Bosnia, as we have seen, it was the three Western permanent members, the United States, the United Kingdom and France, who could not agree among themselves. The creation of an open society coalition ought to prevent a recurrence of that sorry spectacle. The non-permanent membership could also become more cohesive if the selection were confined to adherents of the open society coalition.

The General Assembly is a talking shop at present. It could become more like a legislature in charge of making laws for our global society. An assembly of sovereign states may be ill-suited to carry out executive functions but it is eminently qualified to serve as an international legislature. The laws would be valid only in the countries that ratify them, but members of the open society coalition would pledge themselves to ratify the laws automatically, provided they have been ratified voluntarily by a qualified majority. What would qualify as a majority would have to be carefully defined. There could be a triple test, namely two thirds of the countries, two thirds of the population, and two thirds of the UN budget.* Countries that do not abide by their commitment to accept the decision of a qualified majority would be excluded from the open society coalition. In that way, a body of international law could be developed without infringing on the principle of national sovereignty. The General Assembly could decide what laws are needed and how to enforce them. The International Criminal Court is a step in the right direction. The fact that the United States is the main opponent of the court shows what a radical change in U.S. attitudes would be needed to establish the rule of law in the international arena.

The Secretary General would be appointed by the open society coalition. He would be in charge of the Secretariat, which would guide the legislative work of the General Assembly. His position would be roughly equivalent to the elected leader of a democratic party. In view of his greatly enhanced powers it would be desirable if he could be dismissed at any time when he loses the confidence of the open society coalition.

There have been many studies and proposals for reforming the

---

*"The Binding Triad" as proposed by Richard Hudson, director of the Center for War/Peace Studies in New York.

United Nations but none have come to pass. The only way changes could come about is through the pressure of public opinion, particularly in the United States. What makes the idea of an open society coalition realistic is that democratic governments are responsive to the demands of their citizens. But first people must subscribe to the idea of open society. I hope this book will have furthered that goal.

A Domestic Agenda

I end this book with a brief review of my foundation's domestic agenda in the United States. My purpose in doing so is to show that the abstract concept of open society can be translated into concrete action.

Four years ago, I felt that the revolutionary moment created by the collapse of the Soviet empire had passed and it was no longer appropriate that I should concentrate all my philanthropic efforts on formerly or currently closed societies. The mission of my foundation, as I formulated it in 1979, was to help open up closed societies, render open societies more viable, and foster a critical mode of thinking. It was time to move on to the second and third item on the agenda. The United States, as a paradigm of the open society, had its own shortcomings. What could the foundation do about them? Within a few years, a coherent policy emerged.

My foundation's programs in the United States can for the most part be grouped under three major themes derived from the concept of open society: challenging the intrusion of marketplace values into inappropriate areas; addressing the adverse unintended consequences of perhaps well-intended policies; and dealing with the inequities in the distribution of wealth and social benefits that arise from market fundamentalism.

The first theme is that the profit motive has penetrated into areas where it does not properly belong. In particular, I am concerned about the ways in which market values have eroded professional values. It turns out that ethical standards once thought intrinsic are not standing up very well to market pressures. I have established programs to address this problem in law and medicine, which in recent years have come more and more to resemble businesses rather than professions. I found it easy—and gratifying—to provide support for public interest and public service work that upholds the best traditions and standards in law and medicine. It has proved harder, for a foundation coming at it from outside the professions (albeit with the advice and participation of many insiders), to affect the core, or mainstream, of these disciplines. Here the foundation is still striving for an appropriate means of influencing events, but we are beginning to make some progress. The pressures of the marketplace are also affecting journalism, publishing, and professional and ethical behavior in finance, but we have not yet found appropriate entry points.

The second major theme is what I call "unintended adverse consequences." There are some insoluble problems where the refusal to accept the fact that they are insoluble makes the problem worse than it needs to be. The most obvious and the most threatening of these problems is death. American culture is characterized by a denial of death. Doctors, families, and patients have great difficulties in confronting the issue, and by avoiding it they increase the pain, suffering, and isolation involved.

The problem of death preoccupied me as an adolescent. As a young man, I found a way of dealing with it that satisfied me, although it may not satisfy others. I distinguish between the idea of death and death as an actual occurrence. Death itself is a fact of life, but the idea of death is anathema to my consciousness. I shall never be able to accept the prospect of death but I may come to terms with the fact of dying, especially if it comes late in life. There is divergence between the thought and the reality, so that the *idea* of death is not what is actually going to happen. I find consolation in the insight that the thought is much more terrifying than the reality.

Love can also be a consolation for the prospect of death, as I discovered on the occasion of my mother's death. She had an experience, which is apparently not unusual, of walking up to the gates of heaven, and I was accompanying her, holding her hand while she described what she saw. She told me she was worried that she might take me with her. I reassured her that I was firmly ensconced on this earth and she need not worry. Her dying was really an uplifting experience for all of us because of the way she handled herself and the way the family, not just me but particularly my children, could participate in it. It also gave me the impulse to embark on the Project on Death in America, which promotes palliative care and a better understanding of the problem of death. It has made tremendous inroads in reducing both the physical and psychological pain involved in dying.

Another case where the remedy is worse than the disease is the war on drugs. Drug addiction is a serious social problem that could be alleviated, but not eliminated, by treating it as a public health problem. But we treat it as a crime. As a result, 338,000 adults were behind bars for drug law violations on June 30, 1995, compared with 51,950 at the end of 1980. It costs $9 billion a year to keep them there. In addition, billions of dollars are spent on trying to interdict supply, without making much progress.

The war on drugs is the worst case of fundamentalist, either/or thinking in the United States. Those who dare to oppose it are branded as legalizers. That is what happened to me when I supported (with after-tax dollars) the legalization of marijuana for medical purposes. Fortunately I can take the abuse. In fact, I do not advocate drug legalization. People who become addicted to drugs are no longer in charge of their destiny and need to be protected against their own addiction. Marijuana is not addictive, but it is harmful to children because it affects short-term memory and interferes with the learning process. What I advocate is not legalization. In other words, we should stop equating drugs with crime. Treating drug addicts as criminals is not the best way to treat addiction.

The foundation's engagement in campaign finance reform touches on both major themes. Politics is another arena where the values of the marketplace have intruded. Politicians spend most of their time and effort on raising money and the discussion of issues has been replaced by paid political messages. As part of its effort, the foundation made a substantial grant to an organization that promotes a "clean money option," particularly in state and local elections. The experts feel that federal elections will be much harder to reform. At the same time, we gave a smaller grant to the Brennan Center of New York University to monitor the unintended consequences of *all* campaign reform efforts, including our own. Regulations always have unintended consequences and past attempts at campaign reform have actually provoked worse abuses in the form of soft money contributions and special interest advertising.

The third major theme is the inequality of wealth distribution. This leads us to the more traditional areas of interest of U.S. philanthropy: welfare, the poverty trap, teenage pregnancy, inequality in education, and so on. We look for a niche where other foundations might be reluctant to tread or where our support can be strategically employed to influence public policy. For instance, when Congress deprived legal immigrants of some of their welfare entitlements in 1996, I established with $50 million the Emma Lazarus Fund to help immigrants disadvantaged by this benighted policy. I did so to highlight the unintended adverse consequences of welfare reform—hoping that policy makers might get the message—as well as to help a significant number of victims with naturalization assistance, English language classes, legal services, and so on. At this writing, Congress has restored over $14 billion in benefits, but much remains to be done.

On another front, I provided a challenge grant to spur public and private donors to create after-school opportunities for all children in New York City. We know that giving children something worthwhile to do from the hours of 3 to 6 P.M. will improve their educational performance, help their working parents, and keep them out of trouble. Our aim is to spend $1,000 per child per year and see what difference it makes. The response from federal, state, and local officials has been encouraging.

My foundation has used similar leverage in Baltimore, where our challenge grant is helping the mayor assemble a plan to provide drug treatment slots for all addicts who desire to break their habit but up to now have faced long waiting periods for the handful of places available. In Baltimore, we are also trying to deal with a range of urban problems, from drugs and crime to failing schools and unemployment, by a different approach from what other foundations have tried—the empowerment of a local board to make substantial decisions about grants and priorities, a model somewhat like the one I developed in the formerly communist countries.

The programs of the foundations do not relate directly to the policies that the United States ought to follow because there are many things that a foundation can do and there are many things that a government can do and the two are not identical.

An International Agenda

A global open society cannot be brought into existence by people or nongovernmental organizations acting on their own. Sovereign states have to cooperate and this requires political action. Public opinion and civil society have important roles to play because in a democracy politicians must be responsive to popular demands. In well-functioning democracies statesmen may even provide leadership in mobilizing public opinion. We need such leadership to form a coalition of like-minded countries committed to the creation of a global open society.

Index

ABOUT THE AUTHOR

GEORGE SOROS was born in Budapest, Hungary in 1930. In 1947 he emigrated to England, where he graduated from the London School of Economics. While a student in London, Mr. Soros became familiar with the work of the philosopher Karl Popper, who had a profound influence on his thinking and later on his philanthropic activities. In 1956 Soros moved to the United States, where he began to accumulate a large fortune through an international investment fund he founded and managed.

Mr. Soros currently serves as chairman of Soros Fund Management L.L.C., a private investment management firm that serves as principal investment advisor to the Quantum Group of Funds. The Quantum Fund N.V., the oldest and largest fund within the Quantum Group, is generally recognized as having the best performance record of any investment fund in the world in its twenty-nine-year history.

Mr. Soros established his first foundation, the Open Society Fund, in New York in 1979 and his first Eastern European foundation in Hungary in 1984. He now funds a network of foundations that operate in thirty-one countries throughout Central and Eastern Europe and the former Soviet Union, as well as southern Africa, Haiti, Guatemala, Mongolia and the United States. These foundations are dedicated to building and maintaining the infrastructure and institutions of an open society. Mr. Soros has also founded other major institutions, such as the Central European University and the International Science Foundation. In 1994, the foundations in the network spent a total of approximately $300 million; in 1995, $350 million; in 1996, $362 million; and in 1997, $428 million. Giving for 1998 is expected to be maintained at that level.

In addition to many articles on the political and economic changes in Eastern Europe and the former Soviet Union, Mr. Soros is the author of *The Alchemy of Finance, Opening the Soviet System, Underwriting Democracy*, and *Soros on Soros: Staying Ahead of the Curve.*

Mr. Soros has received honorary doctoral degrees from the New School for Social Research, the University of Oxford, the Budapest University of Economics, and Yale University. In 1995, the University of Bologna awarded Mr. Soros its highest honor, the Laurea Honoris Causa, in recognition of his efforts to promote open societies throughout the world.

PUBLICAFFAIRS is a new nonfiction publishing house and a tribute to the standards, values, and flair of three persons who have served as mentors to countless reporters, writers, editors, and book people of all kinds, including me.

I.F. STONE, proprietor of *I. F. Stone's Weekly*, combined a commitment to the First Amendment with entrepreneurial zeal and reporting skill and became one of the great independent journalists in American history. At the age of eighty, Izzy published *The Trial of Socrates*, which was a national bestseller. He wrote the book after he taught himself ancient Greek.

BENJAMIN C. BRADLEE was for nearly thirty years the charismatic editorial leader of *The Washington Post*. It was Ben who gave the *Post* the range and courage to pursue such historic issues as Watergate. He supported his reporters with a tenacity that made them fearless, and it is no accident that so many became authors of influential, best-selling books.

ROBERT L. BERNSTEIN, the chief executive of Random House for more than a quarter century, guided one of the nation's premier publishing houses. Bob was personally responsible for many books of political dissent and argument that challenged tyranny around the globe. He is also the founder and was the longtime chair of Human Rights Watch, one of the most respected human rights organizations in the world.

. . .

For fifty years, the banner of Public Affairs Press was carried by its owner Morris B. Schnapper, who published Gandhi, Nasser, Toynbee, Truman, and about 1,500 other authors. In 1983 Schnapper was described by *The Washington Post* as "a redoubtable gadfly." His legacy will endure in the books to come.

Peter Osnos, *Publisher*